OPERATION AGREEMENT

OSPREY
PUBLISHING

OPERATION
AGREEMENT

JEWISH COMMANDOS AND
THE RAID ON TOBRUK

JOHN SADLER

This one is dedicated to both my regular co-authors,
Rosie and Silvie.

Sung to the tune of *British Grenadiers* –

You may talk of famous sieges of Lucknow and Cawnpore
Of men like Wellington, Nelson and Admiral Rooke
There was Ladysmith, Mafeking and fierce fighting at Lahore
But none to rank as famous as Heroic Tobruk.

Blue waters to the north, to the south lie desert sands
Huns and Dagoes whichever way we look
But brave men all and free did leave their native lands
And now they stand defending Heroic Tobruk.

Brave youths from Australia and from India's sunny site
From England – and all to their guns have stuck
Daily they are defying Germany's might
The Empire will be proud of Heroic Tobruk.

When all this world is freed from Hitler's boast
And bloody battles are written in a book
Then all free men shall rise and say, 'a toast
To the gallant defenders of Heroic Tobruk.'

J. Campbell, *Heroic Tobruk*

First published in Great Britain in 2016 by Osprey Publishing,
PO Box 883, Oxford, OX1 9PL, UK, 1385 Broadway, 5th Floor, New York, 10018, USA
E-mail: info@ospreypublishing.com
Osprey Publishing, part of Bloomsbury Publishing Plc
© 2016 John Sadler

Every attempt has been made by the Publisher to secure the appropriate permissions for
material reproduced in this book. If there has been any oversight we will be happy to rectify
the situation and written submission should be made to the Publishers.
A CIP catalogue record for this book is available from the British Library
John Sadler has asserted his right under the Copyright, Designs and Patents Act, 1988, to be
identified as the Author of this Work.

ISBN: 978 1 4728 1488 3
PDF ISBN: 978 1 4728 1489 0
ePub ISBN: 978 1 4728 1490 6

Index by Zoe Ross
Typeset in Adobe Garamond Pro
Originated by PDQ Media, Bungay, UK
Printed in China through World Print Ltd

16 17 18 19 20   10 9 8 7 6 5 4 3 2 1

Front cover and title page: Soldiers from the LRDG on patrol in the Libyan desert in 1941.
(akg images)

Osprey Publishing supports the Woodland Trust, the UK's leading woodland conservation
charity. Between 2014 and 2018 our donations will be spent on their Centenary Woods
project in the UK.

www.ospreypublishing.com

IMPERIAL WAR MUSEUM COLLECTIONS
Many of the photos in this book come from the Imperial War Museum's huge collections
which cover all aspects of conflict involving Britain and the Commonwealth since the start
of the twentieth century. These rich resources are available online to search, browse and buy
at. www.iwmcollections.org.uk. In addition to Collections Online, you can visit the Visitor
Rooms where you can explore over 8 million photographs, thousands of hours of moving
images, the largest sound archive of its kind in the world, thousands of diaries and letters
written by people in wartime, and a huge reference library. Imperial War Museum
www.iwm.org.uk

Please note that for several of the Imperial War Museum images in this book, and both images
from the Jewish Museum, while every effort has been made to obtain copyright permission
from the original copyright source it had not always been possible to contact them.
Any queries about copyright should be addressed to the Publisher.

CONTENTS

CHRONOLOGY
SEPTEMBER 1942

6 SEPTEMBER

Force B to move out from Kufra Oasis and march to forming up area outside Tobruk defences

10 SEPTEMBER

Midday: Sudan Defence Force elements to march towards Bahariya Oasis in readiness for the attack on Siwa – Operation *Coastguard*

13 SEPTEMBER

Force A sails from Haifa aboard Tribal Class destroyers

Force C MTBs and Launches sail from Alexandria

Midday: Force B reaches Sidi Rezegh

2130 hours: Air raid on Tobruk begins

2145 hours: Force B secures its immediate objectives to prepare beachhead for Force C to land

14 SEPTEMBER

0130 hours: Allied bombers cease dropping flares

0140 hours: Submarine HMS *Taku* gets Folbot section into the water off Tobruk

0200 hours: Folbots reach shore and mark landing beach for Force A

0200 hours: Force C enters the Mersa Umm Es Sciausc cove provided the appropriate signal has been detected

0230 hours: Force C comes ashore in the inlet

0300 hours: The destroyers arrive off the coast

0340 hours: The first wave of marines to be ashore, followed by second flight

0340 hours: Bombing now ceases but RAF continues to run diversionary flights

0415 hours: All air operations cease

0415 hours: Force C MTBs and launches enter Tobruk harbour to attack shipping

0900 hours: The destroyers now enter the harbour

Force Z leaves Kufra to attack Jalo Oasis

16 SEPTEMBER

Force Z to have secured Jalo

MAP 1: THE NORTH AFRICAN THEATRE OF WAR, 1940–43

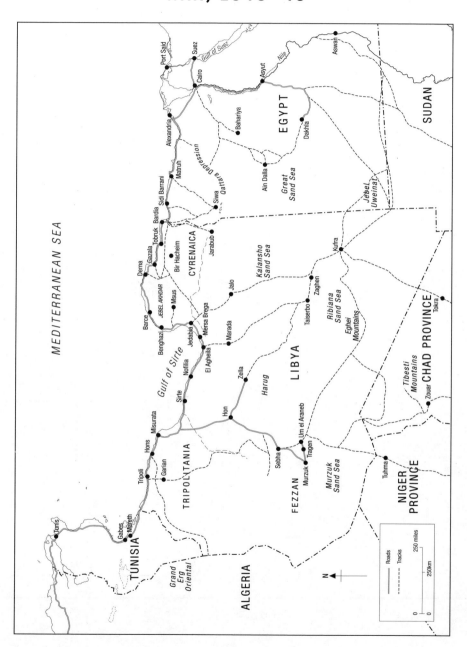

MAP2: THE BIG RAIDS, SEPTEMBER 1942

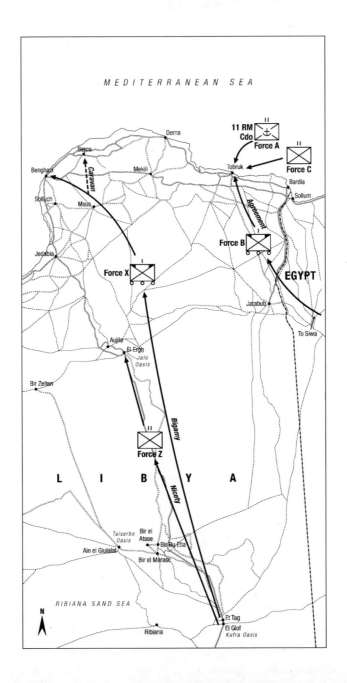

MAP 3: THE BARCE RAID, SEPTEMBER 1942

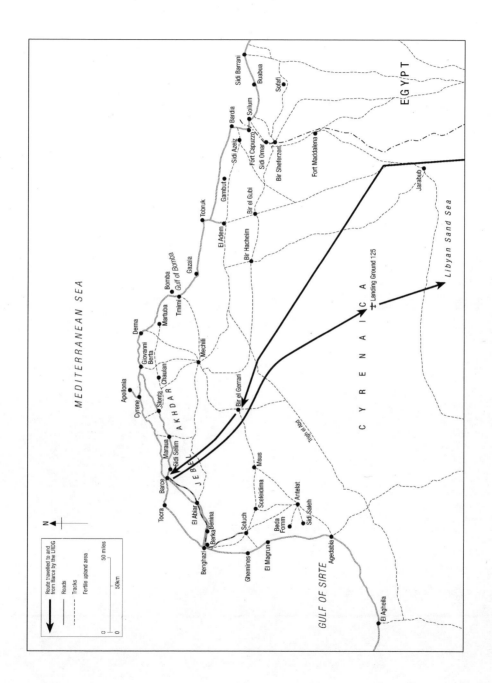

ACKNOWLEDGEMENTS

Anyone writing about Operation *Agreement* immediately owes a debt to Gordon Landsborough's *Tobruk Commando* (London, Cassell, 1956), the first and probably best account of the raid. This is followed by Peter C. Smith with *Massacre at Tobruk* (London, W. Kimber, 1987, reprinted by Stackpole Books in 2008) and David Jefferson's *Tobruk – A Raid Too Far* (London, Robert Hale, 2013). I do, of course, rely upon many of the very good books written about the Desert War generally and as listed in the bibliography. In terms particularly of the Jewish soldiers of SIG (Special Interrogation Group), I rely heavily upon Martin Sugarman's *Fighting Back* (London, Valentine Mitchell, 2010). Much of the primary source material has been included in a compendium volume published by the National Archives, *Special Forces in the Desert War* (2001), and which reproduces two earlier works by Brigadier H. W. Wynter. I have relied upon the latter of these, *The History of Commandos and Special Service Troops in the Middle East and North Africa – January 1941 to April 1943* (CAB 44/152).

Verse extracts are as follows: Frontispiece: *Heroic Tobruk* appears by kind permission of the Fusiliers Museum of Northumberland. Introduction: *Vale* appears by kind permission of Joan Venables. Chapter One: doggerel sung to the tune of *Onward Christian Soldiers*; Leslie Hore-Belisha was the butt of a good deal of marked anti-Semitism. Chapter Two: *Hitler has only got one b* sung to the tune of *Colonel Bogey*. Chapter Three: This extract is from the wartime poet Keith Douglas MC (Military Cross) who served in the desert and was finally killed in action in Normandy. Chapter Four: *Casus Belli*, anonymous, provenance is unknown. Chapter Five: *Libyan Handicap* is included by kind permission of the Fusiliers Museum of Northumberland. Chapter Six: *Christmas at El Agheila* also appears by kind permission of the Fusiliers Museum of Northumberland. Chapter Seven: *Untitled* appears by kind permission of the Fusiliers Museum of Northumberland. Chapter Eight: *Christmas Parade Service on Deck* is included by kind permission of County Durham Record Office. Chapter Nine: *Beach Casualty* is included by kind permission of County Durham Record Office. Chapter Ten: *The Unknown Soldier* is included by kind permission of Samantha Kelly.

Furthermore, this book could not have been written without the generous assistance of a number of organizations and individuals, particularly The Long Range Desert Group Preservation Society, Yael Robinson of Yad Vashem, Roz Currie of the Jewish Military Museum, Peter Hart and the staff of the Imperial War Museum Sound Archive, Eleanor Johnson Ward and Nigel Taylor at the National Archives and Amy Cameron of the National Army Museum, Andras Zboray of FJ Expeditions, the archive staff of the Defence Academy of the United Kingdom at Shrivenham, Liz Bregazzi and Gill Parkes of Durham County Record Office, David Fletcher of the Tank Museum, Bovington, Roberta Goldwater of the Discovery Museum, Rod Mackenzie of the Argyll and Sutherland Highlanders Museum, Thomas B. Smyth of the

Black Watch Museum, Paul Evans of the Royal Artillery Museum, Ana Tiaki of the Alexander Turnbull Library, New Zealand, John Stelling and Tony Hall of the North East Land, Sea and Air Museum, Dr Martin Farr of Newcastle University, Barry Matthews of Galina Battlefield Tours, Trevor Sheehan of BAE Systems Plc, John Rothwell, James Goulty, Sir Paul Nicholson, Major (Retired) Chris Lawton MBE, Arthur W. Charlton, Colonel Anthony George, John Fisher, John Shepherd, Mary Pinkney, Brian Ward, Jennifer Harrison, Neville Jackson, the late Nigel Porter, Timothy Norton, Kit Pumphrey, Captain Sam Meadows of 2RGR. Many thanks to Chloe Rodham, as ever, for the maps and to Marcus Cowper and the editorial team at Osprey for another successful collaboration.

As the author I remain, as ever, responsible for all errors and omissions.

John Sadler
Mid-Northumberland, summer 2015

I am forever haunted by one dread
That I may suddenly be swept away,
Nor have the leave to see you and to say
Goodbye; then this is what I should have said.
I have loved summer and the longest day
The leaves of trees, the slumberous film of heat
The bees, the swallows and the waving wheat,
The whistling of mowers in the hay.

I have loved words which left the soul with wings
Words that are windows to eternal things
I have loved souls that to themselves are true
Who cannot stoop and know not how to fear
Yet hold the talisman of pity's tear:
I have loved these because I have loved you.

Anon, *Vale*

INTRODUCTION

In the late summer of 2014, as the chaotic Libyan civil war raged and all the hopes of a fruitful Arab Spring faded into the bitter dust of murderous sectarianism, it was reported that the Council of Deputies, the nearest to any legitimate basis of civil government, had set up shop on a Greek car ferry moored in Tobruk harbour. For all of us who were born in the immediate decades after the Second World War, here was a name we were bound to recognize. Tobruk and the epic siege were the stirring stuff of desert legend. The story of Operation *Agreement*, which occurred in September 1942, is less well known but represents one of those great 'what if' questions. It was an operation of great audacity, daring and innovation. It was also too complex and its failure proved very costly.

Despite disaster, the attempt marks a milestone, not just in the Desert War, where it had little real impact on the course of the campaign, but in the history of special forces. Modern British units like the SAS and SBS champion the *K.I.S.S.* (for 'keep it simple, stupid') principle when planning operations. This is an important mantra, for certain post-war special forces operations have indicated that, as so tragically demonstrated by Operation *Agreement*, simplicity is indeed key.

In April 1980, the US attempted to free its diplomatic hostages seized by Iran. Operation *Eagle's Claw* ended in disaster, a costly fiasco. Thirteen years later, having seemingly failed to digest necessary lessons, the grandiosely named Operation *Gothic Serpent* in Mogadishu unravelled in bloody chaos, leaving 18 US personnel dead, dozens wounded and several hundred Somalis killed. Both these failed enterprises were backstairs plans involving compromise and complexity. They were not simple.

Along the narrow littoral of the North African shore, with the vast, barren interior of the Sahara to the south, Tobruk constitutes the finest natural harbour, nearly three hundred miles from Benghazi to the west and further still from fabled Alexandria and the Nile delta in the east. It is almost a coastal oasis, the higher ground behind being stripped and bare, home only to the Bedouin. An ancient colony of enterprising Classical Greeks, it became an important Roman garrison on the boundary between the provinces of Cyrenaica and Tripolitania (still a natural fault line in the current civil war).

During the nineteenth century the town was an important bastion of the Senussi sect.* If the British intervention in Egypt had largely been driven by expediency and overriding commercial imperative, then the Italian invasion of the twin Ottoman provinces of Tripolitania and Cyrenaica in 1912 was a blatant act of imperialism. Italy, newly unified, was a relative latecomer to the race for overseas territories. Her early attempts in Abyssinia ended in disaster at Adowa. The Italians claimed to act as liberators in North Africa, but the peoples of what had been classical Libya soon found their new masters equally tyrannical. From

---

* The Senussi were a Muslim sect of the Sufi order created in 1837 by the Grand Senussi Sayyid Muhammad ibn Ali as-Senussi at Mecca.

the outset the Senussi sect fought the invaders, but the Ottomans were forced to cede control under the terms of the 1912 Treaty of Lausanne.

Though King Idris of the Senussi was forced into exile, armed resistance, under Omar Mukhtar*, prolonged a bitter war throughout the 1920s. Italian General Pietro Badoglio and his successor Marshal Rodolfo Graziani had no regard for humanitarian considerations. Murder, mass deportations and the establishment of concentration camps ensued. Up to 80,000 Libyans died. In tandem with this ruthless repression, something like 150,000 native Italians were settled in Libya, mainly clustered around Tripoli and the coastal towns. They did prosper and undertook significant improvements to the limited local infrastructure. In 1937 Mussolini himself came on a state visit to celebrate the opening of the new arterial highway, the Via Balbia. This subsequently proved very useful to the British in the Desert War.

For the armies that would live out the dramatic swings of the Desert War pendulum, Tobruk would be a fulcrum and the prize would be the harbour. This is some 2¼ miles long and just less than half that distance in width. It possesses a deep-water basin with numerous quays and jetties. There is nothing really comparable on the 800-mile-long coastline between Tripoli and the Nile Delta. The town itself was never extensive, being several streets of white-walled Mediterranean-style buildings, facing the highway of the sea rather than the inhospitable expanses inland. Most of what was standing there in 1940 was of Italian construction, built as an outpost of empire; a church, hospital, barracks and school were its civic buildings, with an extensive range of port facilities.

The place scarcely looked warlike. A sleepy port, an isolated bustle of commerce and maritime traffic clinging to the shore of the mighty

---

* He was executed by the Italians at Benghazi in 1931.

continent, it was more a reflection of Europe than Africa, positioned at the rim of the timeless Mediterranean bowl. Intense white light glared from the surface of walls and perfect jewelled waters, striking from the harsh, lunar surface of the escarpment behind. The port nestled in the curve of a natural amphitheatre bounded, both east and west, by steep-sided defiles or *wadis*. Nearest to Tripoli is the Wadi Sehel, while towards Alexandria ran the wadis Zeitun and Belgassem. These features were the natural anchors for any defensive circuit thrown around the port.[1]

Inside this ring, two shallow escarpments rise like natural shelving, the first a mere 50 feet in height, the latter double that. Along the southern flank a third level butts in, reaches away and then swings back again south-westwards. The fringe of desert beyond remains relatively flat and open. Southwards, the real desert begins; stretching, it seems, into a wide infinity, lifting in the haze, with heat so stifling, space so vast, that it casts a blanket of torpor.

Along the coast ran the smart tarmac highway of the Via Balbia, a monument to the new empire of Rome, linking the coastal settlements to Tripoli and Tunis far to the west. Motoring westwards, the Derna Road section would take you straight into the town before looping southwards, one arm heading towards El Adem and the other striking east along the coast towards Bardia. The junction subsequently became known to Allied forces as King's Cross. Access to the escarpments was by a series of tracks leading up from the port. These were unmetalled and connected the outpost lines. Atop the first rise stood Fort Solaro with Fort Pilastrino covering the higher level beyond; Pilastrino stood at the hub of a network of tracks which linked key points in what would become the defensive ring. Beyond the perimeter was a moonscape of great slabs of shattered stone, whipped and scoured by the hot rasp of swirling dust that swept unchecked, on a daily basis in the furnace of summer, out of the deep heart of the desert beyond.

This ring covered some 16 miles, at any point 8 or 9 miles inland from the harbour, marked by wire and an incomplete anti-tank ditch. The line was studded with no fewer than 128 strongpoints, comprising an outer and inner series. The interior posts supported the front line, where the bunkers were grouped together as redoubts, 16 in all, with telephone lines linking them both to each other and the HQ (headquarters) position burrowed into the foot of the inner, Solaro escarpment.[2] Over this generally unassuming canvas some of the highest drama of the dramatic Desert War would be waged. For the Allies, Tobruk would be an objective, an inspiration, the pit of despair and scene of a brave but doomed folly – Operation *Agreement*.

There was also the Jewish Question. The sea passage from Tobruk to Alexandria covers 315 nautical miles; a further cruise of almost exactly the same distance will take you to Haifa, at that time in Palestine. Prior to 1918 and the collapse of Ottoman rule, the whole region was ruled from the Sublime Porte. Jewish settlers had begun to appear in Palestine in the nineteenth century and relations with their Arab neighbours were never particularly cordial. Zionism, the desire amongst certain Jews to create or recreate their traditional nation state in Palestine, was viewed as a threat. After the end of the First World War and the dismemberment of the Ottoman Empire, the threat increased.

In 1800 there were no more than 6,700 Jews in Palestine. By 1931 this number had increased 20-fold. The Balfour Declaration and the first phase of the British post-war mandate gave impetus to demands for a Jewish homeland. Zionists saw this as more of a British than an Arab problem. After all, it was they who now ruled. It was inevitable that tensions between the two communities, Jews and Arabs, would be ratcheted up as more Jewish immigrants arrived.

Quite early on the Zionists had resorted to forming a para-military wing, the Hashomer or 'Guardian', to protect their settlers from

Arab aggression. This developed into the Haganah.[3] After 1931, a group of more extreme Zionists founded the National Military Organization or Irgun. British efforts to cobble up some form of communal council foundered as attitudes hardened on both sides. In 1929 riots and bloodshed erupted. Having suffered pogroms in Hebron and other locations, the Jews relied more and more upon self-defence and on a belief that they could not share what they saw as their homeland with their Arab neighbours. The notion of partition with a mass expulsion of Arabs from an exclusively Jewish territory was in part supported by the Peel Commission of 1937.

Naturally, the whole business of Jewish immigration and the Zionist impulse was dramatically fuelled from 1933 by the developing terror in Nazi Germany. Jews in Germany had never been popular but were tolerated. In *Mein Kampf*, Hitler's incoherent, rambling manifesto, he set out his ambitions to cull the twin-headed hydra of Judaism and communism, which he happily bracketed together. In this, Hitler was playing to national paranoia and the 'stab in the back' theory that blamed European Jewry, particularly the banking cartel, for Germany's defeat in 1918. For a militarist, intensely nationalist state humiliated and maimed by Versailles, this provided some solace.

Eugenics, a popular perversion of science, had transformed the medieval intolerance of Judaism, based purely upon religion, into anti-Semitism, founded more upon principles and characteristics of race. There could be no redemption through conversion; the Jew was a different species, cancerous and unalterable. On 1 April 1933, a mass boycott of Jewish-owned businesses was imposed, with swaggering Sturmabteiling (SA) bullies intimidating those who might be tempted to ignore it. 'Jews, Out! Go to Palestine' and other slogans together with the Star of David were daubed on shop windows. It had begun.[4] This was the slide into mass murder that would reach its terrible nadir in Auschwitz and the other death camps.

As the Nazi death grip intensified, thousands of Jews fled to Palestine. By the end of 1933, some 5,392 Jews had sought exile in Palestine. Arab reaction was bloodily crushed by the British, further fuel for Nazi anti-British propaganda.[5] Despite a rising tide of hate across the Arab world, ably fanned from Germany, nearly 7,000 Jews reached Palestine in 1934. By the end of the following year, the year of the Nuremburg Laws that viciously enshrined anti-Semitism as a valid principle of German law, some 30,000 had fled there.[6]

The young Palestinian Jews who would fight for Britain in North Africa and play so important a role in Operation *Agreement* were not natural allies. Their cause, an independent state of Israel, brought them into direct conflict with the British and militant Zionists would revert to violent opposition to the British mandate after the war. For the moment however, both shared a common enemy, one sworn to obliterate the Jewish race. It was war to the death.

Sung to the tune of *Onward Christian Soldiers*

Onward Christian Soldiers,
You have nought to fear.
Israel Hore-Belisha
Will lead you from the rear.
Clothed by Monty Burton,
Fed on Lyons pies;
Die for Jewish freedom
As a Briton always dies.

CHAPTER ONE

LIONS OF JUDAH

On the balmy Mediterranean evening of 13 September 1942, a Royal Navy flotilla steamed towards the port of Tobruk. Much battered already, this ancient fortress town of Cyrenaica, home to the Senussi dynasty and Rommel's vital harbour, seemed still the invisible umbilical cord that connected his forces to supply from Italy. Sleek men of war, the destroyers *Sikh* and *Zulu* in the van and a gaggle of lesser craft jammed with Royal Marines, infantry and supporting specialists. The heat of the flaming late summer day had waned, mellowed by dusk and offshore breezes. The RN contingent was designated as Force A, the raiders Force C. Force B was already ashore; in fact it had never left land. Force B had trekked over 1,800 miles through enemy territory over hostile ground for the last seven days, their vehicles disguised with Axis decals.

A picked half-dozen commandos went immediately into action. Captain Herbert Cecil 'Bertie' Buck, with privates Rohr, Rozenzweig, Opprower, Goldstein and Hillman (for confusion over names, see chapter five), kicked down the doors of a coastal villa, an Italian trader's holiday home, their actions immediately persuading the handful of Mussolini's crack troops stationed there to depart with some urgency. Buck's squad belonged to the Special Interrogation Group (SIG), a suitably innocuous brand for what was a very irregular unit. If the men's names sound German, most of them were, but they were also Jews and likely Zionists. They had little cause to like the Germans of course, but were mainly at odds with the British. One thing was for sure, surrender was out of the question. They would fight, win or die.

Most of the generation who enjoyed war films in the 1960s will remember *Tobruk*, with Rock Hudson and George Peppard. This was a true blockbuster with lashings of violent action and a spectacular inferno of a finale when Rommel's entire fuel supply was blown off the screen. Whole chunks of this movie were borrowed for the later, lacklustre *Raid on Rommel*. This starred Richard Burton, in a far from memorable role.

The truth was very different and far more interesting. Operation *Agreement*, which forms the historical core behind *Tobruk* and the novel by Peter Rabe from which it was taken, is a very remarkable story indeed, virtually unique in the annals of war. The strap line for Rabe's book was *The impossible mission which turned into an incredible adventure*, and for once the blurb rang true. Two mutually antagonistic fighters, the British on one hand, Zionists on the other, came briefly together to defeat a common foe. Each recognized the manifest evil of Nazism. Once Germany was defeated, the battle for Palestine could be rejoined.

On 13 June 1942, British intelligence in the Western Desert intercepted the following message:

Most secret document – only to be opened by an officer – from Supreme Commander of the Army to Panzer Army Africa – are said to be numerous German political refugees with Free French forces in Africa. The Fuhrer has ordered that the severest measures are to be taken against those concerned. They are therefore to be immediately wiped out in battle and in cases where they escape being killed in battle, a military sentence is to be pronounced immediately by the nearest German officer and they are to be shot out of hand, unless they have to be temporarily retained for intelligence purposes. This order is NOT to be forwarded in writing; commanding officers are to be told verbally.[1]

The success of early raids, the actions of the commandos at Dieppe and a pinprick raid on Sark were later said to have provoked Hitler's infamous *Kommandobefehl* or Commando Order of 18 October 1942.[2] Commandos, even in uniform, were to be treated as spies and saboteurs and shot out of hand. When captured, they were to be handed over to the intelligence branch of the SS (Schutzstaffel), the Sicherheitsdienst or SD for short. The murder by firing squad of survivors from Operation *Frankton*, the Cockleshell Heroes, provided chilling clarity – this was no mere threat.

As a romantic from the school of G. A. Henty, Winston Churchill loved the idea of commandos, their mission to 'develop a reign of terror down the enemy coast'. After the humiliations of France and Norway, the prime minister's bulldog temperament demanded that Britain should not be supine. Harrying the enemy would force him to disperse his forces and give heart to those living under the jackboot. Most of his professional officers disagreed. 'Special Forces' was by no means a universally popular idea. Jews from Palestine were certainly not universally popular and the idea of a Jewish Special Forces unit was distinctly unpopular among the British military establishment.

The Balfour Declaration in November 1917 provided the framework for a Jewish homeland in Palestine. The British government was under swelling pressure from Zionists and anxious to keep Jewish money flowing into Allied coffers. Between the wars, relations between Jews, Arabs and the British in Palestine had deteriorated. Significant swathes of the British establishment were markedly pro-Arab, and the web of conflicting and ambiguous undertakings the war had spawned combined to place limitations on Jewish settlement. The Arabs were no more content. Serious confrontations broke out in 1922, 1929 and 1936, largely orchestrated by the rabidly anti-Zionist Haj Amin, mufti of Jerusalem.

As mentioned, frustrations with the British had led to the formation of what would in time become the Israel Defence Force (IDF), the Defence Organization or Irgun Hahaganah.[3] An underground faction, the Irgun Zvai Leumi (National Military Organization), or Irgun for short, was led by Menachem Begin, latterly head of state, and would, after 1945, be branded as a terrorist organization. An even more radical extremist faction, the Lehi or Stern Group, was prepared to carry out attacks against British servicemen.[4] Only the outbreak of war in 1939 prompted a form of truce. The more extreme Zionists remained opposed to British policy but recognized that Nazi Germany represented a far worse evil. The confrontation in Palestine would therefore be deferred. British and Zionists were allies by necessity only. Despite such a yawning divide, over 30,000 Palestinian Jews saw service with the Allies.[5]

Recruits into what would be No. 51 Commando, raised in October 1940, mostly came from the Auxiliary Military Pioneer Corps.[6] These commandos, commanded by Lieutenant-Colonel Henry 'Kid' Cater of the Royal Scots Greys, formed a battalion sized unit* and fought against the Italians in both Abyssinia and Eritrea before being absorbed into

---

* A typical commando battalion comprised 450 soldiers, divided in troops of 75, subdivided into 15-man sections: see T. R. Moreman, *British Commandos 1940–46* (Oxford, Osprey, 2006), p. 18.

what became Middle East Commando. This was a compromise notion of Churchill's, born out of a reorganization late in 1941. This followed on from the unfortunate experiences of 'Layforce'* on Crete where Bob Laycock's men had been thrown into the battle as an ad-hoc reserve that was both too little and too late. Miserable consequences followed and the commandos suffered accordingly.

Nonetheless, Churchill persisted with the commando concept. In late 1941, Middle East Commando was formed to sweep up earlier remnants into six troops. The first two went to David Stirling (the origins of what would become the Special Air Service (SAS)). Sixty members of 11 (Scottish) Commando formed a third troop. Two more troops made up 51 Commando and the final contingent went into the Special Boat Service (SBS).[7]

A significant number of the Jewish volunteers were native German speakers who had fled Hitler's persecution in the 1930s. Lieutenant-General Terence Airey from G(R) Branch or Military Intelligence Research was one who recognized the potential uses for Germans who were both implacable enemies of the Reich and already trained. Such attributes and such motivation formed a significant pairing.

Airey advised that these Jews could be:

... formed into a Special German Group as a sub-unit of M.E. Commando ... with the cover name 'Special Interrogation Group',[†]

---

* Colonel Robert Laycock had been given command of a rather ad-hoc formation of some 2,000 commandos, to all intents and purposes brigade strength. It had a perceived role carrying out raids in Axis territory, but the changing strategic position undermined this brave intent and the commandos were used very much as infantry.

† Some ambiguity exists as the force has also been called the Special Identification Group; see P. Smith, *Massacre at Tobruk* (Stackpole, PA, 2008) and Special Intelligence Group; see also E. Morris, *Guerrillas in Uniform* (London, Hutchinson, 1989). Morris refers to 'Identification Group' in the text but also to 'Intelligence Group' in his index.

to be used for infiltration behind the German lines in the Western Desert under 8th Army ... the strength of the Special Group would be approximately that of a platoon ... The personnel are fluent German linguists, mainly Palestinian Jews of German origin. Many of them have had war experience with 51 Commando ... It is essential they be provided with transport (a) one German staff car (b) two 15–cwt trucks.[8]

It is unlikely the SIG, now to form part of D Squadron 1st Special Service Regiment, ever reached full platoon strength. Maurice Teifenbrunner ('Tiffen') suggested to Martin Sugarman during an interview in 1997 that the actual ration strength was 38. Other veterans thought rather less.[9] From the outset they were an eclectic bunch; some came from the Free Czech forces (perhaps eight), the French Foreign Legion (maybe two), others from the ranks of the Free French. Several, Dov Cohen, Bernard Lowenthal and Israel Carmi, were former members of the Irgun. Of these, Carmi later served in the IDF.[10]

On 17 March 1942, 51 Middle East Commando, having returned from operations in Eritrea, was based out of the line at Burgh el Arab near Suez. Here Tiffen and his comrades first made the acquaintance of a British officer who was seeking fluent German speakers, Captain Herbert Cecil Buck MC of 3/1 Punjabis & Scots Guards. This meeting would prove significant.

Buck, of impeccable imperial stock, was already fluent in German, since he had been part educated there in the heady, hedonistic days of the Weimar Republic. His battalion, forming part of 4th Indian Division, trained in troubled Palestine. Whilst commanding a truckload of his Muslim soldiers, driving on the hot and dusty road between Tel Aviv and Haifa during the previous summer, he'd ordered his driver to stop and make room for two young female hitchhikers. Leah

Schlossberg was only 13, but she and Buck chatted amiably about the delights of peace and culture. Buck missed the opera but burgeoning Tel Aviv had claims to refinement. Bertie was invited home for tea.[11]

Parents today might be concerned when an officer in his twenties calls to escort their teenage daughter, but the Schlossbergs were enchanted. Bertie was captivating and cultivated, cosmopolitan and fluent: he was described as 'quiet, intellectual and absolutely brilliant. He spoke eight or nine languages'.[12] Buck's interest was not entirely social. A realization that German speakers could be found in Palestine had sparked the idea that would become SIG. Haganah already possessed a German-speaking section within its more militant wing, the Palmach.* Bertie wanted to get in touch with them, and Leah's older sister was dispatched to source collections of German martial songs, scouring Tel Aviv's second-hand bookshops.[13]

Buck's plans might have been derailed when, serving in the Western Desert, he was captured at Gazala late in the year. Despite being wounded and a long way behind enemy lines, he escaped, stripped the uniform from a dead Axis officer and made his way back to safety. This may have been an epiphany moment. A German speaker in a German uniform could bluff his way through virtually with impunity. The war diary for 51 Commando simply records the arrival of 'a Capt. Buck, to select German speaking personnel with a view to certain work.'[14] His second-in-command was Lieutenant David Russell of the Scots Guards, another fluent linguist with a guardsman's extravagant habits, including a preference for bespoke cognac foot-baths.

'Certain work' meant deploying German-speaking Jews, dressed as Axis soldiers, operating deep behind enemy lines. To describe

---

* Raised on 15 May 1941.

this as high risk would be something of an understatement. All armies take exception to their enemies assuming friendly guises for nefarious purposes, and Buck was under no illusions as to what fate lay in store for any who might be captured. A firing squad might be the least of their worries. High risk indeed, but Airey very much liked the idea.

As John Bierman and Colin Smith remind us, Churchill wanted 'ungentlemanly' warfare, and this was ruffianly in the extreme.* Airey reported:

> It is intended that this sub-unit should be used for infiltration behind the German lines ... They will frequently be dressed in German uniform and will operate under the command of a British officer who has already proved himself to be an expert in the German language.[15]

Airey now involved Major John ('Jock') Haselden, who despite having begun his wartime career with the Libyan Air Force (his civilian job was as a cotton trader), had transferred to a staff post involving him in early commando-style operations. At this time he was a temporary lieutenant-colonel leading SAS 'D' Squadron at Siwa. Airey's rather Heath Robinson idea was to have SIG posture in a captured Axis truck bristling with concealed weapons as a kind of Trojan Horse, which would open up on unsuspecting targets of opportunity, particularly staff cars, then roar off into the sunset, Bonnie and Clyde fashion.[16] This was indeed most ungentlemanly.

Buck was not looking to recruit exclusively from Middle East Commando or indeed from within Palmach; he also toured POW

---

* During the Ardennes Campaign in 1944, German commando impresario Otto Skorzeny infiltrated English-speaking commandos behind the lines in disguise as US soldiers. The Americans shot all they took prisoner.

camps. Here, he struck gold, or at least thought so. Feldwebel Walter Essner and Unteroffizier Heinrich Bruckner had both previously served in the French Foreign Legion before being drafted into the German forces. Each had served in 361st Regiment of Deutsches Afrika Korps (DAK) before being captured in November 1941. In the POW camp both had acted as informants, sufficient to convince military intelligence they were seriously anti-Nazi. Buck was taking an enormous gamble, but their inside knowledge of the DAK was of incalculable value in educating the fledgling SIG, helping them fit into the skins of their adversaries. Bluff, after all, was everything.

Tiffen, a native of Wiesbaden, had in fact only arrived in Palestine as an 'illegal' a few days before the war began.[17] Israel Carmi, also German by birth, was a senior NCO. Having won his spurs in the Palestine police, he had graduated to the Special Night Squads[18] and served with that most eccentric of charismatic visionaries, Orde Wingate. Ariyeh Shai was one of those who volunteered from 51 Commando.

Neither Tiffen nor any of his comrades was under any illusions as to the dangers they faced. Their preliminary training was arduous, as they recalled later:

Situated somewhere at the far end of an isolated group of desert encampments. We received no promises. Captain Buck had warned us that lives would depend on our ability to wear our disguises faultlessly, to learn to perfection the slang prevalent among the soldiers of the Afrika Korps, and to drill in accordance with all the German methods. 'If your true identity is found out,' said Buck, 'there is no chance for you.' [19]

One visitor to their otherwise highly secret training area was the 8th Army's senior Jewish chaplain, Isaac Levy. He later recalled his visit.

> I had been told that a somewhat unusual outfit was to be found in the vicinity of a vague map reference. Picking our way through a fairly clearly marked minefield, my driver and I ultimately discovered a special commando unit undergoing intensive training. Except for the CO [commanding officer], all were Palestinian Jewish volunteers. I met the men in a shed which was crammed full of German uniforms and equipment.
>
> I learned to my intense surprise and profound admiration that this unit was destined to be taken behind enemy lines for special commando operations and sabotage. All their activities were conducted in German, daily orders were published in that language and often in the dead of night a man would be suddenly awakened and he had to speak in German. None must be caught by surprise. These men knew the risks were they to fall into enemy hands, denied POW status. They would be shot out of hand; the most painfully distressing aspect of my encounter with these superbly brave men was the confidential information transmitted to me by several of them.[20]

Reveille was to the tones of 'Kompagnie anfsteher' – 20 minutes' exercise followed, then weapons training, demolitions, unarmed combat, random mock interrogations, enlivened by goose stepping and bursts of martial singing. They became accustomed to driving and maintaining captured Axis vehicles. They wore German uniforms, carried German kit, and their photos all showed suitably Teutonic girlfriends.*

---

* In fact, these were ATS volunteers, chosen for their suitability.

The SIG lived apart. They were, in every sense, separate. Their weapons were German, MP 40s, Walther and Luger automatic pistols. Whatever their doubts about the two defectors, both Shai and Carmi recognized their worth as instructors. They revered Buck but considered him 'a little naive'.[21] In this they were to be proved correct.

Life in Mersa Matruh during their three months' intensive training was not entirely devoid of creature comforts. Buck travelled to Palestine with the blond twenty-something Bruckner in tow. Leah Schlossberg was impressed and motored with the pair to Jerusalem, where they dined with Major Aubrey (Abba) Eban, latterly Israeli Foreign Minister. This rather *laissez-faire* attitude to security appears archaic, and Buck's trust in the ex-legionnaire was to reap a bitter harvest.

The group's initial forays into the field were fairly low key. Utilizing German transport, they penetrated behind the lines near Bardia, setting up dummy roadblocks. Such irksome inconveniences were part and parcel of daily life in the Afrika Korps. In the guise of Feldgendarmerie they questioned vexed drivers and garnered useful information. This ostensibly humdrum work could provide valuable dividends. Tiffen confided to Martin Sugarman that the SIG would pull over at desert halts and engage in conversations. They'd infiltrate groups of POWs and, on one occasion, he had the nerve to queue for wages from an Axis quartermaster. Churchill would have loved it! Whether any active sabotage was undertaken remains unclear, but at least one author believes this was the case.[22] This was the proving time. The stakes were about to be dramatically raised.

SIG was to graduate from intelligence gathering to offensive operations in June 1942. David Stirling was planning a raid against Axis coastal aerodromes, Derna and Martuba, a hundred miles west of Tobruk. Attacking enemy planes not only assisted in the desperate battle to save Malta, but obliged the Axis to shift more resources into airfield protection. Buck, when approached, was enthusiastic; this was a mark his group was coming of age.[23]

Siwa Oasis was fixed as the rendezvous (RV) and the attacking force was to depart no later than 8 June, to be in position by the night of the 13th/14th. The Free French Squadron would provide 14 troopers and a single officer, Lieutenant Augustine Jordain. The SAS would lurk in the rear of captured trucks with one command vehicle, probably a Kubelwagen.[*] The shroud of secrecy over SIG operations continued to lie so thick that there is some dispute as to the number of SIG personnel, which varies from eight to 12.[†]

On 6 June, the combined force rumbled out of Siwa, guided by a New Zealand patrol from the LRDG.[‡] Having set their dangerous flock on course, the LRDG shepherds would wait at an agreed RV to guide them back. After four days in the desert, the SIG changed into their Axis uniforms, a decisive act, moving them beyond the pale of the Geneva Convention, from soldiers to saboteurs. From this point on they could expect no quarter. Bertie Buck dressed as an enlisted man, driving the VW with the two ex-legionnaires as NCOs. Ariyeh Shai and Adolf Schubert made up the team. Each of the trucks had an SIG, well armed, as mounted lookout and the Free French 'prisoners' kept hidden grenades and .45 pistols. Machine guns, discreetly under cover, were at the ready.[§]

---

[*] A militarized version of the ubiquitous VW Beetle.

[†] Sugarman (p. 159) summarizes the conflicting views. Cowles asserts that there were four vehicles, the jeep, two German trucks and a captured British lorry used by the Germans (entirely plausible). Tiffen, however, remembers a dozen SIG, four in each of two 'captured' trucks and the rest in the VW. He also recalls that the Jews were posing as Afrika Korps and the SAS as their prisoners. Morris follows Tiffen in this.

[‡] Patrol designated R1 under Captain A. I. Guild.

[§] Cowles, pp. 136–37. It seems the SIGs had MP 40s and 9mm Luger Parabellum pistols and that bayonets had been filed to offer a double-edged blade, suitable as a fighting knife. Sugarman (p. 159) refers to the French having 'automatic revolvers', clearly a misnomer, and it is unlikely they were carrying the Webley-Fosberry; it probably refers therefore to Colt .45 pistols.

The 'captured' British truck broke down and Buck was obliged to provide a tow. This was just the beginning of their difficulties. They came to a roadblock, manned by Italians who demanded the current password. Buck did not have a password. The obdurate private at the barrier summoned his superior and despite much geniality and hospitable *vino*, would not let the raiders pass. Buck and Bruckner stuck to their cover story: they had just emerged from the desert and had to get their vehicles and prisoners back to Derna. Finally, Bruckner exploded in a well-staged burst of Germanic fury, something not unfamiliar to their hosts, and, suitably cowed, the Italians raised the barrier. The bluff was working.[24]

As dusk fell, the column ran into another checkpoint, this time manned by a portly German NCO who offered a helpful warning that 'British commandos reach even out here' – any irony was clearly unintentional. They were advised to leaguer in a nearby transit camp. Dutifully Buck complied. Here they fuelled up, took on stores and generally mingled, while Corporal Schubert cheekily queued for his Afrika Korps supper of lentils and dumplings. Not wanting to push their luck, they discreetly moved beyond the leaguer and sought less crowded overnight accommodation.[25]

On 13 June in the afternoon, just as shadows began to deepen and the furnace heat had abated, the commandos prepared to recce their designated targets. Bruckner, with four of the Free French led by Lt Jordain, spied out one aerodrome, home to a squadron of Messerschmitt Bf 110s* and another with Junkers Ju 87s.† Having made a reconnaissance of the Derna fields they were more circumspect and did not venture too close to Martuba for fear of arousing suspicion, though the aerodromes

---

* A twin-engine heavy fighter.
† A two-man ground attack aircraft or dive bomber, the infamous 'Stuka'.

here appeared to house more ME 110s. By 1730 hours the recce patrol was back. They would attack that night.

Having the right password was essential. They couldn't rely on simply blustering their way out of another tight corner. As ever, there are two versions as to what happened next. The first is that Bruckner and Essner simply walked up to a German post and asked (the challenge was 'Siesta' and the reply 'Eldorado'). Cowles insists that Buck typed a letter of request which two SIG took to the stout NCO they'd encountered the day before. The corporal, who clearly took a relaxed attitude, couldn't remember the right words, which all found amusing, or pretended to. A passing Italian was accosted. He obligingly consulted his codebook for orders of the day and provided the correct answer.

As they made ready, concealed some five miles from the targets at Derna, at the location which would provide the post-operation RV, they passed the tipping point. There was no going back. They were now fully committed. Buck, Shai and Essner, and three other SIG with five of the Free French, would strike at Martuba. Jordain, Bruckner, three SIG* and nine Frenchmen, divided into two squads, would hit Derna. Tiffen is clear that Buck went with the assault group to Martuba (Swinson disagrees[26]), whilst it was Tiffen himself who remained behind with a single SIG comrade as the base/liaison team.

Buck and Essner got away without difficulty. The second group did not set off till 2100 hours. Jordain's section would be the first to deploy on target and then Corporal Bourmont's party would hit the second aerodrome. As the truck chugged through Derna itself, Bruckner, who had been driving, stopped the vehicle, ostensibly as he thought (or claimed to think) it was overheating. The ex-legionnaire, ex-Afrika-Korps SIG, alighted and disappeared into what was either an Axis post

---

* These were Peter Hass (Hess?) and Peter Gottlieb.

or possibly garage/workshop. They'd pulled up just outside a makeshift cinema and apparently the sound of the projector running was clearly audible inside the truck.[27] Another account states that Bruckner got out on the pretence something had dropped off the back and needed to be retrieved. Off into the night he went. Those who had been uneasy previously were uneasy still, and rightly so.

Suddenly, the truck was surrounded by heavily armed Germans. 'All Frenchmen out!' they yelled. Jordain, in the cab, was dragged out.[28] The SAS were not about to submit; they preferred, despite the odds, to shoot it out, and a savage fire-fight erupted. Inevitably, this was very one-sided, but Jordain managed to get clear. Hass/Hess was last seen chucking grenades at the enemy, saving the final one for himself. Brave as the SAS/ SIG might be, the outcome was never in doubt. Again accounts differ as to whether Jordain, certainly wounded, was alone when he stumbled back to the RV. A number of the Free French might have got away in the dark, but all were later captured.[29]

Unaware of the tragedy unfolding behind, Buck's section had completed their mission, destroying a score of Axis planes. Any exultation was short-lived, though, a bitter pill for Bertie Buck that his men's fears about Bruckner had been so fully justified. The survivors drove off back towards Siwa. For a week they camped at Baltel Zalegh, hoping for stragglers; none came. Tiffen remembered they managed to dupe a prowling Axis aircraft by laying out a souvenir Swastika flag.[30]

Corroboration of Bruckner's treachery came from two downed Luftwaffe pilots, Leutnant Friederich Korner and Oberleutnant Ernest Klager.* Both aviators claimed that the DAK already knew of the planned raid and were on high alert. Lt Korner confirmed this:

---

* Both flew ME 109s and were shot down during the First El Alamein battle, in early July 1942: PRO WO 201/727.

Bruckner got out of the truck, saluted the German NCO and stated that he was a German soldier acting as driver of a German lorry containing a party of heavily armed English troops in German uniform with explosive charges to destroy aircraft. The CO was rather suspicious at first but the driver pressed him to organize as many men as possible with all speed and as heavily armed as possible to disarm the raiding party. The lorry was immediately surrounded and the occupants forced to get out. A few seconds after the last one had got out there was an explosion inside the lorry and it was completely destroyed. A melee developed and it was believed that all the raiders had been shot.[31]

The captured fliers confirmed that a wounded man had attended Derna Field Hospital the following morning. He was interrogated after the medical staff (for whatever reason), became suspicious; he was SIG. Tiffen believed, as he confided to Martin Sugarman, that two SIG had escaped the gun battle but were both later captured and shot. This would appear to confirm that, in at least one instance, he was right.[32]

Bruckner apparently used the story he'd been recruited as a POW (true enough) but that he'd just gone along with Buck so he could get a chance to escape and strike a blow for the Fatherland. Whether this was true or whether he'd simply suffered a crisis of nerves in Derna and defected can only be guessed at. Buck seemed to believe that Bruckner might have died in the exchange of fire, wishful thinking perhaps, though he made the claim in his after action report.[33] It seems more probable he survived and was decorated for his role, possibly by the Desert Fox himself. One account[34] suggests he returned to active service during the Tunisian campaign and was captured again, this time by the Americans, but his treachery still did not catch up with him. After the war, the French simply let him go and he re-enlisted in the Foreign Legion. Fears of retribution stalked him certainly into the 1960s.

Tiffin and Buck had disagreed over the German duo. The former insisted they were useful, even invaluable, for training purposes, but should not be given any operational role. Buck stuck to his guns, according to information now in the National Archives.

> He relied on the clean bill military intelligence had given to both. He believed the admitted gamble was a necessary risk for training purposes and initial operations to have men who had recently been in the German Army and knew the ropes. [Bruckner and Essner] had provided intelligence with very valuable information about German dispositions and had extracted information from many POWs.[35]

Given how Bruckner had performed during the early stages, and the fact that Essner never wavered, it is quite possible he simply panicked in Derna: both were under very considerable stress. Defectors were unlikely to receive a sympathetic hearing.

Essner was damned by association. He had shown no signs of defection, but Buck clearly felt, after his humiliation, that the other ex-legionnaire couldn't be trusted. Carmi later confirmed he and Shai were detailed to take Essner back to a POW camp but that he wasn't intended ever to arrive. He would be 'shot whilst trying to escape' en route, as Carmi recalled. Carmi gave the necessary order; Shai pulled the trigger.[36]

The SIG had been fully blooded and lessons had been learnt; now further and greater tests awaited them.

sung to the tune of *Colonel Bogey*

Hitler has only got one ball,
Goering's got two but very small,
Himmler is very similar,
And poor old Goebbels' got no balls at all.

Frankfurt has only one beer hall
Stuttgart, die Munchen all on call,
Munich, vee lift up our tunich,
To show vee 'Chermans' have no balls at all

Anon, *Hitler has only got one ball*

CHAPTER TWO

WAR WITHOUT HATE

Fighting in the Western Desert was a very different proposition from war in other theatres. Aside from the impact of climate and topography, there was the emptiness; 'pure' war (not involving civilians), as it might be described by theoreticians. All this vast space was home to very few inhabitants and most of those were clustered in the coastal towns and scattering of oases. The nomadic Bedouin were few in number and passed like wraiths over the scarred and scoured wastes, like people from another time. It had not always been so: the deserts used to bloom and man had left tantalizing glimpses of his ancient presence, the imprint of his hand upon the rock. Far-flung raiders would, in the very heart of the desolation, come across traces of cave paintings that whispered man had been here long before, ten thousand years ago, but only those traces remained.

The desert (known as 'the Blue') threw up a whole compendium of horrors to hinder military activity and increase the misery of individual combatants. For these soldiers, British and Dominion, German, Italian, French, Greek and others, it seemed they had arrived in the very cauldron of a particular version of hell. The history of the Desert War from 1940 to the end of 1942 unfolds primarily in the Libyan Desert, a natural amphitheatre, in which large armies wheeled and charged, stood at bay, gave and took ground. Men poured out their lifeblood over featureless, rock-strewn ridges barely showing above the scorched desert floor. Tanks, like dusty men of war, cruised and fought, largely untroubled by the human landscape that defined other battlefields. The war poet Keith Douglas, one of the 'Cairo group' of contemporary poets, described the desert in evocative terms:

> The bald head is a desert
> between country of life and country of death
> between the desolate projecting ears
> move the wicked explorers the flies
> who know the dead bone is beneath
> and from the skin the life half out.[1]

In contrast, along the Mediterranean coast runs a narrow littoral of pleasant and cultivated land, the fertile coastal strip, along which most of the main settlements are situated. Tobruk was one of these, isolated from the desert behind and looking over the sea towards Italy and Sicily. Bernard Spencer, another of the Cairo group, reflects on this sea-scape:

> To sun one's bones beside the
> Explosive, crushed-blue, nostril-opening sea
> (The weaving sea, splintered with sails and foam,

Familiar of famous and deserted harbours,

Of coins with dolphins on and fallen pillars).[2]

This agreeable plain is bounded inland by a line of limestone cliffs, steep and bare, pierced with narrow defiles or wadis. This creates a formidable barrier, impassable to most wheeled vehicles. Atop the cliffs and running southwards in a gentle decline is a bare plateau, scorched by the hot sun and burnished by millennia of harsh winds. The surface comprises rock and layered grit, like the topping on a primeval cake, varying in depth from feet to inches. Where the base rock is denser, low hills have been left, insignificant humps or irregular ridges, possession of which was to be vital to the armies and demand a vast sacrifice in blood and materiel.

Where the limestone is more friable, depressions of varying size create undulations. These can form either obstacles or handy defences. Of all these pits in the desert floor the largest is the vast Qattara, which lies to the south of the plateau, forming an impassable inland sea several hundred yards below the escarpment, bounded by steep cliffs with salt-marsh below. As one moves southwards towards this great depression the unyielding surface of the plateau gives way to a rolling, almost dizzying series of dunes.

This, perhaps, is nearest to the classic image of the desert landscape so beloved of film-makers. Theses dunes arise some 50 miles inland and the ground considerably restricts movement of large forces. Thus the armies were penned into the area between the coast and the dunes, a relatively narrow battlefield in so wide a landscape. This was never more than 70 miles in width but stretched for a thousand miles and more east and west, creating a very thin oblong.

Of man-made roads running east to west there was only one, the Via Balbia mentioned previously. This stretched from Tripoli through

Sirte, El Agheila, Benghazi, Derna, Gazala, Tobruk and Bardia to Sollum. Westwards lay Sidi Barrani, Mersa Matruh and Fuka. West of the Nile Delta stood the insignificant rail halt of El Alamein and three score miles or so to the east the great jewel of Alexandria, gateway to the fertile sweep of the Nile. Among the Libyan coastal settlements only Tripoli, Benghazi and Tobruk had significant harbours.

For transit north–south there were only local track-ways (*trigh*). These were not hard-surfaced but beaten paths linking oases, hammered out by centuries of human and camel traffic.* Clearly, these had never been intended for wheeled vehicles and the passage of motorized convoys punished the surface, leaving a chaos of endless ruts. To avoid these drivers tended to edge their vehicles to the side, thus beating an ever-widening path. When the winter rains deluged the *trigh*, surfaces turned into a glutinous and unnavigable soup. Where these routes crossed, the location naturally assumed a clear local significance often marked by a saintly burial (denoted by the prefix 'Sidi').

Such places became natural foci for area defence or supply stations. Fighting in the largely featureless desert placed a premium on navigation, demanding an exact use of the compass. In this, the work previously undertaken by pre-war cartographers was particularly useful. Mapping the desert had an appreciable provenance, beginning with Herodotus. Classical and medieval travellers were followed by the British. The Italians too had made maps but, in many cases, these were simply grandiose fantasies, inaccurate at best where not actually misleading.

During the inter-war years, much work had been done by an eclectic group including two Englishmen who were both destined to create and also serve in the Long Range Desert Group, Ralph

---

* The trigh had previously only been trodden by travellers and camels.

Bagnold* and Pat Clayton.† One of the more colourful of this exotic bunch was the Hungarian Lazlo Almasy.‡ Thanks to their combined efforts the otherwise empty canvas of the desert was marked out using the network of ancient trails, with every feature in an otherwise bare landscape plotted and surveyed. The white bones of escarpments, sunken depressions, oases, salt marshes and dry wadis that could spring to brilliant life after rains were all shown.

In the pre-war work of these bold pioneers lay the seeds of Operation *Agreement*. The idea of a deep penetration leading to an overland approach from the desert was something Axis commanders would not expect. It wasn't just that Bagnold, Clayton and those who followed had form within the desert: it was their outlook. To conventional soldiers, especially those as literally minded as the Wehrmacht, the idea of a gang of eccentrics in uniform operating out on a limb, hundreds if not thousands of miles from formal command and control structures, was unthinkable to the point of heresy. The desert was a forbidden waste, not a back garden. Even after the failure of Operation *Agreement*, the Axis failed to grasp that part of the attacking force had come from the desert rather than from the sea.

---

* Ralph Algar Bagnold (1896–1990) was the guiding spirit behind and the first commander of LRDG, one of the great pioneers of desert exploration during the 1930s. He laid the foundations for the research on sand transport by wind in his influential book *The Physics of Blown Sand and Desert Dunes* (first published 1941), which remains an established reference in the field. It has been used by agencies such as NASA in studying sand dunes on Mars.

† Patrick Andrew Clayton (1896–1962) spent nearly 20 years with the Egyptian Survey department during the 1920s and 1930s extensively mapping large areas of previously unmapped desert. At the outset of the war he was working as a government surveyor in Tanganyika. Bagnold had him brought back to Egypt because of his detailed knowledge of the Western Desert. He was commissioned into the Intelligence Corps. Clayton was leading T Patrol in a planned attack on Kufra when the patrol was engaged by the Italian Auto-Saharan Company on 31 January 1941 near Gebel Sherif. He was wounded and captured.

‡ Count Lazlo Almasy (1895–1951), the real life version of the fictional character immortalized in *The English Patient*, whose life was, if anything, even more colourful.

Desert is hard on footsloggers; it's also hard on vehicles, both soft-skinned and armoured. That the infantry who fought in the desert campaigns should resent their comrades in tanks is understandable, however. An armoured vehicle could be used to transport a whole range of sought after commodities and offered the crew an easy route back to leaguer or the fleshpots of Egypt. In addition to the normal perils of being under enemy fire and the hidden hazard of mines, there were flies in abundance and numerous forms of disease plus the odd poisonous snake or scorpion. The terrain was barren, scorched, featureless, waterless and invincibly hostile to man.

It must at times have seemed almost unbelievable that such titanic efforts were exerted by both sides to win these arid, seemingly endless acres. For the most part infantry inhabited trenches, much as their fathers had done on the Western Front, though these were less permanent affairs. To dig down into sand was not difficult, but where the surface had been whittled away by wind and the limestone exposed, powered tools were necessary to gouge out shallow trenches and fox-holes that were supported by a rough parapet of stones, called *sangars*.*

Battles were large and terrifying, though relatively rare. Smaller actions at platoon or company level were far more common, and there was a constant need for patrolling, either light reconnaissance or the beefier and bristling fighting patrol. As combatants recalled:

Recce patrols were messy affairs if we had to go through the pockets of some poor devil who had been killed and had been left lying out in the sand for a couple of days. People talk about rigor mortis, but

---

* *Sangar* comes from the Northwest Frontier and denotes any small temporary fortification made up of stone and perhaps sandbagged walls.

after a day or two the limbs were flexible again and indeed, after a week or so, a quick pull on an arm or leg would detach it from the torso. Two day old corpses were already fly blown and stinking. There was no dignity in death, only masses of flies and maggots.[3]

For the raiders, their endeavours were generally far easier to grasp than the role of the ordinary Tommy. LRDG troopers were fully briefed on operations. In specialist units, the distances of rank shrank exponentially for each soldier; officers and enlisted men were specialists in their own right. Patrols carried highly proficient drivers and vehicle fitters, wireless operators, navigators, armourers and paramedics. Every man's survival depended upon the rest and vice versa. On patrol, there was no higher chain of command, no spit and polish, none of the regular 'bull' of army life. Equally, there was nowhere to run and no one to blame, no room for bullshit and nobody to pass the buck to.

For the majority of the young men who served in these campaigns, any form of overseas travel, indeed any travel at all, was a novelty. To such innocents the Levant appeared a distant and exotic place, as driver Robert Crawford remembered:

> Waiting for a taxi, I breathed the spicy, flaccid atmosphere of the city and felt the strangeness of things about me. The street lamps were painted blue. Figures in white robes, like night shirts, flickered through the blue gloom, slippers flapping from heels; the women, bundled in black, were scarcely visible.[4]

Few could deny that their apprehensions were overlaid by a sense of adventure and at first their destination appeared almost delightful, as Crawford shows.

As we clambered ashore we stamped and rubbed our feet delightedly … We ran the sand slowly through our fingers; it was warm and real and comforting. I could never have believed then that I would hate this self-same sand so bitterly; the crumbled, remorseless rock that sucked at the lifeblood of us who tried to master her vastness in the following months.[5]

In such surroundings, the comradeship of war was inevitably heightened. Men might express fine sentiments and extol the nobility of sacrifice, but such poetic expressions soon wilted in the face of reality. This war involved endless hours of tedium, dirty, sweaty, beset by a constant and ravenous horde of flies, troubled by looseness of the bowels and all the other complaints that add endless misery to a soldier's life, enlivened only by odd moments of sheer terror. The code of behaviour that evolved was dictated by pure pragmatism. Terence Tiller described their life:

They sit like shrubs among the cans and desert thistles
in the tree's broken shade and the sea-glare
strange violent men, with dirty unfamiliar muscles,
sweating down the brown breast, wanting girls and beer.
The branches shake down sand along a crawling air,
and drinks are miles towards the sun
and Molly and Polly and Pam are gone.[6]

Discipline was essential, though the fire of combat tempered the parade ground bellowing of peacetime and the drill sergeant into a more business-like focus. Crawford remembered that:

Discipline such as we had formerly known disappeared. In its place came a companionship. Officers no longer issued orders in the old manner. They were more friendly and more with the men. They realized that this was a team. We, for our part, never took advantage of this new association. While orders were given, except in emergency, more in the nature of requests, they were obeyed even more punctiliously than under peacetime conditions. It was a case of every man pulling together, willingly. From what we had seen of the German Army, no such relationship existed, and it was not long before we discovered this was our strength.[7]

*Krieg ohne Hass** was a description attributed to Rommel himself, and insofar as war can ever truly be said to represent chivalry, then it was here. The British had a high regard for the Desert Fox, both as a fighting soldier of the highest calibre and a man of impeccable honour. Soldiers were wryly amused by stories that circulated about Rommel, such as the tale that Hitler had secretly contacted Churchill with the offer to remove Rommel from his command in return for Churchill retaining all his generals in theirs.[8]

Though soldiers in the line observed a strict blackout procedure, the sky to the east was lit up with the rich glow of the Delta cities. The brightness and gaiety of easy living these represented could not have contrasted more tellingly with the drab but dangerous austerity of the front. The contrast between the rigours of the line and the luxury of Cairo, the 'unreal city,' could not have been greater.

For those in command of British forces in the Middle East, before the inspired appointment of General Archibald Wavell,[†] the desert

---

* Translated as 'war without hate'.

† Sir Archibald Wavell, 1st Earl Wavell GCB, GCSI, GCIE, CMG, MC, PC (1883–1950) spent his formative years in India and studied at Winchester and Sandhurst, following his father into an army career and being commissioned into the Black Watch. He served in the South African War, in Russia as an observer and then through the First World War, losing an eye at the Second Battle of Ypres in 1915. He served in a succession of staff roles and in

was something to be feared as hot, limitless and nasty, no fit ground for regular soldiers to fight over. The Axis high command generally maintained a similar view. This was in part understandable. The Western Desert is the size of India and the notion of moving large bodies of men with vehicles and cumbersome gas-guzzling armour over such broken and arid terrain seemed incomprehensible. It was Britain's extremely good fortune to possess a cadre of officers for whom the desert was their natural habitat, a remarkable and formidable band of brothers whose creation, the LRDG, would be both a significant step in winning the Desert War and would also validate the concept of Special Forces.

A commando is defined as 'a soldier specially trained for carrying out raids'.[9] The origin of the term commando probably dates back to the South African War of 1899–1902, where small groups of Boer farmers/guerrillas waged asymmetric and highly effective war on the British after the collapse of their field armies. Over a century earlier, Rogers' Rangers, operating in the untamed American wilderness, had formed a behind-the-lines unit which used stealth, camouflage and field-craft to inflict defeat upon their French and Indian adversaries. These were ad-hoc solutions to local tactical problems, however. Once the wars were over, these lessons tended to be overlooked.

To many a regular martinet the idea of Special Forces equated more to a breed of 'special needs' – mavericks and gamblers who siphoned off good men and precious resources only to hazard both in madcap enterprises, doomed to fail. On the other hand, raiding to harrass the enemy was a well-tried tactic. The idea that British forces should dominate the wider battlefield by attacking the adversary at

---

GSO1 (General Staff Officer Grade 1) appointments during the inter-war years. In 1937 he was promoted GOC (General Officer Commanding) British forces in Palestine and Trans-Jordan. His appointment to GOC Middle East came in August 1939.

all points of the compass made sound tactical sense. On the Western Front, in the previous war, it had been policy to seek to dominate no-man's-land by constant and aggressive patrolling. Such blows were delivered under the hand of senior command, controlled through division, brigade and battalion, down to platoon and section levels. That a company of free lances might be turned loose upon the enemy, behind the lines, free from all restraint, was a very different concept.

Insofar as the desert was concerned, there was a sound operational precedent, again from the First World War. The long umbilical cord of the Nile Valley was exposed to attacks by the Senussi, stirred up by the Turks and coming eastwards out of Libya. These famous desert warriors, fighting almost literally in their own backyard, were hard to beat. Regular columns of infantry and cavalry were too slow, too cumbersome and hard to supply. The solution lay in the creation of the Light Car Patrols. These employed the famous Model T Ford, a variation even Henry Ford might not have dreamed of. Vehicles gave mobility and firepower. The Senussi were impressed and quietened. Aside from the concept of a mobile desert force, the Light Car Patrol contributed two invaluable innovations, the sun compass[*] and water condenser.[†] Both, harnessed and refined by Ralph Bagnold, would empower the LRDG.

A fortuitous accident at sea left Bagnold in the Delta. He quickly penned a synopsis of his idea for a mobile strike force and laid this before Middle East Command. Nobody was listening then, and nobody did so until the Italians entered the war and Wavell took over. This

---

[*] Bagnold had also developed the sun-compass which greatly facilitated navigation in the desert (see chapter six).

[†] A key innovation, unique to the desert and upgraded ingeniously by Bagnold himself, was the condenser, which bypassed the usual steam overflow and piped it into storage tanks on the running boards, from where the liquid could be recycled.

general was ready to listen as Bagnold outlined the risks of a potential enemy raid on Aswan coming out of Uweinat. The distance was no greater than five hundred miles and he himself had covered this in only a day and a half.

The potential for damage was enormous, and in their Major Orlando Lorenzini (an enterprising officer Bagnold had encountered during his desert explorations), the Italians possessed a capable leader who had openly boasted he could achieve just this. As a counter, Bagnold proposed raising a small, specially equipped band of volunteers who would have the capability to cross 1,500 miles of ground without re-supply. Bagnold knew the desert like his own back garden. For him and men like him it held no terrors. The key function of the Long Range Patrol (LRP) as it was first known was quite straightforward.

This new unit's primary role would be to carry out deep reconnaissance and intelligence gathering. Wavell then enquired what would happen if the group discovered little of interest: 'How about some piracy on the high desert?', Bagnold suggested. Bagnold later recalled: 'At the word piracy the rugged face that had seemed a bit stern suddenly broke into a broad grin. "Can you be ready in six weeks?" – I said, "Yes".'[10] Before the end of June 1940, the major's revised scheme was approved and the basic building blocks assembled.[11] As Bagnold put it:

> Although most of us were young army officers, not one of us in the 1920s dreamed for a moment that war would ever come to the vast, waterless and lifeless Libyan Desert. We simply enjoyed the excitement of pioneering into the unknown ... HQ British Troops in Egypt [BTE] was just the same as I had known it. Its role having long been confined to internal security, it seemed as yet to have given no thought to the defence of the country against attack from outside.[12]

Major Bagnold was next handed a potent talisman, *carte blanche* signed by Wavell himself. This was a magician's wand that cut through all of the normal laborious and highly unco-operative channels. A cadre of able volunteers was not hard to find. Many of Bagnold's pre-war contacts were straining at the leash as soon as the green light was given. Experienced hands such as Bill Kennedy Shaw* and Pat Clayton (surveying in Tanganyika) were rescued from mundane assignments and threw themselves into the Herculean task with vast enthusiasm.

It must be stressed that, from the outset, Bagnold's commandos saw their prime role as intelligence gathering rather than offensive action, attacking the enemy. Across this limitless expanse, knowledge of the enemy's strength and likely intentions was invaluable. To undertake such a vital function, both the right men and the right kit were absolutely essential. Regular soldiers, drawn from the urban sprawl, were not ideal, as they tended to be too rigid, too conformist and unused to so alien and harsh a battleground. Far more useful were countrymen and farmers, gamekeepers (and poachers), hunters and marksmen, who were to be found amongst Kiwis and Rhodesians, in British Yeomanry regiments and even within the august ranks of the Guards.[13] As one founding soldier later recalled:

General Freyberg agreed to ask his New Zealand Division for volunteers for an 'undisclosed mission of some danger'. There was a

---

* William Boyd Kennedy Shaw (1901–79). Between the wars Kennedy Shaw contributed to the exploration of the Libyan Desert in the area around the south-western corner of modern Egypt with his particular interest and skills as a botanist, archaeologist and navigator. He made three major trips. Bagnold recruited him as the intelligence and chief navigation officer for LRDG. Kennedy Shaw was transferred to the Intelligence Corps in 1940 and latterly served with the SAS. He wrote one of the earliest books on the LRDG, Long Range Desert Group, immediately after the war.

great response. Two officers and some 150 other ranks we had asked for arrived just as the first trucks were coming out of the workshops – tough, self-reliant and responsible people with many useful skills. They were just what we'd hoped for.[14]

Bill Kennedy Shaw drew up a balance sheet for life in the LRP, pros and cons. On the credit side there were excellent rations, no chance for boredom, blessed relief from normal army 'bull' and little or no 'mucking about'. Desert soldiers were always very aware of just how much they were in fact 'mucked about'. On the debit side of the balance sheet, there was the constant stress of behind the lines action, tiredness (frequently to the point of exhaustion) and all the natural hazards of daily life in the desert, including *cafard* (literally 'cockroach', a condition of apathy and depression brought on by exposure to the sun).[15]

One of the staples of the LRDG, the Chevy 30-cwt truck was the backstairs child of compromise. Begged or borrowed from local dealers in the Delta or from the Egyptian Army, these were standard commercial vehicles that could be heavily customized for the harsh rigours of desert warfare. Stripped down to bare skeletons, their load carrying capacity beefed up to a couple of tons by additional springs, fitted out for weapons and ammunition, wireless and medical gear, rigs welded on to take heavy and medium machine guns and the ingenious adaptation of the radiator condenser, the Chevy went to war. Surveyor's instruments, binoculars and the all-essential sun-compasses were cadged or scrounged from any and every source.

What made the LRDG so successful was not just the courage and fortitude of the individual troopers. This was both considerable and constant. Ultimately, the performance of a unit depends upon the calibre of men who serve, and in the case of LRDG this was very high indeed. They set the benchmark for other Special Forces at the time and since. Having Bagnold, Clayton, Bill Kennedy Shaw and Guy Prendergast (another founder member, drawn from the Royal Tank Regiment) as mentors was an enormous boost, as their combined skills and experiences were prodigious. Moreover, they lived and breathed the desert. It held no terrors for them: rather, they worshipped its open expanses, the heaven-sent dawn and the cool benison of gilded dusk.

What they also possessed were specialized vehicles – not bespoke, to be sure, but the very best compromise, ingenious kit such as the sun compass and water condenser and an abundance of firepower. Their trucks were seriously well armed with .303 Lewis and Vickers light and medium machine guns, .50 cal. weapons, the 37mm Bofors and for choice the 20mm Breda, as well as a real speciality, the twin-mounted Vickers K, capable of devastating rates of fire.

They were desert warriors in the footsteps of T. E. Lawrence but equipped and armed for industrial warfare. They could outrun what they couldn't outfight and outfight what they couldn't outrun. They punched well above their weight and consistently delivered first class intelligence. Their attacks on enemy positions and transport, 'beat ups' as they called them, inflicted only minor actual damage but produced a morale effect on both sides that was infinitely greater. Rommel praised them: as endorsements go, they don't come much better.

By any standards the LRDG was a remarkable and utterly professional fighting force, a perfect complement to regular operations. Yet Bagnold and his buccaneers were not completely alone. A slew of other units jostled for a place in the unconventional underbelly of desert warfare. First amongst these were the commandos. Colonel Robert

('Bob') Laycock* commanded Nos 8 & 11 Commando. Laycock was born into a military family, and then commissioned into the Horse Guards. His first wartime appointment was responsibility for chemical warfare during the battle for France, an inauspicious beginning. Actor David Niven later claimed to have been the facilitator for Laycock's transformation to commando.

The Middle East Commandos were what might most kindly be described as a mixed bunch. Some had fought in the Spanish Civil War on the losing, Republican side and so had a strong personal motive for fighting fascism. Others volunteered for less idealistic reasons, as Terence Frost, a yeomanry trooper who joined because he wanted some real fighting, found out:

> I didn't know that the volunteers from the regulars hadn't actually volunteered at all. They had been kicked out for getting drunk or socking the sergeant-major and I had the shock of my life when I found this out. I was amongst a real shower of tough blokes.[16]

On the night of 19/20 April 1941, the commandos mounted an amphibious raid on the Axis port of Bardia. The assault was a partial success. Considerable damage was inflicted on German stores and materiel. Nonetheless, not all the commandos could be got off by the single landing craft that pitched up to extract them, and the rest were left on the beach. Inevitably they were forced to surrender. The prisoners were inspected by the Desert Fox himself, who pronounced them 'very foolish but very brave'.[17] Many in the Allied camp would have agreed wholeheartedly with this pithy analysis.

---

* Major General Sir Robert Edward Laycock, KCMG, CB, DSO (Distinguished Service Order), KStJ (1907–68), a British Army officer, most famous for his service with the Commandos during the Second World War.

After the Bardia raid, Laycock's unit 'Layforce' was dispatched to Crete as a strategic reserve during the Axis invasion of the island. This was hardly a Special Forces role. Wavell had thrown in the commandos largely because there was simply no one else. By this time the fight was virtually lost and Layforce's job was simply to provide a rearguard as the Allies withdrew over the bare spine of the high mountains towards the south coast. Evelyn Waugh was Laycock's aide-de-camp and with his CO was one of the last to be lifted from the beach at Sphakia. This conventional action cost the unit some 600 casualties, around 75 per cent of its fighting strength. Many commandos, fearing capture, wisely dumped their array of fighting knives and knuckle dusters.[*]

From the Boer War onwards the Lovat Scouts[18] had formed the kernel of Special Forces within the British Army. Brigadier Simon Fraser, 15th Lord Lovat, was one of the war's most distinguished commando officers. His first cousin was David Stirling of the Scots Guards, initially attached to Layforce. The latter, an immensely tall and charismatic Guards officer, was the very stuff of Hollywood derring-do. He attempted a self-taught course of parachute training which very nearly brought his career to an end, resulting in two months' hospitalization.[†] His convalescence, enthusiasm undimmed, was spent in preparing ideas for a parachute force descending from the skies upon unsuspecting enemy targets. Neil Ritchie, Commander-in-Chief Middle East General Claude Auchinleck's deputy chief of staff and a long term friend, proved receptive.

---

[*] Waugh used his experiences in Crete when writing his *Sword of Honour* trilogy.

[†] David Stirling (1915–90) founded the SAS. Stirling was indefatigable, bold and often brilliant. His style of aggressive raiding contrasted with LRDG's more low-key, intelligence-led approach. Nonetheless, in the 15 months before his capture, the SAS had destroyed over 250 aircraft on the ground, shot up and bombed dozens of supply dumps, sabotaged railways and all manner of enemy communications. Hundreds of enemy vehicles were put out of action. He ended the war in Colditz.

Stirling's plan was simple. Operations should be undertaken by a mere handful of specialists rather than company sized or larger raiding parties. The Scot was deeply unconventional and wary of the army's byzantine and frequently obstructive ways. He reported only to the commander-in-chief and his fledgling force was designated as 'L' Detachment, Special Service Brigade – latterly the Special Air Service (SAS). This was indeed the birth of a legend.

Gainful employment was soon forthcoming. As a curtain raiser to Operation *Crusader*, Auchinleck's bold gambit intended both to drive Rommel backwards and relieve beleaguered Tobruk, two particularly daring raids were conceived. In the first, Lieutenant-Colonel Geoffrey Keyes, at 24 the youngest officer to hold so senior a rank, would lead No. 11 Commando in an attack on the former Italian prefecture at Beda Littoria. This lay 250 miles behind enemy lines and was believed to be Rommel's HQ. 'Jock' Haselden,[*] an experienced desert hand, had been dropped in by parachute to confirm that the Fox was actually in his lair. He was convinced this was indeed the place and that he'd sighted Rommel himself.[19]

On the night of 13 November 1941, Keyes led a force of raiders whose intention, put quite simply, was to kill or capture the Desert Fox. The rather oddly branded Operation *Flipper* got off to a bad start and fared worse. Keyes was fatally wounded in the initial stages of the assault.[†]

---

[*] John ('Jock') Haselden (1903–42). Jock Haselden was born in Ramleh near Alexandria. Before the outbreak of war, he was employed by Anderson, Clayton & Company, a cotton trader. Haselden was fluent several languages including Arabic, French and Italian. Initially, on joining up, he was posted to the Libyan Arab Force. From 13 July 1940 he served on the GR Staff Middle East, specializing in commando-type operations. He was then appointed as Western Desert Liaison Officer at 8th ArmyHQ, working very closely with LRDG. He was killed in action during the final abortive phase of Operation *Agreement* on 14 September. His name is engraved on the Alamein Memorial at the Commonwealth War Cemetery in Alamein, Column 85.

[†] Keyes won a posthumous VC (Victoria Cross) for his role in Operation *Flipper*, the ill-starred attempt to kill Rommel.

Casualties overall on both sides were light, but there was no sign of Rommel. In fact he wasn't even in the theatre at that point; Haselden had indeed sighted him but this was only a routine visit, as his actual headquarters was far nearer the front line.

Stirling led the second attack. His objectives were the two Axis airfields at Timini and Gazala. Bad weather, which had already contributed to Keyes' failure, scattered the drop. One planeload actually came down onto an enemy runway and all aboard were captured. Another crew was pitched out over the wastes of the Great Sand Sea and none survived. Stirling's group lost most of their kit including vital explosives and detonators. When survivors limped back to the RV with LRDG, only 21 out of 54 made it.[20] The raid was a costly fiasco, but Stirling was undeterred. He did however decide that his commandos, following the example set by LRDG, would now travel by vehicle.

By the summer of 1942 the SAS had some 15 customized jeeps in action in North Africa. SAS jeeps were stripped, like their Chevy predecessors, of all superfluous features including the windscreen, most of the radiator grille bars and even sometimes the front bumper to increase effective load carrying capacity. Condensers, following LRDG precedent, were fitted, and the durable jeep could cart an impressive payload of ammunition, kit, fuel and supplies.

They were ideal, fast moving gun platforms, bristling with a formidable array of Browning and Vickers K machine guns. The latter were stripped from aircraft, generally mounted in pairs. Their combined firepower was phenomenal, a cyclic rate of nearly five thousand rounds per minute. A potent mix of ball, armour-piercing and tracer ammunition could devastate lines of parked enemy planes: as many as a dozen were destroyed in a single five-minute raid.

It was against vulnerable enemy aerodromes that the SAS proved its worth, not just in the total of enemy aircraft destroyed (this amounted to some 400 by November 1942) but, by launching these sudden strikes, the SAS forced the Axis to allocate more and more troops to purely defensive roles. This is perhaps the most enduring image of SAS/LRDG: a patrol of heavily armed jeeps, crewed by bearded, piratical commandos, storming along lines of parked Axis aircraft. Engines racing and jeeps spewing fire, a volcano of noise and fury, planes shuddering and sagging, the raiders cause a brief exultant burst of satisfying destruction and roar off into the desert night.

One of the leading lights in these operations was Robert Blair 'Paddy' Mayne,* a pre-war sportsman of renown, brave to the point of foolhardiness and often in trouble as a result of drunken brawling. When Stirling recruited him, he was in the guardhouse after striking Geoffrey Keyes, his CO! Despite his instability and propensity for binge-fuelled violence, Mayne was formidable. His leadership of a jeep-mounted raid on Tamet airfield on the night of 14 December 1941 did much to re-establish the unit's credibility after the initial fiasco and at a time when disapproving regulars would have been happy to see the SAS fold. Mayne was to claim he'd personally destroyed nearly a quarter of the regiment's total score.

Success earned Stirling promotion to major and inspired a stream of recruits. Inevitably, such an unorthodox unit attracted unorthodox soldiers including Free French and members of the Greek Sacred Squadron, all united by a hatred of the Axis and a burning desire to make an impact. From an inauspicious beginning, Stirling built a highly professional force able to complement the LRDG, with whom they often worked in tandem. Captain Pleydell, the unit's medical officer (MO), commented on this very unconventional brand of warfare:

---

* Robert Blair 'Paddy' Mayne (1915–55) was from Northern Ireland, a highly successful rugby union international and amateur boxer. He was an early recruit into David Stirling's fledgling SAS. Highly decorated and distinguished as a soldier, he had a dark and mercurial side exacerbated by heavy drinking.

Although life was free and easy in the mess, discipline was required for exercises and operations. On the operations in which I was involved, our patrol would make long detours south of the battle line and then loop up north to within striking distance of an airfield or similar target. Camouflage had to be expert, so that when you hid up you couldn't be detected – even at close distance, slow flying enemy aircraft could follow our tracks to our hiding places and they represented a real threat. It was a hit-and-run, hide-and-seek type of war.[21]

One of the more colourful characters in the Allied order of battle was Vladimir Peniakoff. 'Popski', as he was nicknamed, was a Russian émigré who had fought for the French in the previous war and then worked in Egypt as a civilian. He managed to secure a British commission and began his clandestine career by stirring up anti-Italian sentiment amongst Libyan Arabs. Teaming up with LRDG, he graduated to demolition with some success, as one of his raids destroyed 100,000 gallons of enemy fuel.

In contrast, for those handful of members of SIG, this habitual chivalry, a war without hate, was a distant dream. These young men were fighting a very different battle. Hatred defined their war. They were Jews; the normal rules did not apply. To their enemy, they weren't human. They fought against a creed that promised not just their destruction but the extinction of the whole of European Jewry. Hitler and the Nazis were intent upon genocide, the worst, most clinical, most comprehensive ever attempted in man's very long history of intolerance of other men. In Germany and across Hitler's vast satrapy, mass murder was fast becoming a nationalized industry. The SIG were very few but they were fighting back.

But by a day's travelling you reach a new world
The vegetation is of iron
Dead tanks, gun barrels split like celery
The metal brambles have no flowers or berries
And there are all sorts of manure, you can imagine
The dead themselves, their boots, clothes and possessions
Clinging to the ground, a man with no head
Has a packet of chocolate and a souvenir of Tripoli.

Keith Douglas

CHAPTER THREE

SWINGS OF THE PENDULUM

The high drama of Operation *Agreement* was played out in mid-September 1942, by which time the armies had been fighting in North Africa for two years. To understand how this mission came about it is necessary to grasp the contextual background. Hitler never wanted to become embroiled in his Italian ally's imperial fantasy. It was a distraction, a sideshow. After victory, or what appeared to be victory, in the west, the Fuhrer only had eyes for the east. At the end of the war, in 1945, Hermann Goering admitted that 'not invading Spain and North Africa in 1940 had constituted a fatal blunder'.[1]

From the British perspective and to hard-pressed Dominion forces in the post-Dunkirk gloom of 1940, the situation appeared very far from rosy. Wavell's resources were stretched perilously thin and he was palpably short of materiel. 7th Armoured Division possessed only four tank regiments. 4th Indian Division was short of a full brigade of infantry and generally deficient in guns. The New Zealand Division was scarcely at more than brigade strength. Of the 27,500 troops deployed in Palestine, there was only a single British brigade and two extra battalions already marked out for service elsewhere. These difficulties notwithstanding, General Richard O'Connor,* when he assumed command of Western Desert Force in June 1940, found the commander-in-chief already had ideas for an offensive.

To create a viable infrastructure to fuel such an enterprise, it was necessary to construct port, rail and road facilities, lay hundreds of miles of water piping, lay out desert airstrips, establish supply dumps and depots, stockpile vast quantities of petrol, foodstuffs, clothing, tentage and all manner of supplies. Hospitals, workshops, tank repair facilities all had to be planned and constructed. This vast tail of the rear echelon, orchestrated by the Royal Army Ordnance Corps and Royal Army Service Corps, was the very lifeblood of desert warfare without which the mobile columns at the front could never have functioned.

This vast logistical effort was underpinned by supplies from the UK, USA, Canada and India. British shipping could not move freely in the Mediterranean, whilst the Axis, sailing from Brindisi or Taranto, had easy access to Tripoli, Benghazi or latterly Tobruk. Easily but not securely, however, British submarines, warships and planes could issue from Malta and Alexandria. In May 1941, an attempt by the Germans to reinforce their airborne landings on Crete by sea met with disaster beneath the guns of British warships, but those same ships paid a fearful price running the gauntlet of German fighter-bombers.

---

* General Richard Nugent O'Connor, KT, GCB, DSO and Bar, MC, ADC, 1889–1981. Born in India, achieved outstanding success leading Operation *Compass*. On 6 April 1941, in confused conditions, he and General Sir Philip Neame were taken prisoner by a German patrol near Martuba.

The distance from Britain, around the shoulder of Africa, past the Cape of Good Hope and then via the Red Sea to Suez, was 12,000 miles, a huge distance but less perilous than the Mediterranean, particularly once the menace of Italian submarines cruising the Red Sea had been dealt with.* From the USA the distance was only 200 miles greater than from the UK; even India was 3,000 miles away. The small and constricted port of Suez was not the end of the chain, either, as supplies still had to reach the front.

Marshal Graziani† arrived in North Africa towards the end of June 1940, his predecessor Balbo being already dead.‡ The Italian *generalissimo* was under pressure from Mussolini to begin offensive operations, but remained hamstrung by the same perceived difficulties as had afflicted his predecessor. He therefore confined his deployment to a slow build-up of forces between Tobruk and Bardia. On 10 August, he received a communication from the dictator intimating that the invasion of Britain had been decided upon. Il Duce was losing out in the scramble for fresh laurels. After all, he considered he was the senior partner in the cabal of fascist dictators. Something had to be done to maintain the prestige of the New Rome. His idea was to attack Egypt.

A campaign without objectives has limited appeal. The Italians were set for a grand advance but without any clear strategic goals. Both Wavell and O'Connor, despite the odds and apparent difficulties, were becoming clear in theirs. O'Connor was an officer of known dash and initiative, undaunted by the task which confronted him. Offensive operations had already commenced. 11th and 7th Hussars, with the élan of their light

---

* This was accomplished by spring 1941.

† Marshal Rodolfo Graziani, Marchese di Neghelli, 1882–1955. The youngest colonel in the Italian army during the First World War, he commanded Italian forces in Libya in the 1920s, where his uncompromising policies earned him the unfortunate sobriquet of 'Butcher of Libya'.

‡ Balbo's plane was brought down by 'friendly fire' over Tobruk; foul play was suspected.

cavalry forbears, had been enthusiastically attacking the enemy. At home in the desert, the cavalrymen used their armoured cars as the eyes and ears of O'Connor's army. In a succession of raids they beat up enemy quarters at forts Maddalena and Capuzzo. The former fell virtually without a fight, though the latter proved a much tougher nut.

Churchill didn't really like Wavell. The latter's son conceded after the war that nobody would call his father a chatty general. Wavell's reserve clashed with Churchill's loquacity and unfortunate penchant for dishing out tactical instructions. These were matters for the commander-in-chief at any time, were and generally based on Churchill's limited understanding. For his part, the prime minister found Wavell aloof and independent, though the latter responded to Churchill's enthusiasm for offensive action in North Africa and to his boldness when he subsequently diverted supply. Nonetheless, the level of interference in tactical matters rankled, as Wavell thought Churchill did not trust him to run his own show and was set on his own ideas. Even the brilliant success of Operation *Compass*, the first large Allied military operation of the Western Desert campaign, did not affect the prime minister's view. He dealt both churlishly and unfairly with a subordinate whose abilities and conduct merited far better treatment.

In the event, Wavell used those elements of Churchill's instructions that made tactical sense and disregarded the rest. His thinking was already more aggressive than that of his political superior, and he was actively planning a thrust into Cyrenaica. He advised the prime minister that he needed adequate air cover both to defend Egypt and Alexandria and he urgently required a second armoured division. O'Connor was assisted in his detailed planning by Major-General Eric Dorman-Smith ('Chink'),*

---

* Brigadier Eric ('Chink') Dorman-Smith, 1895–1969. Dorman-Smith was a controversial character. Opinions amongst his contemporaries varied. Sir Basil Liddell Hart regarded him very highly, Montgomery did not.

who was intellectually gifted, a friend of such eminent writers as Ernest Hemingway, but lacking in patience with those less favoured and was generally not well liked. His penchant for seducing other men's wives may have contributed to this.

Nonetheless, the planning for *Compass* was bold and imaginative. No lesser critic than Rommel was later to intimate he thought Wavell's handling of this initial campaign showed real genius. Churchill was already fretting, as the British had now been forced out of Somaliland in the face of enormous odds and the Italians were attacking both in the Sudan and on the fringes of Kenya. Admiral Alan Cunningham's ships were making their presence felt and denying the Axis any hegemony in the Eastern Mediterranean, but the Italian navy remained a potent threat.

The forthcoming offensive, Operation *Compass*, had four clearly defined objectives:

1. The capture of Sidi Barrani
2. The capture and occupation of Bardia
3. The capture of Tobruk
4. An advance on Derna.[2]

O'Connor's forces were mainly dug in around Mersa Matruh as, on 13 September 1940, Graziani finally lumbered into action. The Italian 10th Army advanced some 60 miles into Egypt to reach Sidi Barrani and Sofafi. No major clashes occurred and the Italians seemed, having reached their objectives within three days, in no hurry to advance further. From the British perspective, this loss of ground would have been trifling except that the forward air bases were forfeit. This was serious in that British fighters would no longer be able to reach Malta, necessitating the island's reinforcement with additional planes.

Graziani now proceeded simply to dig in, constructing a series of forward camps and establishing his HQ and rear echelon.

This was not quite what Il Duce had intended, but of course the planned invasion of Britain was now stillborn and the Italian dictator was beginning to focus on his enmity upon Greece, where he espied potential for another easy victory. In November, he received a rude check when the British raid on Taranto inflicted grievous loss on his warships. Wavell meanwhile continued with his planning, favouring a short, sharp offensive of perhaps five days' duration to eject the enemy from the Sidi Barrani, Buq Buq and Sofafi area. His subordinate O'Connor was, however, already thinking in terms of a more decisive blow.

Italian forward defences at Nibeiwa were overrun in fine style, though elements of the garrison, including its gallant commander, died at their guns; 4,000 prisoners were taken. So swift was the Italian collapse as the British chased them down their own newly constructed highway, the Via della Vittoria, that the frequently used foxhunting metaphors seemed justified.

The campaign was one of a series of sweeping encirclements and successful assaults on defended positions unable, due to their siting, to provide mutually supporting fire. Here was a lesson for the British, one that wasn't learnt soon enough. On 5 January 1941 Bardia fell, with a further 40,000 prisoners taken. Not even the determined commander of the doomed garrison, Lieutenant-General Annibale 'Electric Whiskers' Bergonzoli,* could delay the collapse. On 22 January, Tobruk was stormed, capturing a further 25,000 Italians. The port changed hands for the first but not the last time.

---

* On account of his luxuriant forked beard!

O'Connor had also established all-arms co-ordination. Having taken and kept the initiative he now he had the opportunity to destroy the fleeing remnants of 10th Army. 7th Armoured Division, with the dashing 11th Hussars, led the flanking charge through Mechili, Msus and Antelat towards Beda Fomm and Sidi Saleh, whilst the Australians, who had replaced 4th Indian Division,* pushed forward along the coast. The Italians appeared to have a particular horror of the Australians whom the British had unleashed into the desert. These 'barbarians' were certainly astonished at the level of creature comforts their enemies had enjoyed till their rude awakening. Or, as one Digger more earthily commented, 'the Tel Aviv police gave us a better fight'.[3]

By noon on 5 February, the Hussars had interdicted the enemy's line of retreat, firmly astride the road along which the Italians had to pass. The odds were formidable, at least ten to one, but the light cavalry held their ground in bitter fighting until the 7th Hussars came up and the jaws of the trap closed inexorably. The next day witnessed more desperate attacks to break the ring. A hundred light Italian tanks were knocked out. Their frantic assaults continued in darkness and into the following day before white flags began to appear, steadily and then in droves. The battle was over.

In the two months' duration of *Compass*, British and Dominion forces had advanced over 500 miles, captured a staggering total of 130,000 of their enemies, taken 400 tanks, twice as many guns, destroyed 150 enemy aircraft and secured all of their objectives. Total losses were around 2,000 killed, wounded and missing. O'Connor was desperate to capitalize on the moment and sweep

---

* The 4th Indian Division had been pulled out from Abyssinia and replaced there by the Australians.

onward to Sirte and Tripoli, but the emerging demands of Greece and the Balkans acted as a brake. Wavell was dead against the ill-starred intervention in Greece, which led to a massive debacle and was followed quickly by another on Crete: two mini-Dunkirks in a row with thousands left captive and mountains of gear lost.

Far worse, a very new breed of fox was set to emerge, one whose presence would transform the nature of the Desert War. By the time the dust had settled over Bardia on 5 January, Hitler had taken the decision to intervene on behalf of his crumbling ally. He could not countenance a total collapse of the Italian position in North Africa. Major-General Hans von Funck was sent to carry out an analysis and gloomily reported that the proposed injection of German forces would not suffice to stem the rot. Hitler had already issued Directive no. 22 on 11 January, determining that Tripolitania must be held and that a special military blocking force would be deployed, Operation *Sonnenblume* (Sunflower).

This infusion of German troops would enjoy air support from X Fliegerkorps, which was to be moved to Sicily. This formation was already trained in air attack upon shipping and quickly made its presence felt, inflicting considerable damage on the aircraft carrier *Illustrious*. The Luftwaffe squadrons could also strike at British depots and targets in North Africa. If the British could strike at the Axis in the Eastern Mediterranean, deprived of any other opportunities in the west, Hitler could riposte effectively and stiffen his failing ally.

The Fuhrer had decided to send 5th Light Motorized Division, which was equipped with anti-tank guns, and later added 15th Panzer Division to the deployment to beef up its offensive capabilities. A further two Italian divisions, Ariete Armoured and Trento Motorized, were to be dispatched to make up, at least in part, the Italians' catastrophic losses during *Compass*. In February, the Fuhrer appointed

Rommel to command. The Desert Fox thus entered the stage, a player who would tax the hounds rather more sorely than his predecessors.[*]

Rommel was not destined to enjoy good relations with the Italians. That necessary talent for patient diplomacy was simply not in his nature. Italo Gariboldi,[†] who had succeeded Graziani, was not in favour of early offensives and chided Rommel on his lack of desert experience. Nonetheless, the newcomer's position was strengthened when Il Duce instructed that all motorized Italian units should be placed under Rommel's immediate command.

The Fox was already in action, parading his armour in a caracole around the streets to convince British eyes that he was stronger than he was. Soon, he had Volkswagen cars padded and disguised to fool aerial observers. The three divisional formations, 15th and 21st Panzer (forming DAK), with 90th Light Division,[4] were already fully mechanized all-arms units[5] and blessed with the inestimable advantage of superb communications.[6] These men were already part of an elite force, one which had won such stunning victories in Poland and France, the Panzerwaffe.[‡]

OKW (Oberkommando der Wehrmacht) had cautioned Rommel not to contemplate serious offensive action until 15th Panzer arrived in May. Wavell too believed no attacks could be launched just then. In this both he and the senior German General Franz Halder were mistaken, as both had equally underestimated Rommel.

---

[*] Field Marshal Erwin Johannes Eugen Rommel, 'The Desert Fox', 1891–1944. Born in Wurttemburg, the legendary general showed early promise as an engineer and, throughout his life, displayed an amazing grasp of technology. During the battle for France in 1940, he showed his trademark energy, dash, fire and utter ruthlessness, though this was always tempered by chivalry.

[†] General Italo Gariboldi, 1879–1970. In March 1941 he was appointed to replace Graziani but was subsequently removed due to his poor relationship with Rommel.

[‡] Panzerwaffe = 'armoured force' or 'armoured arm'.

General O'Connor had been evacuated from the front to undergo treatment in Egypt for a stomach condition and his replacement was Sir Philip Neame VC.* As he did not expect an attack before May, Wavell considered that a single infantry division, supported by one armoured brigade, should be sufficient to consolidate the British grip on Cyrenaica whilst forces were diverted to Greece and Abyssinia. Wavell's chief difficulty was the vast sphere of his fiefdom, where demands were coming in from so many quarters.† The campaign in Abyssinia was followed by others, firstly in Iraq and then in Syria.

In March 1941, then, Neame had 2nd Armoured Division's support group around Mersa Brega, with 3rd Armoured Brigade stationed some five miles north-east. The British tanks were in poor shape, worn out by the rigours of earlier fighting. Many were non-runners, the rest in urgent need of servicing and repair. A quantity of captured Italian light tanks had been pressed into service, but these were of limited effectiveness. Two brigades of infantry from 9th Australian Division were dug in east of Benghazi, whilst a third occupied Tobruk. An Indian motorized brigade held Mechili. Rommel was poised to strike. He had 5th Light Division with 80 PzKpfw Mark III and IV tanks,‡ the Italian Ariete Armoured Division, additional Italian infantry and support from advance squadrons from X Fliegerkorps.

Wavell was convinced Rommel would not be in a position to attack before May. His trust in Neame's abilities was limited, as was later reported:

---

* Lieutenant General Sir Philip Neame, 1888–1978. In August 1940 he was made General Officer Commanding British Forces in Palestine and Trans-Jordan in the acting rank of lieutenant-general. He was captured along with O'Connor.

† The fall of Crete had been so costly in terms of losses amongst Axis paratroops that attacking Malta in the same way became unattractive.

‡ The Mark III, Mark IV and Mark IV Special were the workhorses of the DAK throughout the Desert War.

I found Neame pessimistic and asking for all kinds of reinforcements which I hadn't got. And his tactical dispositions were just crazy; he had put a brigade of Morshead's[7] 9th Australian Division out into the middle of the plain between El Agheila and Benghazi, with both flanks exposed … I came back anxious and depressed from this visit, but there was nothing much I could do about it. The movement to Greece was in full swing and I had nothing left in the bag. But I had forebodings and my confidence in Neame was shaken.[8]

On 24 March, Rommel launched a probing raid on the British positions at El Agheila. This was entirely successful and justified his confidence in a more ambitious undertaking. By 31 March, Rommel was about to confound both Neame and his own superiors at OKW. His advance began on that day, columns sweeping along the coastal route in the north, striking for Mechili through Andelat and Msus in the centre. He sent Ariete cruising to the south in a wide flanking movement, converging on Mechili. These dispersed, all arms groups were ideally suited to desert warfare and their deployment gave the lie to any assertion Rommel did not understand the nature and demands of the terrain. Like a battlefield conductor he led from the front, flying overhead in his Fiesler Storch light spotter, constantly urging his formations to 'push on'. His style was one of relentless insistence, backed by personal leadership and intervention.

Such close and constant contact enabled him to direct the flow of battle to exploit opportunities. By 5 April, Rommel had decided to concentrate his drive upon Mechili. The day before, his troops had entered Benghazi and Neame was focusing upon withdrawal. This at least was sound, as there was more to be gained from keeping forces intact than clinging on to ground. As Benghazi fell, Wavell had sent the recovering O'Connor to bolster Neame. On 7 April, a fresh reverse hit the Allies when both generals, together with Brigadier John Combe, were captured.

Also on 7 April, Wavell reported gloomily to London and Churchill was quick to pick up on the commander-in-chief's earlier and outwardly more confident briefings; he claimed that the War Cabinet decision regarding assistance to Greece had largely been founded on this appreciation. This was untrue: Wavell had opposed the Greek fiasco from the start and the prime minister was now preparing to offload responsibility for defeat in Cyrenaica. Churchill and Wavell were in accord, however, that the place which must be held was Tobruk.[9] The chiefs of staff were in full agreement and Morshead, with 9th Australian Division, was entrusted with the defence whilst the shaken British regrouped around Mersa Matruh.

Rommel, too, was aware of the significance of Tobruk and decided upon its capture. His own supplies were becoming a matter of acute concern and he couldn't permit a major Allied garrison to remain and threaten his rear. To maintain current efforts the Axis required some 50,000 tons of supplies every month. These were shipped by sea through Tripoli, but less than 30,000 tons were arriving.[10] British activity from Malta and raids by the Royal Navy were taking their toll. The use of Tobruk and the elimination of the garrison would greatly ease this burden.

In attacking the Australians, well dug in and equally well prepared, Rommel discovered this was a new type of warfare, where mobility and firepower were not the determining factors. Each attack was repulsed in turn: in the assault the Axis lost more than 1,200 men killed, wounded and missing, showing how sharply the curve of casualties rises when one reverts from mobile to position warfare.[11] The defence of Tobruk by primarily the Australians and later British 70th Division became an epic of the Desert War, a long, grinding battle of attrition, impossibly hard on both sides, besiegers and besieged locked in a punch-drunk grip.

Wavell was not alone in having critics. Success breeds jealousy in the same way as defeat brings recriminations. Rommel had few friends in OKW and plenty of enemies, Halder in particular. He, like a prissy headmaster, decided to send out Paulus, a member of staff, to rein in this reckless prefect. Rommel could not comprehend why news of his successes was received with at best indifference if not downright disdain. Of course he did not know that a conflict with Soviet Russia was brewing, which would soon assume titanic proportions.

With the imminent arrival of 15th Panzer Division, Wavell recognized that his deficiency in armour would become even more telling. For once he and Churchill were on the same wavelength, and the prime minister took the courageous decision to strip home defence of resources and send these, via the dangerous waters of the Mediterranean, to Alexandria. Operation *Tiger* was thus an enormous gamble and also an unqualified success. Only one transport and its precious cargo was lost, and the rest berthed on 12 May. Wavell would get 238 new tanks and 43 Hurricane fighters. Churchill was inordinately proud of his 'Tiger Cubs' and hoped for great things to follow.

Paulus had reached North Africa on 27 April. Whilst he reluctantly acquiesced to another, and equally unsuccessful, attempt on Tobruk, he reported, undoubtedly as Halder would have wished, that the army was grossly over-extended and should confine its role to the defensive. Paulus, unlike Rommel, was privy to Operation *Barbarossa*, a campaign that would furnish him with his own catastrophic nemesis at Stalingrad. Ultra intercepts picked up on the cable traffic, yielding intelligence that appeared to favour an early counter-offensive. The Official History gives details:

The 'Tiger' convoy would soon be arriving, but without waiting for it General Wavell decided to strike a rapid blow in the Sollum area, and for this purpose allotted all the available armour, such as it was to the Western Desert Force.[12]

Brigadier William ('Strafer') Gott* was entrusted with undertaking Operation *Brevity*. A limited offensive aimed at driving the Axis from Sollum and Capuzzo, wreaking as much havoc as possible and driving forwards towards Tobruk as far as supply and prudence would permit. Any successes would form the curtain-raiser to a far more substantive blow, Operation *Battleaxe*, which Wavell was now planning. 'Strafer' Gott began well, with Halfaya falling, but Axis opposition stiffened and few other gains were achieved. Those that were, including Halfaya, swiftly fell to counter-attacks. *Brevity* was a failure.

General Sir Noel Beresford-Peirse was to have command of *Battleaxe*, with 4th Indian Division (led by General Frank Messervy) now returned from service in East Africa and 7th Armoured Division (led by General Michael Creagh). Messervy, with 4th Armoured Brigade in support, was to attack toward the Bardia, Sollum, Halfaya† and Capuzzo area whilst his open flank was covered by 4th and 7th armoured brigades. The intention was that the British armour would draw the Axis out into a decisive showdown. The date for the offensive to open was fixed for 15 June. Unlike his opponent, Beresford-Peirse maintained his HQ at Sidi Barrani some 60 miles from the action. Rommel was ready. He had some 200 tanks fit for service. He would not be taken by surprise.

---

* Lieutenant-General William Henry Ewart Gott, CB, CBE, DSO and Bar, MC, 1897–1942. 'Strafer' Gott was firm favourite to succeed to full command of 8th Army following Auchinleck's eclipse. He was, however, killed following an attack on the plane in which he'd been travelling, thus making way for Montgomery.

† DAK at Halfaya was commanded by a former pastor, the energetic Major the Reverend Wilhelm Bach.

The objectives of *Battleaxe* were threefold:

- A successful advance against the enemy in the Sollum–Capuzzo area
- An advance towards Tobruk, co-ordinated with sorties by the garrison
- Exploitation of gains as opportunities arose

Thus, Churchill's cherished 'Tiger Cubs' were blooded. 4th Indian Division could make little initial headway and, well dug-in, the dreaded 8.8cm FlaK guns took a fearful toll of both 'I' tanks and cruisers. Having blunted the British attacks on 15 June, Rommel struck back the following day. 15th Panzer Division was stalled in the north but 5th Light Division was able to effect a minor breakthrough and push on towards Sidi Suleiman. Rommel, the master tactician, was quick to see the potential of the turning point of the battle.[13] He ordered 15th Panzer to divert its main effort along the northern flank of the break-in. He also judged that Beresford-Peirse would launch his next thrust towards Capuzzo and resolved to strike first. Again, he was successful, and an intercepted message from Creagh to HQ requesting Beresford-Peirse to come forward, indicated the British were wavering.

Battleaxe notched up another failure. British losses had not been catastrophic, with 122 killed, 588 wounded, 259 missing, and 36 planes and four guns lost. In terms of materiel, however, 64 Matilda and 27 Cruiser tanks had been destroyed or abandoned on the field. In contrast, German losses in terms of tanks were only a fraction, perhaps a dozen in all.[14] Wavell did not hesitate to take the blame upon himself, knowing with full certainty what the consequences must be. He was to be replaced by General Claude Auchinleck ('the

Auk')* with General Cunningham† leading the Western Desert Force, soon to be 8th Army.

Cunningham's plan was that XXX Corps would attack in the north past Fort Maddalena (where the General's HQ would be located) and push on to Gabr Saleh and towards Sidi Rezegh, seeking to pull the Axis armour into a showdown. Once the Panzers had been tamed, then the beleaguered garrison in Tobruk would mount a sally to link up. Meanwhile XIII Corps would advance to the south of Sidi Omar and deal with Axis forces manning the frontier zone. The experience of desert warfare would show that success turned upon two key tactical elements, all-arms integration within formations and the need to concentrate armoured forces. Singleness of aim was necessary to drive the delivery of force.

The army commander's plan had compromised the all-arms role to satisfy concentration of armour; he had no real experience of handling large armoured formations. Fears that the uncovered flank of XIII Corps was unduly exposed were only relieved when an armoured brigade from XXX Corps was detached to provide cover. Cunningham, whose HQ was again many miles to the rear of the main action, was a general who believed that once the plan was translated into action, he depended on his subordinates to bring home the bacon. Rommel, of course, was very much the opposite, a commander who led, in one instance during this battle, literally from the front. This dashing style

---

* Field Marshal Sir Claude John Eyre ('the Auk') Auchinleck, GCB, GCIE, CSI, DSO, OBE, 1884–1981. An Ulster Scot from Fermanagh, his father was a soldier and Auchinleck served initially in the Indian Army, then commanded 5th Corps before being appointed as GOC of Southern Command. His subordinate was Bernard Montgomery, who now had V Corps. The two men did not bond, as Montgomery recorded, 'I cannot recall that we ever agreed on anything.'

† Sir Alan Gordon Cunningham, GCMG, KCB, DSO, MC, 1887–1983. He was appointed to command 8th Army in August 1941 but he proved less effective against the DAK, and hesitancy led to his swift removal, spending the rest of the war in non-combat positions.

also had it limitations, leaving the Panzerarmee virtually leaderless during a critical period in the fighting.

On 16/17 November, as formations of 8th Army advanced to their start lines, something like 100,000 men, 600 tanks and around 5,000 support vehicles were on the move.[15] Any brigade with a thousand vehicles in its train, allowing for no more than ten per mile, would have a tail nearly a hundred miles in length, a vast, slow, choking caravan, consuming terrific quantities of fuel at an alarming rate. Vehicles would also break down, experience punctures and overheat; a planner's nightmare!

Operation *Crusader* burst across the frontier on 18 November and sped forwards in a kind of dummy war. Opposition was minimal and no immediate counter-punch developed. Rommel was still fixated on the impudent garrison of Tobruk and dismissed the offensive as a probing raid. He himself had earlier instigated just such a reconnaissance in force, *Sommernachtsraum* (Midsummer Night's Dream) to learn what he could of Auchinleck's intentions. By evening, 7th Armoured Brigade had reached Gabr Saleh, thrusting forward virtually unopposed. The Desert Fox had been humbugged but, ironically, his very inertia had robbed Cunningham of the decisive clash of armour his plan demanded.

Disconcerted, Cunningham proposed, on the second day, to split his armoured forces and seek out the foe. By now the Fox was alert and began to concentrate his own armour for a counter-punch. Gott, at this point commanding 7th Armoured Division, expressed the view that the moment was now ripe for a break-out from Tobruk. This was contrary to the previous planned assertion that the Panzers must first be humbled. Nonetheless, Cunningham agreed and the move was planned for morning on 21 November. Meanwhile, armoured units were colliding piecemeal in the tanker's equivalent of a 'soldier's battle': not the precise, staff-college business of ordered formations but a swirling, dust-shrouded, grinding melee.

Despite the ferocity of these initial exchanges, the main armoured forces of both sides had yet to engage. Cunningham, nonetheless, appears to have considered that a major fight had indeed occurred and was disposed to believe over-optimistic assessments of enemy losses.* Not only were these wildly exaggerated, but DAK was still far more accomplished at retrieving damaged machines from the field and restoring them to battle-worthiness. Reassured, Cunningham gave the order for the Tobruk break-out, codenamed 'Pop'. This threw into sharp relief the need to hold the tactically significant ridge at Sidi Rezegh, which lay between Gabr Saleh and the town. This otherwise unremarkable feature would now become a boiling cauldron.

Rommel was aware of the significance of Sidi Rezegh, a mere dozen miles from the beleaguered citadel. More and more Axis armour was fed in as the battle for the ridge intensified, drawing in much of 8th Army's own tanks. The fighting was close and frightful. 7th Hussars were decimated whilst tank commander Brigadier Jock Campbell† performed prodigies of valour to rally the troops and co-ordinate counter-attacks by Allied tanks, which earned him his well-merited VC. As tanks surged around the disputed higher ground, the ring of Axis forces besieging the port remained unbroken. Despite the fact that by evening on the 21st the break-out had been contained, Cunningham remained buoyant and Auchinleck was sending confident cables to London.

Though Rommel had been obliged to divide his available forces, he was far from defeated. Even as Churchill was drafting a victory address, the Fox struck back on the 22nd, sending his Panzers in a flanking

---

* The Allies had a tendency to overstate Axis losses, discounting the DAK's remarkable capacity for salvage.

† Major-General John Charles ('Jock') Campbell, VC, DSO and Bar, 1884–1942. He won his VC in November 1941 for a spirited defence of Sidi Rezegh airfield. In February 1942 he was promoted to lead 13th Corps only to be killed in a minor traffic accident barely three weeks later.

arc to strike at Sidi Rezegh from the west. This manoeuvre netted tactical gains and various support units were overrun. Throughout the next day fighting raged unabated, a rough and savage collision of armoured leviathans, wheeling and blazing. Tanks were shot to pieces, others simply broke down and both sides suffered losses; wrecks littered the scarred waste like primeval skeletons. The New Zealanders suffered heavy losses, though fewer than the South Africans. Jock Campbell was still on hand to rally, exhort and lead, but although Allies losses were significant, there was no victory in sight.

With that daring and tactical insight which would guarantee the endurance of his legend, Rommel planned a counter-stroke of breathtaking audacity, one that sent shudders through his more cautious subordinates. He had resolved to draw off some of his forces from the furnace of Sidi Rezegh and strike towards Egypt. This was at the very moment Cunningham was suffering something of a personal crisis. On the 23rd, alarmed by the heavy attrition, particularly in armour, he had broached the possibility of breaking off the action and retreating. This was not something the Auk was prepared to countenance.

By next day the commander-in-chief had decided to remove his 8th Army commander and appoint General Neil Ritchie in his stead. Now Rommel was leading his spearhead eastwards, leading very much from the front, the epitome of daring and gallantry, if not perhaps of prudence. Under his personal command he led the remnants of 15th Panzer and Ariete divisions. The blow threatened to sever XXX Corps' line of retreat and swept through rear echelons like the grim reaper. General Cruewell, his reservations dismissed, was ordered to send 21st Panzer to drive XIII Corps back onto the web of frontier minefields. For both sides this was to be the crisis.

Auchinleck, despite the seriousness of the situation, did not lose his nerve and Rommel's sweeping gambit soon ran into difficulties. Ariete could not get past the 1st South African Division whilst 21st Panzer could make no headway against 4th Indian Division. General Bernard Freyberg and the New Zealanders were fighting hard for Tobruk, though their casualties were high.[16]

On 27 November, union with the 70th Division was effected and the heroic garrison was finally relieved. British armoured forces at Sidi Rezegh, despite their fearful pounding, were re-organizing and still very much in the fight. Rommel's units by contrast were equally battered but now dispersed and vulnerable. At DAK Headquarters Colonel Westphal had already assumed responsibility for the recall of 21st Panzer. Rommel, however, now out of touch, tacitly approved on flying back that evening and began drawing back 15th Panzer as well.

His priority now was to try and re-establish the ring around Tobruk. From 28 November, there was more savage combat around El Duda, Belhammed and Sidi Rezegh. Ground was taken, lost and retaken; both sides sustained further, heavy losses. As November drew to a close, German armour was battering the remnant of the New Zealanders, unsupported by Allied tanks. Freyberg was pushed back, his division's casualties dreadful, and Tobruk was again encircled. The battle was by now one of attrition, a fight in which the Allies were better placed but Rommel was not yet ready to withdraw. On 2 December he threw his battered formations back into the fight for a further five days of murderous intensity.

By 7 December, the pace of this attrition had forced Rommel to recognize the need for a withdrawal. Both sides continued to incur casualties, but the Allies could replenish at a far faster rate, as they had greater reserves. This steady grinding down was not a fight DAK could win. Consequently, Rommel proposed to retire upon a fixed, defensive line running south from Gazala. The British, scenting victory, swooped after him, hard upon the heels of the retreating Axis. By 16 December a further retirement became expedient and by 22 December, as 1941 drew to a close, the Axis forces had fallen back as far as Beda Fomm and Antelat. Further withdrawals, firstly to Agedabia and finally El Agheila, followed and, though constantly harassed, the rearguard provided an effective screen. By now both sides were equally exhausted.

The pendulum had indeed swung, but this placed fresh difficulties in the path of 8th Army. As a direct result of this strategic shift, the Allies were that much further away from their supply base and communications were that much more attenuated. Conversely, the army that had retreated was much closer to its own base, thus supply and replenishment was that much easier. Technically, 8th Army had won the day and so Operation *Crusader* ranks as a British victory. It was dearly bought, however. Allied losses in killed, wounded and missing were in the region of 18,000, whilst the Axis lost 20,000. Both lost heavily in tanks and guns.

'Victory' was largely illusory, and the thinning of British dispositions left the gains in Cyrenaica, so dearly won, again at hazard. Auchinleck was proceeding to plan Operation *Acrobat*, a further attack upon the remaining Axis hold on Tripolitania. Strung out in winter quarters, the army had few fixed defences and small scattered garrisons, a woeful lack of concentration. 7th Armoured Division had been withdrawn for a much-needed refit and 1st Armoured Division, who lacked their fellow tankers' battlefield experience, were put in to plug the gap. Supply lines were tenuous and inadequate, plus there remained the problem of Malta. 8th Army required the island fortress still in British hands to continue the fight, but needed to maintain forward aerodromes in Cyrenaica to protect Malta.

Rommel had also noted these deficiencies and a subtle shift in the balance of resources provided him with an opportunity that he, as arch-opportunist, was not about to ignore. At a staff conference held on 12 January 1942 his senior intelligence officer, Major F. W. von Mellenthin, predicted that for the next fortnight the Axis forces would be slightly stronger than the British immediately opposed to them.[17]

On 21 January, the Desert Fox threw two strong columns into an attack, one advancing along the coast road, the other swinging in a flanking arc north of Wadi el Faregh. Caught off-guard and dispersed, British units began to fall back. General Ritchie was, at this time, far to the rear in Cairo and was disposed to regard these moves as nothing more than a raid or reconnaissance in force. He and Auchinleck did not detect the tremors of disquiet that commanders on the ground were experiencing. Early cables suggested the situation might be ripe for a strong riposte.

It has been said of military matters that 'too often the capacity to advance is identified with the desirability of advancing'.[18] Never was this truer than in the Desert War, and the reality was that Rommel had seized and was maintaining the initiative. By 24 January the Auk was sending signals in an altogether more sober tone. Rommel was still advancing, his own supply difficulties notwithstanding. When one officer had the nerve to point out fuel stocks were critical, he was curtly advised to go and get fuel from the British. Within a day there were plans to evacuate Benghazi. Both Ritchie and Auchinleck flew to the front, but the local commanders, their instincts more finely tuned, were preparing for withdrawal. 4th Indian Division was pulling out from Benghazi as 1st Armoured Division prepared to regroup near Mechili.

Swift as a terrier, Rommel, alerted by wireless intercepts, planned a double-headed thrust. One pincer swept along the coast road, whilst the second, the Fox in the lead, pushed over higher ground to sweep around and come upon the port from the south-east. A dummy lunge toward Mechili was intended to fool Ritchie and succeeded. He dispatched his armour, leaving Benghazi exposed.

If Ritchie was groping in the fog of war thrown up by his brilliant opponent, Rommel himself faced other enemies much nearer home.

General Bastico* had become alarmed because the limited spoiling attack, to which he had agreed, was turning into a full-blown offensive, of which he strongly disapproved. He signalled his fears to his high command and asked that General Rommel should be made to take a more realistic view. This brought General Ugo Cavallero[†] to Rommel's headquarters on 23 January, accompanied by Field-Marshal Albert Kesselring and bearing a directive from Mussolini. In this it was stated that there was no immediate prospect of sending supplies and reinforcements to Africa in the face of present British naval and air opposition.[19]

In short, Rommel was to halt further attacks and establish a defensive position. Despite the weight of the delegation ranged against him, he demurred and reminded his superiors that only the Fuhrer himself could apply restraint. Besides, as he contemptuously added, most of the fighting would be done by Germans. Kesselring, who was inclined to back Cavallero and was no particular admirer of Rommel, could not move the general, and the party were sent packing, 'Smiling Albert' now apparently growling in frustration.

Meanwhile, and without armour, Lieutenant General Tuker, commanding 4th Indian Infantry Division, could not maintain a viable defence and quite rightly withdrew. 7th Indian Brigade was garrisoning the port whilst the remainder of the division was holding a line east of Barce. These troops encountered the sweeping arm of Rommel's flanking move in a series of sharp encounters and escaped the net only with difficulty. On 29 January Rommel rode triumphantly into

---

* General Ettore Bastico, 1876–1972. A native of Bologna, his command in North Africa was diminished with Cavallero's appointment and, after the loss of Libya, became largely meaningless. He was nonetheless made a marshal.

† Marshal Ugo Cavallero, 1880–1943. A Piedmontese, his appointment in North Africa was complicated by his poor relationship with the volatile Rommel. Latterly, he was embroiled in the Italian collapse of 1943.

Benghazi whilst the 8th Army scattered to a defensive position astride the line from Gazala in the north to Bir Hacheim. Rommel's own post-mortem on the fighting up until early February, forming a portion of his official report, whilst allowing for some artful editing, contains a very fair assessment of British shortcomings.

Despite being penned by the enemy, this was by no means an overly harsh assessment. Throughout the 'Msus Stakes' the 8th Army had been hamstrung by inaccurate intelligence, uncertainties of supply, inadequate training and a total lack of flexibility. The retreat resulted in the loss of 1,400 men, 70 tanks and 40 guns.[20] Operation *Acrobat* was now a distant dream and Malta was weakened by the loss of forward airfields. This reverse came at a singularly bad moment for the War Cabinet. It is easy to criticize Churchill for his abrasive and often unreasonable attitude, yet the burden he carried was a mighty one. The entry of the US into the war had yet to make an impact, whilst the crisis in the Far East deepened with Singapore threatened. Malta was under terrific pressure and plans for Operation *Gymnast* – joint Anglo-American landings to capture French North African colonies – had to be shelved. After a week's leaguer, the unthinkable happened and Singapore fell, a savage blow.

Rommel, on the other hand, appeared to have near magic insight, the Nelsonian 'touch and take'. He displayed the remarkable ability to convert limited tactical successes into major gains. His policy of leading from the front, though fraught with risks, had so far paid handsome dividends. Even though 8th Army command might be depressing the War Cabinet with what appeared to be excessive caution, Auchinleck and Ritchie were if anything understating British weaknesses. The policy of senior officers to lead from a distance placed a greater burden on corps and divisional commanders. When the latter painted a sombre picture of the true state of their units, these assessments, though valid, were hardly ever greeted with rapture.

Churchill, though he railed at the bad designs, continued to press Auchinleck for an early offensive and the Auk, to his credit, remained obdurate. A snappish exchange of cables ensued. When the Auk refused to bend and refused to hazard Egypt to succour Malta, he was summarily ordered home. He demurred, leaving Churchill with the choice of either backing him or sacking him. Viscount Alanbrooke, the CIGs and other wise counsels prevailed against the latter course and Auchinleck won his breathing space.

Both Churchill and Auchinleck were right. The pressure on Malta was dreadful and the Russians were in deep difficulties, but for 8th Army to have mounted a hasty and ill-prepared assault would have been disastrous. Lieutenant General Nye, Vice-Chief of the General Staff, was not to be browbeaten either and the commander-in-chief had another eminent and persuasive ally in Brooke, who could argue his case in person. With grudging reluctance, Churchill was persuaded to agree to a date of 15 May as the earliest upon which an assault could be launched.

Rommel was also subject to political restraint. Hitler and Mussolini held a conference in April at which the strategy for Axis moves in North Africa was on the agenda. It was concluded that DAK should launch an attack on the Gazala Line at the earliest opportunity. So far so good, but this was to be a limited offensive. Neither dictator would let the Fox completely slip the leash. Once the line was breached and, as a major secondary objective, Tobruk re-captured, then the attack would be stalled till Malta was dealt with and the overall supply situation improved.

For his part, Auchinleck quickly found that he could not hope to meet his own deadline of mid-May; mid-June looked possible, but a delay till August could not be fully discounted. Even Brooke found it difficult to maintain his dogged defence and his diary recounts an increasing frustration. Churchill was at his most venomous. A further, highly acrimonious exchange of cables followed, but the commander-in-chief refused to be pushed on the basis that Malta's peril justified the risk.

Quite rightly, his attention was focused on defence of the Delta. Rommel, however, was about to decide the matter, as he was planning his attack for 26 May. Auchinleck was aware of his opponent's intention in terms of an offensive, but not how and where he planned to deliver the main blow. The 8th Army was braced to expect an attack in the centre with a diversion to the south. British armour was deployed accordingly.

Rommel, disobligingly, intended his main assault to be directed in the south swinging on the pivot of Bir Hacheim, which he expected to overcome without undue difficulty. The attacks in the centre and north would, in the case of the former, be secondary and in the latter instance a mere feint. The Fox himself would lead the main armoured thrust in the south, which would, having dealt with the Free French at Bir Hacheim, sweep around behind 8th Army and begin rolling up the line. Italian armour would attempt to batter through British minefields in the centre, whilst Cruewell would command joint infantry forces in the north.

General Tuker's lament over wide dispersal of Allied forces was well uttered, but no heed had been taken. Ritchie's deployments were piecemeal and ill-considered. In the north 13 Corps was spread in a series of defensive 'boxes', with 30 Corps to the south disposed by brigades, together with the bulk of available armour. Auchinleck, in all fairness, was not unaware of the current failures in British tactical doctrine.

In qualitative terms the British armour was still deficient. A new version of the Crusader tank had thicker frontal armour but was still plagued by reliability problems.[21] The German armour had also had the benefit of a makeover with improved face-hardened frontal protection. Only the US M3 Stuart tank (dubbed 'Honey' by the British) with its 37mm gun could fire capped ammunition, yet the newest variant of the PzKw III was fitted with a long, highly effective, 50cm gun. The under-gunned Allied tanks were at least now being reinforced by a new American model, the M3 Grant, which carried a 75mm sponson-mounted gun capable of firing both HE (high explosive) and AP (armour piercing) rounds.[22]

Rommel's offensive and the Battle of Gazala, dubbed 'the Gazala Stakes' by 8th Army, can be divided into three phases. (1) 26–29 May: Rommel launches his flank attack, attempting to overrun British defences from behind; (2) fighting in the 'Cauldron' – Rommel tries to re-supply and consolidate his forces; (3) 11–13 June: the reduction of Bir Hacheim and the pounding of British armour, followed by withdrawal from the Gazala Line. A fourth and final phase of this battle was the subsequent storming of Tobruk. In the fighting 100,000 Allied troops, 849 tanks and 604 planes would face some 90,000 Axis with 561 tanks (228 of which were of the inferior Italian sort) and 504 aircraft.

Bir Hacheim, the pivot upon which the Axis southerly attack was to turn, proved a far harder proposition than Rommel had anticipated. General Marie-Pierre Koenig's Free French put up a spirited and resilient defence. The task of hammering these defences into submission was entrusted to Ariete Division. Nonetheless, the Panzers achieved a series of local successes, swatting a succession of badly co-ordinated Allied units. By mid-morning they had swept over Messervy's HQ, netting the general and his staff. Though he soon made good his escape, the resultant confusion was disastrous. Rommel's two more northerly assaults both failed to break in, stalled against minefields and determined resistance.

The new Grant tanks and heavier punch of the 6 pounder AT (anti-tank) guns made their presence felt. Failure to eliminate Bir Hacheim spoilt the smooth execution of Rommel's plan, supply lines were attenuated, vulnerable to marauding columns of light armour and armoured cars. Despite the Axis's potentially exposed position, Ritchie failed to concentrate his armour, an error which amazed his more nimble opponent. Many of the Allied tank officers had been more confident before this battle, believing the improved firepower of their Grants would even the odds.

Thrown into battle in piecemeal fashion, 2nd and 22nd armoured brigades, despite gallant and costly efforts, were insufficient to stem the onslaught. DAK was now within an area known as the 'Knightsbridge Box'. British command failures permitted Rommel to concentrate his forces, whose position, hemmed by mine marshes and Bir Hacheim, could and should have been dire. During the 29th this consolidation proceeded, with Panzers massing between the Sidra and Aslagh ridges, an inconspicuous span of barren desert soon to be dubbed 'the Cauldron', with good reason.

For Rommel this was the crisis. His armour was backed onto the British mine marsh and his support from the west had yet to penetrate. Bir Hacheim was not subdued and the supply situation was critical. Resolute and concentrated attacks by properly directed British armour with artillery and infantry support could have achieved success, but no such concentration seemed possible. Instead, penny packet assaults without the necessary guns and men were fed into the mincer. The Germans too suffered loss: senior officers such as generals Gause and Westphal were wounded and Cruewell himself, recognized by both sides as a 'brave and energetic' leader, was captured on 29 May when his Storch spotter was shot down.

On 30 May, the British 150th Brigade, left horribly exposed, was overrun. It was not till 1–2 June that Ritchie decided to storm the Cauldron. The subsequent attack put in before dawn on the 5th – Operation *Aberdeen* – was a tragedy. 7th Armoured and 5th Indian divisions stormed their objectives only to find they'd missed the enemy and landed a blow in the air: evil consequences were to follow quickly.[23] Exposed to relentless counter-attacks, several regiments and their supporting guns were decimated.

When the minefield barrier was finally breached and Axis support came through, Bir Hacheim was further isolated, with the pressure ratcheted to an irresistible level. On 9 June, the survivors, battered but unbowed, fought their way clear of the trap. Of the 3,600 who had begun the fight, only 2,700 escaped.

With this obstacle removed, Axis forces were freed for a further thrust, this time toward El Adem, with a demonstration to distract the British in 'Knightsbridge'. By dark on 11 June, Rommel had attained El Adem, having, once again, wrong-footed his opponents. Next day he moved in an attempt to surround the remnants of 2nd and 4th armoured brigades. There was now a very real risk the largely static infantry formations to the north could be surrounded, and heavy clashes occurred in the vicinity of Rigel Ridge.

Here the Scots Guards fought tenaciously, earning high praise from Rommel, never an easy general to impress. Nonetheless, relentless pressure and mounting losses forced the British from the higher ground. 22nd Armoured Brigade lost some two thirds of its tanks. On 11 June, Ritchie had been able to field some 300 machines, giving him a numerical superiority of two to one. Within two days, ground down by murderous combat and poor tactics, only 95 runners remained, the odds having thus swung heavily in favour of DAK.

By 14 June, Ritchie was seeking permission to draw off, fall back to the frontier and save his forces from encirclement. Rommel was master of the central battlefield. This would imply the temporary abandonment of the Tobruk garrison, which would again be isolated. Auchinleck was not yet ready to throw in the towel, insisting that further counter-attacks be launched to deny the approaches to Tobruk. As commander-in-chief he had to answer to the prime minister, who was already querying his intentions and pressing for reassurance that there was no question in any case of giving up Tobruk.[24] Rommel felt a surge of confidence, which he transmitted in his daily correspondence to his wife on 15 June: 'the battle has been won and the enemy is breaking up'.[25]

Withdrawal in the face of an aggressive enemy is never a smooth business, and the retreat of 8th Army inevitably produced a semblance of rout. Rommel would not relinquish pressure and struck toward the airfield at Gambut. The rump of 4th Armoured Brigade sallied out but was again badly mauled. Control of events had passed irrevocably beyond Ritchie's grip. For Rommel, there was now the matter of his unfinished business with the defenders of Tobruk.

As early as January 1942, the joint Middle East commanders, Auchinleck, Cunningham and Air Marshal Arthur Tedder had agreed that Tobruk, if isolated, should not once again be defended. Militarily, this was eminently sensible, but the place had become imbued with a great deal of political capital at a time when British arms had endured a series of dismal defeats in Norway, France, Greece and Crete, as well as such sharp reverses in the Western Desert.

By 17 June, Rommel had secured Gambut airfield and beaten off the remnant of British armour. Tobruk was again invested. Two days later there was still some ill-founded optimism that the perimeter could be held in the pious hope that Axis forces would settle down for a lengthy siege. The situation now within the ring was very different from before. Previously strong defences had been denuded and pillaged to meet the exigencies of the now defunct Gazala Line, and the garrison was badly placed to resist a sustained attack.

Rommel, scenting this weakness, unleashed the Luftwaffe, who began blasting the fortress on 20 June as the precursor to a determined attack from the south-east. By 0745 hours the anti-tank ditch, equivalent to the medieval moat, had been breached and the perimeter was collapsing. There had been talk of a breakout should this occur, but in reality no escape route was viable. Auchinleck's report to London, late on the 20th, sounded a note of impending catastrophe:

> Enemy attacked south-east face of Tobruk perimeter early morning after air bombardment and penetrated defences. By evening all our tanks reported knocked out and half our guns lost ... Major-General Klopper commanding troops in Tobruk last night asked authority to fight his way out feeling apparently could not repeat not hold out. Ritchie agreed ... Do not, repeat not know how he proposes to do this and consider chances of success doubtful.[26]

Tobruk fell, and 35,000 Allied soldiers passed into captivity, with 2,000 tons of fuel and as many vehicles falling into Axis hands.[27] It was a disastrous defeat. The debacles in Greece and Crete combined had not witnessed such fearful loss. Churchill was in the United States within the sanctum of the Oval Office when the dread tidings arrived. This was a terrible blow: first Singapore and now Tobruk. It is unquestionably true that a lesser man than Churchill would have been broken. The news could not have come at a worse time, as Britain was struggling to instil some measure of confidence in its ally. There is perhaps no more telling testimony to the prime minister's indomitable genius that he emerged still doggedly defiant even from this latest blow.

The second fall of Tobruk, this time reverting to the Axis, would be the event that brought Operation *Agreement* into being. Control of the port, vital in a war where continuity of supply was paramount, eased Rommel's logistical difficulties. His back door was bolted and he could look forward to greater success, perhaps even triumph. At the same time, Tobruk remained an Achilles heel, vulnerable from the sea and from the air as the Allies gained dominance over the skies. Thanks to LRDG and SAS, it was also at risk from the desert.

A sense of moral duty
Drove Britain into war
When Hitler grabbed for booty
The Polish Corridor.
No man of honour doubted
That we were in the right.
When guarantees are flouted,
The guarantor must fight.
For ours is not the quarrel
By fleeting passion stirred
For us the issue moral
Is — that we keep our word.

Anon, *Casus Belli*

CHAPTER FOUR

FIT ONLY FOR WAR

The swings of the desert pendulum meant that Rommel, whilst he had fought a masterful campaign, was always at risk of out-running his own supply line the further east he advanced. On the Allied side of the hill and despite the scale of recent reverses, 8th Army HQ persisted in a degree of upbeat assessments whose optimistic tone rested on the belief that Rommel, for the moment, was spent and could not maintain his offensive. Given the British deficiency in mobile armoured forces the policy was one that sought to delay the enemy at the frontier while withdrawing the main body of 8th Army to the Matruh defences.[1] 'Chink' had given the assembled war correspondents a bracing and confident briefing on 21 June. This was more propaganda than pragmatism, of course, but reflects his reliance on Clausewitz's principle of diminishing offensive capacity. If Rommel was not minded to agree, then his nominal superiors at Commando Supremo most definitely were.

Bastico, with Kesselring, reminded their impetuous paladin that it was time to draw breath whilst the agreed strategy for Operation

Herkules, the capture of Malta, went ahead. Bastico, who like Rommel, had now attained his field marshal's baton, demanded a halt. The Desert Fox, who modestly ascribed his successes solely to the valour of his troops, and who might have regarded his elevation as rather more hard won than that of his theoretical superior, simply declined this 'advice'. Kesselring, who had met with him on 21 June, achieved no more. Doubtless, he was again left growling.

As before, Rommel appealed directly to Rome and Berlin. For Il Duce, deprived of laurels, there was the dazzling prospect of riding his white charger through the streets of conquered Alexandria. Hitler was receptive; after the Pyrrhic victory on Crete he had little enthusiasm for an assault upon Malta. He cabled his fellow dictator that it would be foolish to break off contact whilst 'the Goddess of Victory smiles'.[2] On 24 June, Rommel received the green light, which was just as well perhaps as his forward units had already been advancing for the last two days!

He was poised to deliver what he believed to be the final blow. Not just his magical touch but hard intelligence supported this decision. In the circumstances, it is difficult to see what other course remained for Auchinleck except to take direct command. Ritchie was floundering and 8th Army was left in a most vulnerable state. Brooke maintained his confidence in the Auk.

Yet it was as if 8th Army had learnt absolutely nothing from previous mistakes. Gott, with XIII Corps, was to hold the perimeter around the port with hastily dug and inadequate defences – inviting a repeat of Tobruk. XX Corps was deployed a score of miles to the south astride an escarpment; Freyberg with his New Zealanders was posted in the middle of nowhere. Remnants of 1st Armoured Division were lurking far to the south, while the yawning gap between the two corps was patrolled by a brace of relatively weak mobile columns.

Auchinleck was painfully aware of the political capital invested in the 'last ditch' position at Matruh. Britain's faltering credibility would slide yet further and there was the inevitable knock-on effect on civilian morale in the Delta, where anti-colonial sentiment was already hopeful of an Axis victory. He had thus decided to make a stand at Matruh whilst allowing his army the necessary flexibility to fall back toward the El Alamein position. This was perhaps the very worst of both worlds as it implied any withdrawal would literally be under the enemy guns. This obvious difficulty would be compounded by the fact the principal corps positions were so far apart.

Battle was joined on 27 June when 90th Light Division pushed past 'Leathercol' Brigade[3] and 21st Panzer brushed aside 'Gleecol' Brigade.[4] The gap between XIII and XX Corps now yawned, with the Littorio Division trailing the German armour and the remainder of Italian XX Corps behind 90th Light Division. Caught in an isolated and exposed position, 9th Durham Light Infantry, part of 151st Brigade, was completely overrun. Auchinleck had intimated to both corps commanders, Gott and Lieutenant General Holmes, in Matruh that, should they deem a withdrawal necessary, they should do so in unison. Given the yawning gap between the two formations and the chronic unreliability of signals, this was highly optimistic.

'Pike' was the code for retreat, and both were to converge on Minqar Omar, which lay some 30 miles east. Gott had already acted, but his disengagement soon ran into difficulties. Though 1st Armoured withdrew smoothly, the New Zealanders ran into opposition. Freyberg had been wounded and Brigadier Inglis took over to find the division boxed in around Minqar Quaim. The Kiwis reacted vigorously and broke through the ring, inflicting loss upon the enemy. In Matruh, General Holmes was completely out of touch and was even planning a counter-attack. This came to nothing and by 28 June his corps was isolated and encircled.

Holmes then planned for breakout. Both 50th and 10th Indian divisions would begin to move after 2100 hours and hasten south for 30 miles before swinging eastwards into the vicinity of Fuka.

British formations, thrown into brigade groups and moving in columns, endured a dangerous passage. Axis forces were already at Fuka, where 21st Panzer had overrun the remnant of 29th Indian Brigade and a series of sharp, confused actions ensued. 10th Indian Division, in particular, suffered considerable casualties. So the decision to stand at Matruh had precipitated a further debacle, and the Panzerarmee seemed unstoppable. In accordance with the notion of diminishing power of the offensive, Rommel should have run out of steam. The rule applied doubly in the desert where supply difficulties imposed such severe constraints, but DAK had in part been sustained by captured materiel in Tobruk and more garnered in the wake of 8th Army's precipitate and frequently headlong retreats.

Prior to Rommel's offensive, supplies had been stockpiled for Operation *Acrobat*, the onward Allied rush into Tripolitania. Now, the hard-pressed rear echelon units of the RAOC (Royal Army Ordnance Corps) and RASC (Royal Army Service Corps) struggled to salvage or destroy their precious stores in the confusion of defeat. Prodigies of deliverance were indeed effected, but such was the scale and extent of the build-up that much still fell into Axis hands.

If the Axis were doing well on the ground, their grasp of the skies was crumbling. Squadrons of Kesselring's planes were being fed into the endless mincer of the Eastern Front whilst sorties from Malta were exacting an increasing toll. For both sides, to be attacked from the air was a most disagreeable experience, as one Allied combatant recalled:

During all these trips there were constant attacks by dive-bombers and Messerschmitts. These were bad enough when the column was at rest, and you could hear or see them coming. But it was much worse when the first indication you had of an attack was when the lorry in front of you blew up or the bullets smacked through your own windscreen.[5]

The Luftwaffe threat was diminishing at a time when the Desert Air Force was coming into its own, soon to be reinforced by USAAF (United States Army Air Force) B24 'Liberator' bombers.[6] Though ground/air communications were still far from perfected, 'Mary' Coningham's[7] squadrons did excellent service. 8th Army was battered and depleted, but more US tanks and self-propelled guns were on their way, together with two fresh UK divisions, 44th (Home Counties) and 51st (Highland). The pendulum had not yet swung for the final time.

Matruh had been another reverse for Allied arms, yet, despite this setback, Auchinleck had kept the army in being. This, as he and Dorman-Smith had identified, was the prime objective. Only by preserving mobile field forces could the British position in the Middle East be saved. He had now gone beyond Wavell's 'worst case' and was considering how best to defend the Delta itself should he be pushed that far. Meanwhile, there was the ground south of El Alamein, a strip of desert some 38 miles in extent that lay between salt marsh and sea to the north and the impassable Qattara Depression, where no tank could tread. Here was ground that favoured a defensive battle, to be fought by an army markedly inferior in armour and less mobile than its opponent, one that needed time to rebuild and replenish.

For the most part this ground is featureless until one reaches the rock-strewn hills that flank the waste of marsh and dune announcing the depression. Even these are no more than 700 feet above sea level, but much nearer the sea are the twin eminences, rounded hillocks or '*tells*' of which Tell el Eisa and Tell el Makh Khad would prove significant. The terrain is everywhere barren; loose, deepening sand alternating with unyielding rock that emerges in the narrow lateral ridges Miteirya, Ruweisat and Alam el Halfa.

These insignificant features would assume considerable importance in the fighting to come and blood would be poured out in torrents to secure them. Once taken, such features were heartbreakingly difficult to fortify, as they were horribly exposed. In places the ground dipped into shallow depressions (*deirs*), natural saucers. That Auchinleck and Dorman-Smith should focus on the potential here was nothing revelatory as the Alamein position had been identified as a natural defence line for the Delta for some years beforehand.

Whilst the debacle at Matruh was unfolding, Churchill had again cabled the commander-in-chief to offer some helpful tips on generalship, tending to indicate how little the prime minister had learnt from the desert campaign. He was incapable of understanding that the fluid and mobile nature of desert warfare was, above all, a battle of competing technologies. Put simplistically, the side that had the best tanks and in adequate numbers, together with commensurate strength in supporting arms, would win. Heroic if pointless calls that 'every fit male be made to fight and die for victory' meant nothing. The Italian collapse in the winter of 1940–41 showed that simply deploying large masses of infantry had no place in this most modern of modern wars. Given the circumstances, Auchinleck's reply was the very model of patient diplomacy.

Any hopes that the swing of the pendulum would cause Rommel simply to grind to a halt proved groundless. His juggernaut, thin on supply, men exhausted, machines overtaxed, still came on relentlessly.

The so-called 'good source' – a leak through diplomatic channels* – was still pumping out vital information. Mellenthin, on 30 June, received confirmation, via an intercept from A. C. Kirk the US ambassador, that a US attaché and noted Anglophile Bonner Fellers felt the Axis could, within days, be at the very gates of Cairo.[8] Rommel was only too happy to oblige in fulfilling this despondent prediction. Victory, as it seemed, was very close indeed. Battered, ground down and in no small part bemused, 8th Army was still far from beaten, however. The Desert Rats[9] were down, but not out, and their morale, despite such repeated pummelling, did not collapse. This resilience was a disappointment to Egyptian nationalists hoping for signs of cracking.

Rommel, on 30 June, was poised for the attack. His men were utterly weary and suffering from a customary shortage of supply, but he did not pause, and instead moved straight into the offensive. His limited reconnaissance was soon to be found wanting, for he had failed to appreciate the strength of the South Africans dug in around El Alamein. His plan was that both 90th Light Division and DAK would charge the gap north of Deir el Abyad. Whilst the Light Division would seek to replicate its earlier success in interdicting the coast road and thus isolating the Alamein garrison, DAK would sprint south to swing around behind XIII Corps. As ever, the Italian formations were given a subordinate role, one division assaulting Alamein from the west, another moving behind 90th Light Division and the remainder trailing the panzers.

Matters did not go according to plan. Foul conditions delayed the progress of German armour and 90th Light Division bumped the Alamein defences and suffered under the intense weight of fire the South Africans brought down upon them. DAK found Deir el Shein

---

* The 'good source' was Bonner Fellers, the acerbic US attaché and no friend to the British. His reports were sneering but also highly detailed. This was good news for Rommel as the diplomatic codes had been cracked!

unexpectedly held by 18th Infantry Brigade and a fierce battle erupted. Newly arrived and inexperienced, 18th Brigade had struggled to dig into the stony surface and had limited support. Nonetheless, the brigade fought hard against lengthening odds within a crumbling perimeter, their few 'I' tanks and guns disabled. Despite a very gallant stand, the survivors were forced to surrender by evening on 1 July. The loss of the brigade was yet another blow and intervention by 1st Armoured Division was so long delayed as to be too late. DAK had won another tactical victory, but at the cost of a badly disrupted timetable.

The 90th Light Division, having extricated itself from this initial contact, sought to resume its headlong dash, but more intense fire from South African positions descended like a storm and stopped any advance dead in its tracks. Desert Air Force was living up to its role as the main striking arm and the Axis sprint was grinding to a halt. DAK had suffered significant reported losses in available tank strength and its supply columns had been bombed incessantly. By 2 July, Rommel was still making no progress and resolved to throw his armour behind the assault on the coast road.

Auchinleck had quickly appreciated that Allied outposts were exposed and moved to concentrate his forces. The Kiwis were given a more fluid role as their 6th Brigade was pulled from Bab el Qattara with only a column remaining. The Indian Division was likewise to quit Qaret el Himeimat. As Rommel massed to attempt break-through at El Alamein, XXX Corps would hold the line whilst XIII Corps launched a blow towards Deir el Abyad. Both sides attacked during the afternoon of 2 July.

In the north, General Pienaar's South Africans again resisted the Axis strike, aided by 'Robcol',[10] an ad hoc force of field and light artillery anti-aircraft with some infantry drawn from 10th Indian Division and led by Brigadier Robert Waller. 90th Light Division was again harassed by the incessant attentions of Desert Air Force and could make no headway. To the south and west, just beyond Ruweisat Ridge, British and German armour were heavily embroiled. At the end of a hard day's fighting, neither side could claim victory, but the Axis offensive had not progressed.

During the hours of darkness air attacks continued till battle was rejoined on the morning of the 3rd. There was yet more heavy fighting south of Ruweisat Ridge. In the south, Freyberg's New Zealanders scored a signal success when they overran the artillery component of Ariete Division, netting a fine haul of prisoners and captured guns. 5th New Zealand Brigade was in action against the Brescia Division at El Mreir. By now the Axis formations were severely ground down. Rommel reported his own divisions could only muster 1,000 or 1,200 men apiece[11] and incessant aerial bombardment was playing havoc with already overstretched supply lines. Skirmishing continued throughout 4 July, but the main German effort was, for the moment, spent. It had been a failure.

Auchinleck, sensing the enemy was severely weakened, began to think in terms of turning the stalemate into a rout, proposing to unleash XIII Corps towards the Axis rear, but the British armour, probing forward, was held by a scratch gun line. Next, he planned a concentrated advance towards Deir el Shein, but again this made little headway. SAS and LRDG were active against enemy airfields, destroying some aircraft on the ground.

Rommel was in fact preparing to draw off his armour and the exhausted 90th Light Division leaving Italians to hold the line whilst the Germans drew breath and replenished. At last the Luftwaffe was able to lend support and the high pitched screaming of Stukas again filled the desert air. Auchinleck, for his part, had now decided his main blow should fall in the north and concentrated his forces accordingly.

This neatly foiled an attempt by 21st Panzer Division to catch the New Zealand Division, and the intended Axis blow fell on empty ground. Meanwhile, Desert Air Force had switched to pounding long-range targets and Axis-held ports, whilst Coningham's fighters embarked on a tactical bombing role.

Having rightly judged the oppositon to be exhausted, Auchinleck launched a series of counter-strokes. The first of these involved XXX Corps making an attempt to seize the rocky knolls of Tell el Eisa and Tell el Makh Khad. Possession of these would facilitate further moves southwards toward Deir el Shein and raids westwards against Axis airfields. XIII Corps was to prevent any enemy reinforcement northwards and be ready to exploit opportunities. On 3 July, Morshead's 9th Australian Division had returned to the line and was now tasked with taking Tell el Eisa whilst the South Africans stormed Tell el Makh Khad. Both had armoured support, and the attack at first light on 10 July was preceded by a hurricane bombardment. Both formations made good progress, taking many Italians prisoner.

Mellenthin, in charge of HQ whilst Rommel was absent and located only a few miles up the coast, collected a makeshift battlegroup and held the line whilst the Desert Fox brought up more reinforcements from 15th Panzer Division. A late counter-attack made some progress but was seen off. The following day, the Australians attacked again in a further attempt to secure the entirety of their objective. Fighting on the ground was matched by the fury of combat in the air, as skies were crossed with trails and bruised by the chatter of guns while Allied fighters duelled with Axis. For the next three days Rommel sought to recover lost ground and eliminate the newly formed salient, but his attacks were repulsed and efforts to drive a wedge between the hills and the Alamein box were equally abortive. The initiative now lay with 8th Army.

Having got the Axis off-balance, Auchinleck decided to maintain pressure by striking southwards against the long, lateral finger of Ruweisat Ridge. This otherwise unprepossessing feature would witness hard fighting through 14–15 July, and again on the 21st The Official History dubs these actions '1st and 2nd Ruweisat', both of which would highlight significant tactical deficiencies in 8th Army, a lack of co-ordination between the attacking arms resulting in tragic losses. The objective was straightforward: to storm the ridge and drive the enemy from ground east of the Alamein–Abu Dweis track and north of the eminence.

The task of securing the western flank of the ridge was given to 13 Corps, whilst 30 Corps was to take the eastern extremity and also strike southwards from this newly created salient to take the hump of Miteirya Ridge. This was to be a night attack. XIII Corps would send in two brigades of New Zealanders whilst XXX Corps deployed 5th Indian Brigade (from 5th Indian Division). Crucial armoured support for the Kiwis was to be provided by 1st Armoured Division, which would come up after first light. Both corps were to be on their objectives by 0430 hours.

To reach their target, the New Zealanders had to cover some six miles of ground in the dark. The attack, even once the enemy was alerted, was driven home with great élan, but in the smoke and dust of a moonlit battle many enemy posts were left un-subdued. Some units became scattered, and digging into the unyielding rock proved near impossible. Supporting arms, a few vital anti-tank guns, were got up, but much had not arrived. The remaining infantry sought to consolidate and, above all, dig in.

Initially, XXX Corps' attack met with stiff resistance and there was some disorder; supporting armour was still distant. Italian defenders from Brescia and Pavia divisions had been caught off-guard and numbers of them bolted.

A passing column of German tanks fell upon the New Zealand 22nd Battalion, swiftly dealt with the AT guns exposed on their portees (guns mounted on the rear of flatbed trucks) and compelled several hundred survivors to capitulate. Efforts were made to get the British armour mobile and tanks were able to support a renewed assault by 5th Indian Brigade, which partially succeeded in securing objectives on the ridge. Efforts to bring up supporting arms were frustrated by fire from enemy posts missed in the first rush. Only with the aid of a barrage were the reserve units able to begin filtering through.

With the Italians in disarray, Rommel had to assemble German units for the inevitable counter-attack, command of which was entrusted to General Nehring. 4th New Zealand Brigade, with little or no support, was eventually overwhelmed and the western end of the ridge lost.[12] Next day, 16 July, the Germans attempted to drive off 5th Indian Brigade, who repulsed this and a subsequent attack. On the 17th Australian troops attacked southwards towards Miteirya Ridge, taking hundreds of Italian prisoners, but were halted by heavy shelling and a German counter-stroke.

In these actions, the New Zealand Division had fought hard and well, but at considerable cost. They had stormed and taken their objectives, but felt badly let down by their comrades in armour, whom they blamed for leaving them so desperately exposed. This grudge and mutual incomprehension between infantry and tanks was to bedevil 8th Army for some time. This was not due to faintheartedness on the tankers' part but to a degree of misunderstanding as to the role and capabilities of armour, which were far more constrained than the infantry might have imagined. Tank commanders, such as General Lumsden, were loath to restrict themselves to the infantry support role at the expense of mobility. Progressive opinion favoured tanks being left free to act as the battle unfolded to seize opportunities whilst artillery and anti-tank guns shielded the infantry.

Despite these costly setbacks, Auchinleck was convinced the Axis was close to breaking. The Italians had lost heavily in men and materiel. Rommel's Panzers were ground down and diminished. The Auk now felt a further heavy blow in the centre might shatter them altogether. Overall, the Allied position was considerably better. Both the Australians and South Africans were in good shape, though the 5th Indian and New Zealand divisions were reduced to a mere two brigades each. 1st and 7th armoured divisions, the latter being developed as a mixed battle-group,[13] were in strength. 7th Armoured Division had a hefty contingent of over 60 Grants, in addition to Crusaders and Honeys. 161st Indian Motor Brigade and 23rd Armoured Brigade were arriving to swell the muster. The British might have initially lagged behind the Germans in developing the ability to recover damaged machines under battlefield conditions, but this was, at last, changing.

For this fresh attack, the main impetus fell on XIII Corps, who would fracture the Axis at Deir el Shein and Deir el Abyad and then drive west. A feint would be launched in the south and XXX Corps would ensure vigorous local action in its sector to keep enemy forces there tied down. Close air support would be provided. Gott was intending that 5th Indian Division would storm the western end of Ruweisat Ridge, where the New Zealanders had previously come to grief. The Kiwis themselves were tasked with taking the eastern rim of El Mreir saucer. Once the infantry were on their objectives, 1st Armoured Division would push westwards to a further goal, whereupon the brigades would follow up and consolidate. 22nd Armoured Brigade was detailed to cover the southern flank of the attack, whilst 2nd Armoured Brigade was to interdict any initial counter-attacks once the attacking infantry were successful.

'Gapping' the minefields (the dangerous task of creating a path through them) was entrusted to the infantry, though both brigades were relatively inexperienced in this most difficult of tasks. Gott's plan appeared sound, but a key assumption was that the minefields could be detected and gapped in time to allow 23rd Armoured Brigade, whose role was to charge forward to the further objective, to pass through. Despite the weight of artillery brought to bear, the New Zealand attack came to possess a sad resemblance to that earlier tragedy.

The infantry managed, in a night attack, to gain their objectives, but were left dispersed and without essential fire support. At first light Axis armour struck back, easily eliminating the few anti-tank guns available. The denouement was inevitable; the infantry were overrun, artillery communications broke down and the brigade suffered some 700 casualties.[14] 2nd Armoured Division did attempt relief, but was stopped by a mix of uncleared mines and Axis fire.

161st Indian Motor Brigade's attack also experienced varying fortunes. After hard fighting, the assault battalions were either short of their objectives or driven off by vigorous counter-attacks. Only when the reserve battalion was thrown in did the attack make headway. Major-General A. H. Gatehouse was now in command of 1st Armoured Division, as Lumsden had been wounded earlier. He was doubtful over committing 23rd Armoured Brigade when it became clear the mines had not all been cleared and a viable gap had not been created. Gott would not countenance calling off this part of the plan, however, as he believed the enemy to be significantly wrong-footed. He therefore proposed that the line of advance should shift southwards to cross an area believed, or rather hoped, to be free of Axis mines.

Two tank regiments were sent in. Both were heavily shelled and struck a host of unexpected mines covering their supposedly clear approaches. Serious loss was incurred before the objective was reached and then the survivors were furiously attacked. When 21st Panzer Division was thrown into the fight, the battered remnants withdrew, leaving 40 tanks wrecked and more badly damaged.[15] An attempt by 2nd Armoured Brigade to get through to the New Zealanders isolated in the El Mreir Depression foundered in the face of intense fire, and a further 21 tanks were lost in the broil.

Another night action, on 22 July, again launched by 5th Indian Division and aimed at finally securing the deadly Point 63 on Ruweisat Ridge, failed after a gallant and costly attempt. The infantryman's frustration with his seemingly Olympian comrades in armour was largely based on the aforementioned ignorance of the tactical role and capabilities of Allied tanks.

On XXX Corps' front, the Australians again attacked on 22 July. Fighting centred as before on the twin eminences of Tell el Eisa and Tell el Makh Khad. Early gains prompted a savage riposte and the Australians battled hard to hold ground won. Though they had some armoured support from 50th RTR (Royal Tank Regiment), equipped with Valentines, liaison between the two arms was again patchy and 23 machines were knocked out for paltry return. Despite these costly reverses, Auchinleck was not yet ready to concede a stalemate, persisting in the belief the Axis forces were on the cusp of disintegration. This time, on 26 July, an attempt was to be launched by XXX Corps, beefed up with additional armour and infantry, to advance through the gap between Miteirya Ridge and Deir el Dhib. For its part 13 Corps, battered by previous exertions, would mount a convincing, full-scale diversion to the south.

To the South Africans fell the task of gapping the enemy's minefields south-east of the ridge. By 0100 hours the Australians were to have seized the eastern flank and would then advance north and west. An infantry brigade would pass through the gaps to Deir el Dhib, gapping any further minefields encountered. Then it would be the turn of the armour to strike westwards. Some initial success was soon shrouded in a mist of confusion. The armour did not come up and, once again, the attacking infantry were left vulnerable, an opportunity the Germans never failed to exploit. 6th Durham Light Infantry and 5th East Yorkshire Regiment were overrun, as latterly were the survivors of 2/28th Australian Battalion. As before, heavy fire prevented supporting arms from getting through and armoured support was ineffective and costly.

By the end of July, the opposing armies were played out. Generals on both sides had demanded great sacrifices from their men and these had been freely made. It is hard to view this battle as anything other than a costly draw. Rommel's seemingly unstoppable run and the dismal series of 8th Army defeats had been halted. Mussolini could leave his stallion in its stables for the moment, as no victorious ride would be needed. Indeed the moment had most likely passed. First El Alamein must rank as an Allied defensive victory, though Auchinleck's efforts to break the Axis had, with the exception of 9th Division's northerly salient, foundered at high cost in men and materiel. Allied infantry, attacking at night, had shown competence and sustained valour, but the vital support from armoured formations at dawn had not been forthcoming, leaving a wide and embittered breach between the two arms.

As the front lines hardened, great belts of mines girded extensive positions and impeded any amount of free movement. Some writers have likened the process to the stalemate of trench warfare in the previous conflagration. It remained to be seen who might break the deadlock. Rommel had described the desert fighting as war without hate, and 8th Army's Official History records that its German prisoners matched this sentiment:

A curious mixture of arrogance, belief in Hitler and surprise that the British had ever gone to war with them. They openly boasted that they were the finest soldiers in the world and then added the British were easily second best.[16]

Auchinleck, though much concerned with the state of 8th Army, could never ignore other threats that loomed over his wide satrapy. An Axis breakthrough in the north would be calamitous, threatening Iran, Iraq and Syria, all volatile regions. As the Soviets were not in the habit of sharing plans, it was difficult to ascertain if the northern front could be secured. The increasing demands of campaigning in the Far East, where one disaster followed another, also drained resources. Auchinleck simply did not have sufficient troops to fight in the desert whilst creating a viable defence to the north.

The question was which constituted the greater imperative, holding Egypt or the Persian oilfields. By 12 July[17] Churchill cabled that as it was impossible to do both, defeat of Axis forces in Cyrenaica must remain the absolute priority. Despite the considerable gains German offensives in southern Russia appeared to be achieving, it was unlikely that a complete breakthrough could be anticipated before the onset of winter halted operations. The question however, remained: could Auchinleck, increasingly perceived as spent force, deliver the long hoped for victory?

Though Rommel had been halted, this was only a check and not a reverse. Allied efforts to assume the offensive in July had been, at best, disappointing. There were significant gaps in 8th Army's tactical competence and these would have to be resolved. Dorman-Smith was confident that a renewed Axis offensive could be successfully countered and that a 'modern defensive battle'[18] could be waged in the El Alamein sector. Rommel did not have sufficient infantry reserves for a blow to the north, therefore he would be obliged to attempt another wide, flanking move from the south. At this time, Auchinleck wished to formally appoint Brigadier Freddie de Guingand[*] as chief of staff, freeing Dorman-Smith to return to his preferred job in the Delta.

Though Dorman-Smith has been credited with much of the vital tactical thinking that proceeded during the latter part of July and early August, this, as Neil Barr points out, would be to underestimate the importance of the work undertaken by the commander-in-chief himself with his two corps commanders. One of the key tenets of Auchinleck's new approach was to try to close the yawning chasm between infantry and tanks. His proposal was to overhaul the divisional structure to improve mobility and co-ordination. Thus the 'mobile' division would include one armoured and two infantry brigade formations.[19] Logical as this might seem, it rather betrays his own lack of understanding of and bonding with his subordinates. Both infantrymen and tankers regarded this new doctrine as heresy.

Major-General Richard McCreery, who commanded the armoured forces in Middle East Command, was vehement. Armoured formations trained together and this developed their particular ethos and comradeship. The idea of beefing up each tank regiment with the addition of a further, fourth squadron was equally unpopular. For once, infantry officers like Major-General Douglas Wimberley, who commanded 51st Highland Division, were *ad idem* with their tank brethren.[20]

In spite of this, Auchinleck was far from being played out. His tactical appreciation of 1 August, whilst conceding that major offensive operations were, for the moment, out of the question, provided that both army corps would undertake vigorous raiding

---

[*] Major-General Sir Francis Wilfred ('Freddy') de Guingand (1900–79). From the time Montgomery succeeded Auchinleck, de Guingand acted as his chief of staff, a post wherein he combined zeal and ability with that flair for diplomacy so noticeably absent in his commander.

involving land sea and air resources. They would also be utilizing the buccaneering talents of the LRDG and SAS. Herein lay the germ of Operation *Agreement*.

Such an active defence would disrupt Rommel's fragile supply lines and prepare for the day, probably not before mid-September, when a serious blow could be delivered. General Gott prepared a further appreciation, focused on the need to counter an Axis offensive that was feared for August. He identified the high ground of Alam Halfa Ridge as vital for any advance down the coast to Alexandria.

Ramsden was also busy looking at plans for XXX Corps. Any battle in the northern sector would resemble 'break-in' battles mounted by the BEF (British Expeditionary Force) in 1918. Ramsden was a veteran of that titanic conflict. He noted that, in the July operations, infantry had generally succeeded in mounting successful night attacks and gaining their objectives. What had then gone wrong was the subsequent failure of armoured support to come up and prevent these gains being overrun by local counter-attacks.

He considered that anti-tank guns must accompany infantry to consolidate a viable defence. Armoured support must not be tardy and pockets of uncleared enemy activity should never be left in the rear. The concentration of artillery effort had paid dividends and should be developed, as should a matching re-organization of sappers. This was a 'tight' battle rather than the fluid, fast-moving offensive, a classic break-in of the 1918 mould.[21]

Auchinleck, when writing up his own further appreciation a day later than the first, took all of his subordinates' thinking into account. He examined the prospects for an offensive in the north, centre and south. Each was fraught with difficulty, but he echoed Ramsden in viewing the vicinity of Miteirya Ridge as most promising. A break-in here could corral the Axis forces in the north and expose those in the south.

In essence, the plan for the forthcoming offensive comprised the following elements:

- A major blow in the north
- Diversionary activity and phoney preparations to the south
- Disruption of enemy supply and communications
- Creation of a defended zone behind the main El Alamein line to defeat any Axis thrust from the south
- Ensuring armoured forces were full prepared to exploit any break-through(s)[22]

This was to prove Auchinleck's legacy. Far from being washed-up, he had, with his subordinates, produced the blueprint for final victory in the Western Desert, even though full credit has traditionally gone to his successor. No sooner was this appreciation committed to paper than 8th Army staff, under de Guingand's able control, began working up detailed plans. This would be the true 'tight' battle, planned in detail and intensively trained for. Previous operations had failed, but the lessons derived from those mistakes would lay the groundwork for final success. It should be noted that Rommel, for all his brilliance, did not appear to learn from past errors.

Hand in hand with the need for intense preparation and training was recognition that key operations, particularly mine clearing, should be standardized. In consequence, a clear doctrine for gapping and clearing mines emerged. This emphasized the need for intense artillery bombardment to smother the enemy gun line, followed by a creeping barrage and the establishment of forward positions enabling sappers to approach their task. Full fire support could thus be directed to cover the dangerous work of the mine clearance teams. As soon as possible, the lead elements of the armour should advance to test the gap, supported by anti-tank guns. Behind this vanguard the main body with infantry support would then move forward, broadening the gap as required.[23]

Dorman-Smith had earlier applied his formidable theoretical capacity to the question of defence and was most ably seconded by Brigadier Frederick Kisch, chief engineering officer. The lessons of Gazala were plain. A series of isolated brigade boxes with little capacity for mutual support and a lack of defence in depth had provided Rommel with a perfect target. Though many thousands of mines had been laid, these were not necessarily under Allied guns and could therefore be gapped with impunity. Breadth and depth were the keys to fresh planning.

In the north, from Alam Nayil to the coast, a dense fortified zone was to be prepared, far thinner defences were employed further south to provide Rommel with the necessary incentive. These minefields would merely delay rather than frustrate. Two brigades from 7th Armoured Division, 4th Light Armoured and 7th Motorized, were deployed as a screen. Their designated task was essentially to impose delay, to avoid being drawn into a battle of annihilation and to lead the enemy on toward their own nemesis.

In terms of this defensive concept, these ideas championed by Dorman-Smith were considered innovative, though, as Niall Barr points out, actually reflected no more than a continuation of the methods devised by Germany in Flanders in anticipation of Haig's summer offensive of 1917. The first line would comprise thinly held outposts intended to do no more than give warning of a major attack. When the blow fell, these forward units would retire into the main defensive positions. These would contain battalion sized groups sufficiently proximate for mutual artillery support. Between these static bastions, mobile groups of guns and tanks would be stationed in readiness for a counter-stroke. As Alam Halfa Ridge was recognized as a key Axis objective, the slopes were heavily fortified. Behind the Alamein position a further major defence web was to be dug in the Delta itself. As sound as these ideas may seem, they were not necessarily welcome, since they were seen as carrying connotations of defeat and withdrawal.

Despite limited successes in the previous battle, Auchinleck had never been able to develop an easy and clear understanding with his subordinates. Dorman-Smith, for all his undoubted abilities, was even more a part of the problem. He appears to have held most of his fellow officers in low regard, his clear intellectual grasp conferring a somewhat Olympian view, untrammelled by the realities and exigencies of actually commanding troops in the field. The instructions given to 30 Corps appeared ambiguous: was 8th Army defending or attacking? To the Australians, the idea of thinning out their positions in the Tell el Eisa salient did not appeal at all. Morshead would be pushed into explaining reasons he did not himself understand as to why his officers and men should give up such hard won ground.[24]

Gott had no such qualms and proposed the New Zealanders would hold Alam Halfa. Inglis could certainly see the logic but was unhappy in the detail, feeling the two brigade sized boxes were vulnerable. Gott in turn accepted the validity of these concerns and, importantly, there was time for Inglis and Brigadier 'Pip' Roberts, commanding 22nd Armoured Brigade, to fully confer and develop a better understanding. 8th Army thus prepared for Rommel; they had not, however, prepared for Churchill.

On 3 August the prime minister had left England bound for Cairo. He was not alone. Brooke, Wavell and Field Marshal Smuts were to join him. Though Churchill had suffered immense frustrations over seemingly endless delays and disappointments, he had always been impressed by Auchinleck's many qualities and soldierly bearing. Nonetheless, in the words of the Official History:

Mr Churchill and the C.I.G.S. [Chief of the Imperial General Staff] now carried out a brisk programme of interviews and inspections in Cairo and the Western Desert. They met many senior army and air officers, including in particular General Gott, and visited the Australian and South African Divisions. On 6 August Mr Churchill discussed his impressions with General Smuts, Mr Casey and General Brooke. He concluded, and his advisors agreed, drastic and immediate changes should be made to impart a new and vigorous impulse to the Army and restore confidence in the High Command.[25]

Auchinleck's perceived failure to deliver a knock-out blow had obviously weakened Churchill's negotiating position with the Americans. With agreement reached, it was absolutely imperative that *Acrobat* be revived. It seemed increasingly that the Auk would not be able to deliver. Even Brooke, his patient champion, was beginning to lose confidence and the downbeat nature of the commander-in-chief's communications further undermined his position. Auchinleck lacked the ability both to weld his subordinates into an effective, cohesive team and also the knack of dealing with his political masters, where a blunt rendition of the true position was not always the best course.

Whatever his limitations, Auchinleck shouldered an immense burden from which he had never flinched. He may not have defeated Rommel but he had stopped him dead in his tracks. His direct command of 8th Army had been a decision forced upon him by circumstances and was undoubtedly the right one. He now recognized the need for a fresh pair of hands and favoured Gott. He reckoned that the officer appointed to command 8th Army must be:

> ... a man of vigour and personality and have a most flexible and receptive mind. He must also be young, at any rate in mind and body, and be prepared to take advice and learn unless he has had previous Western Desert experience.[26]

Brooke was keen to advance Montgomery,[27] something of a protégé but someone who the CIGS believed could deliver, despite his contentious nature. Though it was not immediately proposed to relieve Auchinleck, the 'chill', as Dorman-Smith described the atmosphere,[28] could clearly be felt when the prime minister arrived at Desert HQ; the Auk himself had no gift for courtly diplomacy.

The interview that followed in the stuffy, fly-laden heat of the operations room was not a happy one. Dorman-Smith felt he and Auchinleck were alone with a 'caged gorilla'.[29] Churchill was more on 'transmit' than 'receive' mode, brusquely demanding offensive action without really listening to the matters being explained. Reasoning was mere excuse and Churchill was not disposed to listen; he pointedly went outside with his back to his two senior officers. It was not auspicious.

Progressing to 13 Corps, the prime minister fastened upon Gott and spent some time alone with him, forming a favourable impression. Gott's excellent fighting record, high personal courage and correct soldierly manner impressed Churchill at a time when he was clearly utterly disenchanted with the pairing of Auchinleck and Dorman-Smith. The mere fact the Auk, like Brooke, favoured Montgomery probably helped the prime minister decide upon Gott as new 8th Army commander.

For Auchinleck, the die was cast and he was to be replaced by Alexander, an excellent choice and a general who was imbued with an innate flair for difficult diplomacy. Churchill expected his new commander-in-chief to lead the onslaught against the Axis personally and proposed to hive off the 'northern' or Iraq/Iran sector, leaving the commander-in-chief Middle East better placed to concentrate his energies in the Western Desert. Dorman-Smith and others, who Churchill saw as tainted with the Auk's tarnished brush, were to be cleared out.

On 7 August, Gott carried out his final briefing as a unit commander, ensuring his officers in 13 Corps knew exactly what was expected of them in the coming battle. Perhaps for the first time, 8th Army had a precise understanding of the enemy's intentions with a clear, coherent and cohesive plan. Infantry, artillery and armour understood their roles and the roles of their supporting arms. The senior officers were familiar with each other, confident and ready. It seemed a propitious moment for their charismatic commander to ascend the promotional ladder.

Gott then prepared to fly to Cairo, hoping for a few days' leave before taking up the command he would never exercise. Random fate relegated Gott's command to one of history's tantalizing 'what ifs'. His plane crashed and he was killed.[30] Not all in 8th Army mourned Gott's sudden death.[31] Montgomery thus gained 8th Army as Brooke would have wished, but ironically by default. Auchinleck, having been summarily removed was offered the truncated northern command, more of an insult than a compromise, and one he understandably declined.

Alexander, in taking over his new command, was blessedly free of the peripheral entanglements that had bedevilled his predecessors. He reinstated McCreery, whom Auchinleck had dismissed, and this proved a most judicious appointment. It is hard not to feel, however, that the historical record has been unfair on Auchinleck. Much of what was subsequently achieved was due to his and Dorman-Smith's solid preparation. He had, above all, kept 8th Army in being. Without this, neither Alexander nor Montgomery could have succeeded in their designated roles. 'Monty', it has to be said, was not one to share the limelight.

Alexander's instructions were plain, as set out in a directive on 10 August:

1. Your prime and main duty will be to take or destroy at the earliest opportunity the German-Italian Army commanded by

Field-Marshal Rommel together with all its supplies and establishments in Egypt and Libya.

2. You will discharge or cause to be discharged such other duties as pertain to your Command without prejudice to the task described in paragraph 1 which must be considered paramount in His Majesty's interest.[32]

Monty was nevertheless very much the new broom. Unlike his predecessor he was very much part of the British military establishment and knew which officers he wanted, men who he already knew. He was not shy over getting rid of those who did not fit the bill. Alexander had made it plain that there would be no further retreats and that established divisional formations would stay as they were. Both of these pronouncements produced collective sighs of relief. Morale was not low, but it was clouded by uncertainty. This would now disappear, as the Official History recounts:

General Montgomery ... set to work at once to inspire confidence and enthusiasm in his Army. His address to the officers of Army headquarters made a tremendous impact, of which word soon spread. The defence of Egypt lay at El Alamein, he said, and if the 8th Army could not stay there alive it would stay there dead. There would be no more backward looks.[33]

One of Monty's most remarkable and admirable traits was the air of absolute confidence he exuded, regardless of circumstance. Here was a commander who knew his business inside out, who had an almost Cromwellian faith in himself and his men. In a whirlwind tour of the troops Monty cleared away the fustian and made plain his intentions. If Rommel attacked, 8th Army was ready. When that battle was won another and offensive engagement would follow, and this time the

Allies would, in the words of the Official History, 'hit Rommel and his army for six right out of Africa'.[34] When Monty said it, people believed him. He described his meeting with HQ staff as follows:

> I introduced myself to them [HQ staff] and said I wanted to see them and explain things. Certain orders had already been issued which they knew about, and more would follow. The order 'no withdrawal' involved a complete change of policy and they must understand what that policy was, because they would have to do the detailed staff work involved. If we were to fight where we stood the defences must have depth; all transport must be sent back to rear areas; ammunition, water, rations etc. must be stored in the forward areas. We needed more troops in the Eighth Army in order to make the 'no withdrawal' order a possibility. There were plenty of troops back in the Delta, preparing the defence of that area; but the defence of the cities of Egypt must be fought out here at El Alamein.[35]

With Gott's death a new corps commander was needed, and Monty drafted in Lieutenant-General Brian Horrocks,* with whom he'd previously worked whilst leading South-East Command.

He had in fact given significant thought to the coming 'modern' defensive battle. He had also decided to retain de Guingand, whom he knew well, in place. This was a wise choice as the chief of staff possessed a flair for diplomacy which his commander most certainly did not. Monty wrote:

---

* Sir Brian Gwynne Horrocks, 1895–1985. Something of an all-rounder, Horrocks competed in the 1924 Paris Olympics and latterly enjoyed a second career as a broadcaster. In 1940 he served under Montgomery and by 1942 commanded 9th Armoured Division. He next took over X Corps from General Lumsden and fought with distinction throughout the Tunisian campaign before being badly injured in a bombing raid on Bizerte.

I had pondered deeply over what I had heard about armoured battles in the desert and it seemed to me that what Rommel liked was to get our armour to attack him; he then disposed of his own armour behind a screen of anti-tank guns, knocked out our tanks and finally had the field to himself. I was determined that would not happen if Rommel decided to attack us before we were ready to launch a full-scale offensive against him. I would not allow our tanks to rush out at him; we would stand firm in the Alamein position, hold the Ruweisat and Alam Halfa Ridges securely, and let him beat up against them. We would fight a static battle and my forces would not move; his tanks would come up against our tanks dug-in in hull down positions at the western end of the Alam Halfa Ridge.[36]

As part of his new broom approach, Montgomery proposed to concentrate the whole HQ function at Burg el Arab and promote closer liaison with the Desert Air Force. This had rather slipped during the course of the recent fighting.[37] The Official History states: 'Now the two Services were to work in double harness, and, as will be seen, in their first big test – at Alam el Halfa – their mutual confidence was to be renewed in an unmistakable manner'.[38] In tactical terms, Montgomery was proposing nothing radical. Rather, he was maintaining the careful work done by Auchinleck, Dorman-Smith, Gott and Ramsden. What he did achieve was to give this detailed planning a clear and public face as far as 8th Army as a whole was concerned. In modern terms, he put a positive 'spin' on what, though sound, had appeared confused and inherently pessimistic. Monty was also helped by the fact the flow of armaments and equipment from both Britain and the US was continuing to build.[39]

On the other side of the hill there was less general cause for optimism. As matters improved for 8th Army, the position overall of Panzerarmee Afrika was deteriorating. Rommel continued to suffer supply difficulties. Axis shipping was suffering heavily from the attentions of British planes and warships, and the air route from Crete, whilst less risky, was cumbersome. Most supplies, once unloaded at Tobruk, had to be brought forward by road, and the port received unending attention from British night-bombers, roughly 50 aircraft every 24 hours.[40] Axis intelligence forecast the arrival of a massive Allied convoy due at Suez in early September. If Rommel was to attack, it had to be soon before the disparity became crushing. The full moon was due on 26 August. Clearly this was the moment to strike.

As Gott had predicted, the blow would fall in the south, with a lightning rush through the moonlit dark of the empty desert, sweeping for nearly 31 miles, past the bastion of Alam Halfa to expose 8th Army rear areas. This was to be achieved by dawn and was extremely ambitious. Rommel's right would be covered by his German and Italian mobile formations whilst Ariete and Littorio divisions (Italian XX Corps), both armoured, moved on the left. 90th Light Division, which had been out of the line to recuperate, would take the northern shoulder of the assault. Surprise, speed and guaranteed mobility were the prerequisites of success. Build-up would be accomplished in the hours of darkness with Panzers hidden beneath camouflage during daylight. To keep 8th Army guessing, the Italian forces located in 30 Corps' sector would mount diversionary raids. This was, of course, precisely what Auchinleck, and now Montgomery, had been expecting.

Alam Halfa was, as both sides saw, the pivot. If Rommel could get safely past, his offensive stood a very good chance of achieving success. If he could not, if the Allies remained in possession, then his position would become untenable. The ridge completely dominated his lines of communication. Defences at Alam Halfa were beefed up accordingly and the newly arrived 44th Division was brought up with two brigades (131st and 133rd) deployed, supported by divisional artillery, both field and anti-tank. 22nd Armoured Brigade was massed at the western end of the ridge.

Alam Nayil was garrisoned by Freyberg's New Zealanders, together with 132nd Brigade. Behind, to the north, stood 30 Corps' reserve formation, in the shape of 23rd Armoured Brigade. Eastwards, toward Point 87, was stationed 8th Armoured Brigade. Further south, the deployment of 4th Light Armoured and 7th Motorized brigades had already taken place. As described above, their role was to delay rather than engage. 7th Armoured Division would snap at the flank and heel of any eastward attack. The noose was laid. It merely remained for the Fox to obligingly extend his neck.

The Official History describes the plan clearly:

> The turned-back left flank of the New Zealand Division formed a stiff shoulder which could remain in place without the support of the relatively weak 7th Armoured Division to the south. In rear of the New Zealand Division's position was the Alam el Halfa Ridge, originally chosen by General Auchinleck to be a defended locality, and now strongly fortified and held by the 44th Division. General Horrocks's plan was for the New Zealand and 44th Division to hold their ground to the last, while in the south the 7th Armoured Division, on its wide front, was to delay and harass the enemy as much as possible. It was so likely that the enemy would try to seize the Alam el Halfa Ridge that the 22nd Armoured Brigade was placed in dug-in positions at the western end, where the fire of its tanks and the 6-pdr anti-tank guns of its motor battalion could be united with that of the supporting artillery in a strong defensive fire plan.[41]

As ever, Rommel's prime concern was petrol. Insufficient supplies were available to enable the attack to proceed on 26 August. Kesselring promised to release some 1,500 tons from his Luftwaffe stocks and the Italians promised more, their ships due to reach North Africa on 30 August:

> Consumption had been greatly in excess of the amounts arriving by sea, and stocks of all kinds – particularly fuel and ammunition – were running dangerously low. Rommel reported on the 22nd that, if the Panzerarmee was to attack at the end of August, shipments of about 6,000 tons of fuel and 2,500 tons of ammunition must reach Libya by specified dates between 25 and 30 August. Comando Supremo promised to do everything possible, and sent seven ships, carrying 10,000 tons of fuel, half for the Panzerarmee and half aviation spirit for the Luftwaffe.[42]

In the event, four of the seven ships were sunk. Despite these depressing shortfalls, Rommel could not afford to wait; the offensive would begin on 30 August regardless.

This was to be the date fixed for the attack and everything would hinge upon whether the initial objectives were gained during the night of 30–31 August: the DAK had seven hours in which to go thirty miles and be ready to advance again to the attack.[43] As the tanks rumbled forwards in the dark, they blundered into unseen British minefields of substantial depth. As pioneers moved forward to begin gapping, a storm of fire descended. The Desert Air Force swooped and added a deluge of bombs. The two British harassing formations performed their roles perfectly. When the sun rose over the bare landscape, DAK was still far to the west of its initial objectives. Any element of surprise was now lost. Speed and élan would give way to attrition.

For the Desert Fox, there was no good news. Two of his experienced senior officers were out of action: Bismarck, commanding 21st Panzer Division, had been killed by a mine and Nehring was wounded by a bomb blast. General Fritz Bayerlein assumed temporary command of

DAK as the drive eastwards struggled to gain momentum. Even at this early stage, Rommel contemplated calling a halt, but instead modified his plan of attack. Now, the Panzers would not seek to pass to the east of Alam Halfa but turn north, aiming for Point 132 on the line of the ridge, whilst the Italians made for Point 102 at Alam Bueit. If a breakthrough could be achieved then the Axis forces could continue their drive to the coast, passing the eastern edge of Ruweisat Ridge. At this time, however, around noon on the 31st, both Ariete and Littorio divisions were still held in the minefields and 90th Light Division had halted around Deir el Munassib. It was time to tighten the noose.

Monty now sent 23rd Armoured Brigade to cover the gap between the New Zealanders and 22nd Armoured Brigade. This was just the type of battle he'd intended to fight, his armour hull down and in strength with the Axis doing the 'balaklavering'. Both German tank divisions now smashed into this strong defence and an intense battle raged all afternoon, recorded in the Official History: 'A fierce duel began in which the Royal Scots Greys, the 1st and 104th Regiments R.H.A., and part of the 44th Divisional Artillery joined to give the enemy tanks a hot reception'.[44] The British would not be lured from their positions and the battering cost Rommel dearly. As darkness again fell, the Panzers withdrew. Overall, they had achieved nothing.

Night brought no relief from prowling bombers that hammered the exposed attackers, seeking out transport and supply. The murky dark was suddenly enlivened by the incandescent drop of flares, laying bare the bones of the desert floor, throwing vehicles into stark relief. Montgomery gave credit to the air force for its crucial role:

A most important factor which forced his [Rommel's] eventual withdrawal was the action of the Desert Air Force … Army and Air Force worked on one plan, closely knitted together … A major factor in the overall air plan was Tedder's decision to send his Wellingtons to bomb Tobruk behind Rommel's attack, in that his last quick hope of re-supply vanished.[45]

On 1 September, 15th Panzer Division attempted to outflank 22nd Armoured Brigade but found its advance barred by 8th Armoured Brigade. Other Axis armoured formations scarcely moved, and the Italians were still mired in mines. Trieste and 90th Light divisions, further north, managed some limited gains, insufficient to affect the outcome. It was now stalemate. As darkness fell Desert Air Force began its nightly activities.

Montgomery, true to his expressed doctrine, refused to be drawn, but with all Axis forces committed, he could afford to deplete 30 Corps to stiffen the line at Alam Halfa. South African 2nd Brigade was shifted to a position just above the line of the ridge, whilst 5th Indian Brigade was placed under Freyberg. From the Delta, he moved up 151st Brigade (50th Division) toward the eastern rim. The noose was tightening. British armour in the south was already nibbling at Rommel's exposed flank and Freyberg was ordered to prepare for a southwards thrust. On 1 September the Australians mounted a major raid from their salient, attacking the German 164th Division and netting a haul of prisoners, some 140 in all, though at the cost of sustaining 135 casualties.[46]

Desert Air Force led relentless sorties, reinforced by American bomber squadrons. The US Mitchells added the massive detonation of their 4,000lb bombs to the wailing chorus of destruction. Rommel's difficulties increased when his promised fuel failed to materialize. The Italians had suffered further losses at sea and what was delivered remained on the dockside. Kesselring also failed to make good on his promises. On 2 September, the Fox conceded the game was up and began a phased withdrawal through the maze of the British minefields. He expected to be attacked in force but Montgomery held back, confining his armour to harassment and cutting up stragglers.

Though Rommel might have judged his opponent overly cautious, the British attacks in July had indicated that 8th Army was not yet ready for the offensive. Much additional training and preparation was needed and time was on Montgomery's side. The Official History gives a succinct summary:

> Although it was clear to General Montgomery that Rommel had shot his bolt, he resisted the temptation to start a general counter-attack. He judged the 8th Army to be unready, and going off at half-cock would only make it harder to prepare for the decisive blow he had in mind.[47]

Even Freyberg's push, set for the night of 3–4 September, had very limited objectives, intended to do no more than close the minefield gaps as the Axis withdrew. At 2300 hours on the 3rd the attack went in, with the inexperienced 132nd Brigade suffering heavily from enemy fire.[48] Montgomery recorded that 'the reaction was immediate and violent'.[49] The newcomers had 'much difficulty' in reaching their start lines, being nearly an hour late, by which time the Axis had had ample notice: the Official History states 'there was much straggling and general confusion, which took some time to sort out.'[50] This may be something of an understatement. Brigadier Robertson was disabled by wounds and Brigadier Clifton, commanding 6th New Zealand Brigade, was captured when he ran into enemy positions whilst undertaking reconnaissance.

5th New Zealand Brigade, tried veterans of desert warfare, reached their objectives after heavy fighting. Indeed, the Maoris overran enemy rear areas, wreaking havoc. Next day the Axis counter-attacked in strength. This assault was seen off, as was the next, guns and aircraft piling into the advancing enemy. Such was the intensity of the combat that Freyberg rightly concluded any further attempts by his Kiwis were pointless, as casualties were already high.[51] His subsequent request to withdraw survivors was accepted by both Horrocks and Monty.

In assessing the results of this battle,[52] the Official History defines the effect on morale as being of greater importance than the material gains which were indeed insignificant: 'To the Axis the battle seemed to put an end to their hopes of reaching the Delta. To the British it appeared as a clear cut victory in which Rommel had been defeated at his own game'.[53] This must substantively be correct. 8th Army had won no new ground nor destroyed the Panzerarmee Afrika, but it had fought Rommel to a standstill and obliged him to withdraw. The limited offensive operation with the closing of the minefield gap as its objective had failed, but it had demonstrated advantages, as the Official History records:

> What had been plain for all to see was the benefit of concentrating resources, which was made possible by a particularly accurate forecast of what Rommel was going to do. This meant that the enemy's striking force could be met on ground of the defenders' choice by a tremendous volume of fire: from the air with a rain of projectiles ranging from machine gun bullets to 4,000lb bombs, and from the ground with the concentrated fire of field and medium artillery, anti-tank guns and the guns of dug in tanks, notably the Grants.[54]

8th Army had scored a significant defensive triumph. The task now was to convert this new confidence into an overwhelmingly successful attack. If a blow could be struck at Rommel's over-stretched and precarious logistics, this could significantly affect his ability to stand. Fuel was critical. The obvious target had to be Tobruk. The logic of striking a major behind-the-lines blow at the enemy's logistical tail was inescapable. Translating that wish into reality would be the trick.

Sung to the tune of *Blaydon Races* –

We were told to go to Libya, one December afternoon
After ice-cream merchants, the fighting fifth did run
Engineers, infantry and Tank Corps chaps as well
Graziani and his crowd, they ran like blinkin' 'ell.

Chorus:

Oh me lads you should have seen us gangin'
Past the Eyeties on the road, with their hands up they were standing
Their officers wore posh uniforms; the rank and file wore rags
But every prisoner we did see was sporting large, white flags.
We flew past Sidi Barrani, past the Capuzzo fort
We stopped outside of Bardia and a battle there was fought
We broke up their defences
And lots of prisoners we did take
Then on the road to old Tobruk with all haste we did make.

Chorus

Tobruk was the next objective, that's what we were told
Supporting Australian infantry went in the old and bold
We made the attack at the crack of dawn
And broke through their front line
Then through the Dagoes we did go, just like a number nine.

Chorus

R. J. Luke, 1st Royal Northumberland Fusiliers, *Libyan Handicap*

CHAPTER FIVE

OPERATION TOPSY

'Never in the whole history of human endeavour have so few been buggered about by so many.'[1] So some unknown wag from Middle East Commando quipped. And he wasn't wrong. Special Forces are by no means popular with regular commanders. Montgomery had little time for them, and whilst he wasn't involved in the planning of Operation *Agreement* and bears no responsibility for its failure, he wasn't slow to add his own stridency to the universal recriminations.

This author's own introduction to the raid came, as mentioned above, via Hollywood. As a boy, I thrilled to the screen version of Peter Rabe's book *Tobruk* with Rock Hudson and George Peppard. Being from the USA the storyline had to cast an American as hero and the sub-plot involving the SIGs bore no resemblance worth speaking of to history. It was a very good film though. Nigel Green and Jack Watson, with a host of British actors, played the commandos, though none really resembled Haselden.

In the film, Rommel's fuel supply went up in a blaze of biblical proportions and the legions of the fearful Axis were suitably decimated.

Earlier, and though set in the Dodecanese (a later disaster), Alistair Maclean's brilliant *Guns of Navarone* carried clear resonances of the raid on Tobruk. That's the beauty of fiction, the good side always wins. It could be said those who planned the actual operation were similarly inspired, except their cast comprised real flesh and blood and the dead would not be rising at the end.

Winston Churchill liked commando raids. He liked the Henty-esque derring-do and the idea of clandestine assaults on the enemy where he least expected to be attacked. The prime minister also liked the idea that, despite the many reverses Britain had suffered and despite the ongoing crisis in the Western Desert, the constant tale of woe from the Far East and the parlous position of our almost-allies in Russia, we could somehow hit back. Besides, the Germans didn't really understand the whole commando concept: amphibious operations and peripheral strategies were not really their style. Tobruk was also dear to Churchill's heart. The Great Siege rated as an Allied victory when these were very scarce indeed. The final, humiliating fall was a massive blow. He wanted the place back or at least convincingly denied to the Axis.

The idea of attacking the Axis at Tobruk was by no means a novelty in the summer of 1942. Operation *Agreement* probably owed its genesis to a scheme put forward in October 1940 at the very start of the Desert War. The aim of the first proposal was much the same, to destroy fuel dumps and harbour facilities. There was no shortage of suitable targets: four large oil tanks by the harbour, each of 32,000 gallon capacity, another four Benzedrine vats nearby, petrol stores north of the local settlement, and a dump seven miles south of the town and the El Adem junction. The power station, magazines, wireless stations and distillery were all ripe for destruction.[2]

All of the main jetties projected from the north flank of the harbour, together with a slipway. Water depth at the end of the piers was between 14 and 20 feet.[3] The coaling jetty and boom jetty provided anchor points for a brace of booms cordoning the harbour. One of these stretched from Marsa Agaisa to a bunker on the northern flank, whilst the other reached from the southern side 400 yards west of the Marsa Sciarfa up to the coaling pier.[4] The entrances were mined and the fighting strength of the garrison around 17,000 strong; a formidable defence. The port was guarded by numerous coastal guns. One vulnerable feature was the access to the port area from the lower of the escarpments ringing the town. Two fairly narrow tracks came running downhill; blocks placed across these could create a bottleneck and halt the flow of enemy reinforcements.

There were two alternatives: a classic hit and run night attack or a prolonged occupation that would breach the daylight hours. It was recognized that, as ever, with raids, surprise was the key element. For that reason it was deemed essential that the raiders be brought in by fast destroyers. This was logical, but there weren't enough of the sleek warships to be found. Another essential was overhead fighter cover to facilitate the withdrawal, tricky at best. Again, fighters were scarce.

***

Four groups of raiders were to be deployed. Group 'A' would land to the west and hit the fuel dumps north of the aerodrome. The second, Group 'B', would land simultaneously at the same spot, then attack those installations east of the naval barracks and take out any planes that happened to come within their sights. Group 'C' were to hit the coastal guns north of the settlement and possibly the fuel stores in the same vicinity. The last group would simply attack the town itself and generally 'cry havoc'. This would sufficiently distract the defenders and prevent them being a nuisance to the other groups. This last formation,

Group 'D', would comprise a single Special Service Company, and they would target command and control centres during their spree.[5] The men would carry weapons and ammunition only.

To convey the raiders only a modest naval flotilla was required: four destroyers, the same number of motor torpedo boats (MTBs) and a single submarine. The approach, however, would require the involvement of the entire Mediterranean Fleet as a grand diversion. The ships would sail as though preparing to shepherd a Malta convoy, and the attack force would peel off towards the Libyan coast. By the time they were steaming towards the hostile shore, the lone submarine would have marked the landing zones and guided the laden warships in. Meanwhile, the MTB flotilla, coming westwards along the coast probably from either Alexandria or Crete, (still in Allied hands at that point), would make smoke to cover the actual landings. As soon as the troops were onshore, the landing boats would withdraw and be re-hoisted onto the destroyers, which would then stand clear, safely out of range of the coastal guns, until needed to take the raiders off.[6]

Here was the critical point. All amphibious operations may be said to succeed or fail according to how efficiently and swiftly the men are put ashore. The Allies did not, at this stage in the war, possess sufficient specialized landing craft. They relied, as ever, upon innovation and making do generally. Making do could take one of two forms. The normal ships' boats could be used. These were tried and sturdy, but clearly would be insufficient in terms of available numbers. Additional boats could be found and more davits fitted. Alternatively, some form of lightweight specialized craft could be built. This seemed reasonable. The boats would have to be seaworthy and reasonably easy to navigate, but making do like this rather depends upon the seas being co-operative. The Mediterranean is rarely so obliging.

Though they opted for the second choice, the planners of Operation *Waylay*, as the scheme was dubbed, were aware of the limitations. Calm seas and light northerlies would be vital. It would take the raiders five hours to accomplish their allotted tasks with a further period of three and a half hours needed to complete the landings. Near-total darkness was clearly another essential. What the *Waylay* team proposed was that the air raid should take place *after* rather than prior to the raid. This and a naval bombardment would provide the shield behind which the commandos would re-embark. We cannot say exactly what influence the early idea exerted over those planning *Agreement*, but in hindsight we can say it was probably a better plan, or at least less flawed.[7]

When Tobruk fell to Rommel, it wasn't just a blow to Churchill's pride and Britain's tottering esteem, but it netted the Axis a significant haul of booty. The Allies had reaped a similar harvest when prising the place away from the Italians. Hitler had written encouragingly to his ally Mussolini, sufficiently so for Il Duce to plan his own triumphal entry into Alexandria as the new Caesar, even if any such entry would largely be effected on the back of German efforts. In fact, Rommel had failed, but the hot desert summer of 1942 saw Allied fortunes at very low ebb. The Desert Fox had stumbled at the final hurdle, but he was still unbeaten. With hindsight, it is possible to see how the position had in fact shifted. The Allies, in Montgomery, would finally have a general of equal worth, and the build-up of strength, facilitated by Britain's American allies, would finally tilt the balance Monty's way.

Admiral Andrew Cunningham* had commanded the Mediterranean Fleet with great élan and considerable success. Il Duce had been thrashed at sea as comprehensively as on land. His successor, Admiral

---

* Admiral Browne Cunningham (1883–1963, widely known simply as ABC, was probably the most outstanding British naval commander of the war. He commanded the Mediterranean Fleet during the early stages of the North African War.

Sir Henry Harwood,* faced a difficult challenge. His ships had taken a fearful pounding trying to succour Malta. He had neither battleships nor carriers and the RAF could provide only very limited cover. The savaging meted out to Royal Navy ships salvaging survivors from the mess on Crete had shown just what damage sustained aerial attack could do. Churchill was still expecting the reduced fleet to achieve prodigies, and, at the same time, to arrange blocking operations against Tobruk and Benghazi.

This was a favourite obsession of the prime minister – using blockships to bottle up enemy ports. It was highly difficult, dangerous, of dubious long term value and bound to be expensive in terms of both ships and men. Cunningham had vigorously resisted any such notions. In mid-April 1941, he had been urged to commit one of his only battle-cruisers, HMS *Barham*, in an attempt to block Tripoli.[8] Cunningham considered the idea crazy and resisted. Churchill personally intervened to press the scheme. The admiral ignored the exhortation.

Once Tobruk had fallen to Rommel, such daft ideas were resurrected. On 21 July, Harwood received a message from Whitehall (undoubtedly inspired or even drafted by the prime minister) that he should send a destroyer to attack shipping in the harbour: the signal did admit 'this is a desperate measure'.[9] Hysteria was the order of the day, a mood ably caught by the well-known commando Fitzroy Maclean:'In Cairo the staff at GHQ Middle East were burning their files ['Ash Wednesday'] and the Italian colony were getting out their black shirts and fascist badges in preparation for Mussolini's triumphant entry'.[10] It was in this heated and fearful context that the idea for Operation *Agreement* took root and began to grow.

Whilst the notion of the earlier concept, Operation *Waylay*, may have formed a viable precedent, both Stirling and Haselden had put

---

* Admiral Sir Henry Harwood (1880–1950) took over the Mediterranean Fleet in April 1942.

forward ideas for limited attacks against Tobruk and Benghazi. These were plans for clean, surgical strikes involving land forces only, SAS, LRDG and other raiders. What would become the plan for Force B was Haselden's idea, a group of commandos, sneaking through Tobruk's defended perimeter, attacking fuel installations, then withdrawing swiftly across the desert. This would be something on the scale of the actual LRDG attack on Barce, which did achieve some gains, though these came at a high price.

When suggesting an attack on Benghazi, Stirling had, unwittingly, opened a Pandora's Box by proposing to add a naval element including a blockship. Fitzroy Maclean, always a *beau sabreur* of the cut likely to appeal to the prime minister, found himself dining with Churchill in Cairo. He recalled:

> The plans for a raid on Benghazi had been greeted with enthusiasm at GHQ. With such enthusiasm that by the time they came back to us they were practically unrecognizable. The latest scheme envisaged a major operation against Benghazi, to be carried out in conjunction with similar large scale operations elsewhere.[11]

Another commando element was added by the Special Boat Service (SBS). This unit was the brainchild of Lieutenant Roger Courtney, who had joined the commandos in mid-1940. He had the idea of specialist raiders who would approach from the seas using folding kayaks. Initially nobody seemed interested, so he adopted the bold and unorthodox tactic of launching his own private raid against HMS *Glengyle* moored in the Clyde. He got aboard undetected and wrote his initials on the door of the captain's cabin, seizing some booty as further proof. He flung his gains at the astonished feet of his superiors then dining in the Inverary Hotel. Message received, he was promoted and given a dozen men to nurture his new unit.

The Folboat was some 16 feet in length, a rubberized canvas surface stretched over a timber frame with front and rear buoyancy bags. These handy, folding kayaks took two men and their kit. The Folbot troop became No 1 Special Boat section early in 1941 and the team was deployed to the Mediterranean as part of Layforce. Courtney's raiders successfully carried out a series of missions and returned to the UK in December to recruit a second formation. The original bunch were grafted onto Stirling's SAS as the Folboat Section and carried out a further series of raids during the early summer of 1942.[12] It was felt by the Directorate of Combined Operations that up to half a dozen teams, taken in by three subs, could paddle into Tobruk Harbour and fix limpet mines to Axis vessels there. Once their charges were planted, they would slide out of the harbour and get back by moving only at night and hugging the coast till picked up by MTBs. The idea foundered, however, as there weren't enough submarines available.

Rommel's Achilles heel was his supply route. If both Tobruk and Benghazi were hit and successfully put out of action, even temporarily, then his logistical troubles would multiply, forcing him to extend his supply lines even further. Such a deprivation of resources at a time when both sides were girding their loins for what would be the decisive clash could reap a huge dividend for the Allies, though by no means all of the planners were convinced.

On 3 August the Joint Planning Staff (JPS) set out their initial considerations in Paper 106. The prime objective was to destroy harbour facilities and installations at both ports, as it was thought that this may well lead to the rapid defeat of Rommel by land forces.[13] This was wildly optimistic at best, wishful thinking embodied in tactical planning. Operation *Agreement* began with a wish that was built up into a plan; pious hopes, fed by frustration and desperation, led from the start. The planners went on to detail the units that could be employed to find sufficient forces without pinching from 8th Army. This was fine by Monty, as the operation wasn't his and the resources would not be his. If it went well, he could look to grab some of the credit; if it failed, he could simply stand clear.

Ideally, both places should be attacked simultaneously, if the forces available were sufficiently strong. If not, then Tobruk would remain the prime target. In each case the tactics would be similar. The landward party would be responsible for rushing the coastal guns, taking these under new management and turning them against their previous owners. Amphibious raiders would be responsible for most of the demolitions, which would be blown in daylight. The whole lot would re-embark at dusk. This draft was then reviewed by the Director of Military Operations General HQ Middle East Forces (DMO GHQ MEF). He broadly concurred and 8th Army would not be placed to start attacking before 30 September. Rommel was getting new tanks through Benghazi plus some 1,200 to 2,000 tons of supplies per day; rather less was coming in through Tobruk.[14]

If the raids could be carried out by the middle of August, then Rommel might be seriously embarrassed. The initial drafts highlighted the risks and advised that losses might be heavy. The final draft acknowledged casualties could be as a high as one hundred percent of those taking part in the landings.[15] It wouldn't be feasible to launch the raids until the first week in September and the JPS were never more than lukewarm. The commander-in-chief, however, seized upon the idea and his reaction to Paper 106 was galvanic; 'I am in NO rpt NO doubt that it is essential rpt essential that these operations take place in August and that probable losses must rpt must be accepted'.[16] It doesn't get much plainer than that. Operation *Agreement* was now pretty much assured, and there wasn't going to be room for doubters.

If this wasn't emphatic enough, the commander-in-chief went on to stress how important the psychological aspect would be, uplifting for the Allied troops and depressing for the Axis. If any lingering qualms persisted, the JPS were exhorted 'to adopt a more vigorous and offensive habit of thought'.[17] The die was cast, and the operation would be vigorous and aggressive. It is probably not entirely coincidental that Churchill was in Cairo at this time. The tone of the communication does rather suggest his style. GHQ got the message and agreed their planners were falling short of the bulldog temperament. If the PM was so adamant, who were they to object?

To deliver before September was problematic, even with the most snappish of bulldogs barking. It couldn't be done during the dark moon period in August, though Admiral Harwood did not apparently consider that full darkness was necessarily vital. Overland elements would have to approach via Kufra, an immense distance to cover, and some of those among the raiding parties might not be fully trained up. As Peter Smith points out, Operation *Agreement* had become *Topsy*; it just kept on getting bigger. A further strand, Operation *Hoopoe*, an attempt to recapture Siwa Oasis, was now bolted on. An all-arms force there could create merry hell with enemy transport and oblige the DAK to detach substantial forces to remove the threat. The bigger the threat, the bigger the response, so the idea was to beef up the attacking force, providing AA (anti-aircraft) cover and giving the enemy something really massive to worry about.

It was known that the Italian garrison at Siwa was quite small, at best a weak battalion, with no armour and only a quartet of 37mm Breda AA guns. It could be attacked by LRDG/SAS, with some armour to add a heavier punch, and then the main force could move up and take ownership. This would be a hefty contingent including a regiment of Honeys, Bren carriers, transport, signals, guns, engineers, medics,

RASC and RAF detachments.[18] Happily, the commander-in-chief wisely decided against such a commitment and *Hoopoe* went in the basket. Popski, most irregular of irregulars, summed up the comic opera of GHQ in unflattering terms:

> Friends joined in with suggestions picked from boyish books that they had pored over in earnest only a few years before, Drake and Sir Walter Raleigh, Morgan and the Buccaneers were outbidden; new stratagems poured out in a stream of inventiveness.[19]

This is probably not such a gross exaggeration. Lieutenant-Colonel Calthorpe on the planning staff undertook a review of the planning process as it stood in the latter part of August. He stressed that the prime objective at both ports was to take and hold the enemy's defensive ring or those elements that could fire on the demolition parties. As with Operation *Waylay*, the prime factor was surprise. Where Calthorpe differed was in the timing of the air raid. He wanted this before and not after, to cover the approach rather than screen the withdrawal. The reasoning behind this is understandable, but what price surprise? The enemy would not require high levels of tactical insight to twig that they were being softened up prior to an attack.[20] There was also the matter of timing; it had to be either mid-August or from 8 to 13 September when moonlight was minimal.

As planning moved beyond feasibility into detail, it was recognized that both attacks should ideally go in on the same date. Surprise only comes around once. As the assault on Benghazi could not be staged before the end of August, it made compelling sense to deliver both the following month. The delay would allow for sorely needed training and preparation. Destruction of enemy supplies would be as damaging in September as it would have been in August.[21]

Broadly then, the plan for Tobruk was that a land-based element would attack the coastal guns at the south-east end of the harbour before moving westwards to seize the additional guns on the south side. This would have to be accomplished in darkness, so detailed local knowledge of the tricky and broken ground east of the port was clearly essential. Assuming this part of the operation succeeded and the requisite signal was given by 0200 hours, a flotilla of MTBs with around 200 reinforcements would slide into the cove at Mersa Umm Es Sciausc, previously secured as a beach head. The full complement would then advance westwards to silence the southern battery and destroy the various dumps and facilities that lay in their path.

To the west at Mersa Mreira, a strong party of marines would come ashore and sweep along the northern flank, dealing with the guns and facilities there, gathering in a shoal of lighters. Once the flanks were secure the MTBs would pull out of the cove and accelerate into the harbour itself, where they'd torpedo any targets of opportunity, hiding themselves amongst the debris. With all of the enemy guns in British hands, the MTBs would cut out or sink lighters. They'd be joined by the two Tribal Class destroyers, which would take precautions to disguise themselves as a ruse against air attack while the shore party manned captured AA defences. The whole force would ship out at dusk.

This was the plan for Tobruk, bastard child of Operation *Waylay*. It marked a very significant leap from the modest spoiling raids proposed by Stirling and Haselden. It was bold, certainly, but reliant upon a whole series of disparate groups being able to coalesce on time and in the dark. It counted upon a weak enemy garrison, stunned by the ferocity of the air raid and yet not on alert. The seaborne elements were dependent on the right weather conditions. Good communications between the interlocking units was essential, but British radios didn't always work.

It was very complex. At Benghazi, rather surprisingly, it was decided that Stirling's 'L' Detachment could manage the job without amphibious support. He would have a small naval party along, but ensuring the raid was more hit and run obviated the need to take and hold coastal guns. It scaled down the complexities a very considerable extent and minimized the potential loss of men and ships. As Peter Smith points out, this reasoning could as easily have been applied to the attack on Tobruk.[22] That process did not occur.

***

The final orders for Operation *Agreement* were set out in the commander-in-chief's Combined Operation Instruction No. 1, dated 21 August and issued to Captain Micklethwait, lieutenant colonels E. M. H. 'Mit' Unwin (Force A) and Haselden (Force B). The overall tactical aims were to destroy petrol and oil installations, to sink enemy shipping, degrade harbour and dock installations and to bring away port lighters. Those that could not be 'cut out' were to be shot up and sunk.[23]

Exact orders of battle (ORBAT) are as shown in the appendix, but Unwin's seaborne invaders would comprise his own unit, 11th Battalion RM (Royal Marines), with attached AA and Coastal Defence gunners, sections of engineers, signals and medics. The naval elements would be led by Captain Micklethwait, commanding two Tribal Class destroyers, HMS *Sikh* and *Zulu*, which would deliver the marines and their cumbersome, improvised landing craft.

Haselden's Force B was to come out of the desert, the most daring part of the plan. He would have a squadron of Major Campbell's 1st Special Service Regiment, Y Patrol of the LRDG, led by Captain Lloyd Owen, a squad of Buck's SIGs commanded by Buck himself, plus Lieutenant Russell with further detachments of AA and CD artillerymen (Lieutenant Poynton), engineers signals (Captain Trollope) and RAMC

(Royal Army Medical Corps) (Captain Gibson). Force C, which was to land in support of Haselden east of Tobruk, would be formed by a company of the Argylls under Captain Macfie, a machine-gun platoon of the Northumberland Fusiliers, two sub-sections of engineers, AA gunners and medics. The force, coming in from Alexandria, would be conveyed in 15 to 20 MTBs.[24]

Additional naval support would be provided by Forces D and E, which comprised the light AA cruiser HMS *Coventry*, several Hunt Class destroyers from No. 5 Destroyer Flotilla and a single submarine HM *Taku*, responsible for delivering the pathfinder or 'Folbot' party. The entire show would be preceded by a massive RAF raid, bombing the northern shore of the harbour from 2130 hours on Saturday 13 September until 0340 hours the next morning. This opening deluge would be Haselden's cue to begin his attack inside the perimeter, targeting the AA and CD batteries at Mersa Umm Es Sciausc, a cove which lies toward the south-eastern extremity of the main harbour. It was here that Force C would disembark once Haselden signalled the beach head was secure.

Force C had to be in position by 0200 hours at the latest. Besides bringing in the assault troops, they were to beat up enemy shipping beyond and inside the harbour. An hour later the destroyers transporting Force A were to land their marines 1½ miles north of the town at Mersa Mreira. The invaders would then deal with the gun emplacements guarding that flank, fight their way into the port and generally enjoy themselves blowing things up. The warships too would enter the harbour to add the weight of their guns.[25]

Of the three main elements, the role of Force B was most critical. If Haselden's commandos failed to secure the batteries and beach head, then the whole plan would have to be aborted. Force B would have to send the signal for success before 0200 hours on the 14th. If this wasn't picked up, both Forces A and B would withdraw. The original RAF element was to involve additional air raids on 12, 13 and 14 September on selected targets not only along the North African coast but also on Crete. Low flying aircraft would come in close on the night of the 13th to distract and confuse enemy radar and lookouts.[26]

It was whilst the whole of Force B was concentrated at Kufra on 1 September that Haselden issued his operational orders. The force would march out from the oasis on 6 September piled into in eight 3-tonners (in addition to Y Patrol's vehicles) and motor across the desert to a forming up area in the vicinity of Sidi Rezegh of evil memory by 1200 hours on D1. Moving out at dusk on the 12th and less the LRDG contingent the commandos would sneak into the Tobruk perimeter via the eastern approach. Here they'd come through camouflaged as depressed and scruffy Allied POWs, guarded by DAK *abteilung* who would in fact be Buck and his SIGs posing as Germans.

Assuming the ruse worked and they passed through without being rumbled, they'd approach the cove at Mersa Umm Es Sciausc through the maze of wadis cutting through towards the shore. A track was known to run down past the aerodrome at El Gubi. Lieutenant T. B. Langton from the Irish Guards and 'borrowed' from the SAS would be the pathfinder. Force C had to be safely ashore by 0230 hours.[27] Once the bombs began to fall (and it was hoped the roar of engines and explosions would drown the MTB approach), Force B would split into two assault groups.

One contingent with the artillerymen and engineers would descend upon enemy gun positions on both flanks of the cove. They'd deal with any opposition and turn the captured ordnance on any ships trying to get clear of the harbour. Three sections were to take the eastern positions and the remainder those to the west.[28] Taking these guns was deemed vital. If they could not be silenced, then the whole operation should be called off. Both German and Italian passwords were known and the attackers would use the name 'George Robey'.[*]

David Lloyd Owen and his piratical crew would not be left idle. Their task was, two hours after the commandos had got through the wire, to follow on and attack a radar station. The place was to be thoroughly destroyed before midnight, and at dawn LRDG would fall upon the Axis landing fields at El Gubi and wreak their customary havoc. Having had their fun, they'd then set up a block astride the Bardia road to deal with any enemy reinforcements coming up from that direction.[29]

Whilst Tobruk was being attacked, the second raid, Operation *Bigamy*, would target Benghazi. This group, dubbed Force X, would comprise Stirling himself leading L Detachment of 1st SAS marching in 40-odd jeeps, supported by two LRDG patrols (S1 and S2) with a further detachment of Royal Marines. Their objectives were still substantial – to block the inner harbour, sink ships and blast port installations. Mission accomplished, Force X would retire only as far as Jalo Oasis and launch more raids over an intense, three-week period.[30] At one point, it was proposed to ferry in a full battalion from Malta and throw in a couple of Honeys. This enlargement was, happily, soon mainly forgotten.

Another LRDG patrol would guide a unit of the SDF (Sudan Defence Force) to Jalo Oasis (then in enemy hands), on the night of 15/16 September, in Operation *Nicety*. It was thought the place was weakly held by Italians and the SDF was to be beefed up with howitzers, anti-tank and AA guns. The RAF would bomb Benghazi as well as Tobruk. Planes would sow a harvest of dummy 'parashots' over Siwa,

---

[*] Though largely forgotten today, Sir George Robey was one of the most celebrated music hall performers and pantomime dames of the early twentieth century.

which would be ostensibly threatened by a feint mounted by SDF. Two more LRDG patrols, led by Captain Jake Easonsmith, would also attack Barce, purely their affair. This merest of mere sideshows would be the only successful operation.

Lieutenant Colonel Unwin would lead 11th Battalion Royal Marines in the amphibious assault. The CO, a mature officer recalled to service, was described as 'taciturn but a good leader, bold in nature and concerned to turn 11 RM into an aggressive commando force'.[31] His battalion had endured a frustrating war. They'd been raised as part of the Mobile Naval Base Defence Organization (MNBDO). Their function was to provide and secure temporary naval havens wherever the need should arise. Employment had been found for them on Crete in the superb anchorage of Suda Bay, but 11th Battalion had arrived too late for this deployment; a blessing as it turned out after the skies over Crete darkened with General Karl Student's *Fallschirmjäger*.

Throughout the remainder of 1941, the marines trained around the Bitter Lakes, possibly once an extended finger of the Red Sea, but they spent a depressing amount of their time guarding Morscar Barracks. In 1942 they spent long periods at Haifa, a crucial port and link to the lifeline of Anglo-Iranian oil. On 15 April they finally went to war in earnest when Unwin led a company sized force in an amphibious raid on the small island of Kuphonisi off the south-east tip of occupied Crete.

Their mission was to destroy an Axis wireless station. It became very lively but they got the job done and left the place wrecked. An enemy collaborator in the pleasing form of an ample swine was made captive (POW = 'pig of war'). This was rich booty indeed. Ironically, the codes and ciphers they'd filched had already been cracked, but the marines' larceny prompted the enemy to change these.[32]

The marines trained aboard the two Tribal Class destroyers *Sikh* and *Zulu*. These were larger type destroyers but they were well above reasonable capacity when 200 marines and their boats were embarked.[33] Land-based fitness training took place in Palestine, Trans-Jordan and Egypt. The men were strong and they were ready. The difficulty lay in how they might be got ashore. Clearly, this is the critical element in any amphibious operation, and has exercised commanders since the Siege of Troy. The plans for *Waylay* had favoured purpose built timber craft as opposed to ships' boats. On paper this made sense. In practice it did not, as Major Mahoney recalled:

> The selected small craft dumb lighters towed by small powered craft, and these small three ply power boats with their dumb lighters were all the contemplated boats for the landing. They were pathetically slow and subjected mainly to fouled propellers in shallow waters during exercises.[34]

Nobody liked the boats, as Gunner Wilson stated:

> We first practiced the landings at Cyprus with these special boats built in Lebanon, and the 'Sikh' could carry about half a dozen of these I think. They were built with green Lebanon wood and were extremely fragile and far from handy … As far as I can remember they were not very long, about fifteen to sixteen feet and very lightly built of wood on steel frames.[35]

Here lay the problem, the fatal flaw. The concept for getting the marines ashore was wrong from the start, as it involved cheap nasty little boats, barely seaworthy in calm water, far less so in rough. This tactical design failure would come back to haunt the execution of Operation *Agreement*.

The marines did not fail, but these shoddy excuses for landing craft, or 'shoeboxes', did for them as surely as any Axis guns.

This was bad, but the security situation was worse, as Fitzroy Maclean remembered:

> For obvious reasons, secrecy was vital, and only a very small number of those taking part in the operations were told what their destination was to be. But long before we were ready to start there were signs that too many people knew too much. At Alexandria a drunken marine was heard boasting in a canteen that he was off to Tobruk; a Free French officer picked up some startling information at Beirut; one of the barmen at the hotel, who was generally thought to be an enemy agent, seemed much too well informed. Worse still, there were indications that the enemy was expecting the raids and taking counter measures.[36]

If surprise was the key, then so was secrecy. If the enemy got wind of the plan, the game was effectively up. That Tobruk was a likely target required no hint of genius. Intelligence is at the heart of all successful operations. So far the Allies, thanks to the brilliance of the Bletchley code-breakers, were doing rather well. The arrival of Rommel in the North African Theatre coincided with the establishment of a special signals link to Wavell and Middle East Command in Cairo. Hut 3 at Bletchley could now transmit reports directly to the GOC. Ultra intelligence was not able to identify Rommel's immediate counter-offensive, but Hut 6 had broken the Luftwaffe key now designated 'Light Blue.' Early decrypts revealed the concern felt by OKH (Oberkommando des Heeres) at Rommel's maverick strategy and indicated the extent of his supply problems.

Though the intercepts were a major tactical gain in principle, the process was new and subject to delay to the extent that they rarely arrived in time to influence the events in the field during a highly mobile campaign.[37] Equally, Light Blue was able to provide some details of Rommel's seaborne supplies but again in insufficient detail and with inadequate speed to permit a suitable response from either the RN or RAF.

Then, in July 1941 a major breakthrough occurred. An Italian navy cipher, 'C38m', was also broken, and the flood of detail this provided greatly amplified that gleaned from Light Blue. Information was now passed not just to Cairo but to the RN at Alexandria and the RAF on Malta. Every care, as ever, had to be taken to ensure the integrity of Ultra was preserved. Jim Rose, one of Bletchley's air advisors, explains:

> Ultra was very important in cutting Rommel's supplies. He was fighting with one hand behind his back because we were getting information about all the convoys from Italy. The RAF were not allowed to attack them unless they sent out reconnaissance and if there was fog of course they couldn't attack them because it would have jeopardised the security of Ultra, but in fact most of them were attacked[38]

Ultra thus contributed significantly to Rommel's supply problem. On land a number of army keys were also broken; these were designated by names of birds. Thus it was 'Chaffinch' that provided Auchinleck with detailed information on DAK supply shortages and weight of materiel including tanks. Since mid-1941 a Special Signals Unit (latterly Special Liaison Unit) had been deployed in theatre. The unit had to ensure information was disseminated only amongst those properly 'in the know' and that, vitally, identifiable secondary intelligence was always available to mask the true source.

Experience gained during the *Crusader* offensive indicated that the best use of Ultra was to provide detail of the enemy's strength and pre-battle dispositions. The material could not be decrypted fast enough nor sent on to cope with a fast changing tactical situation. At the front, information could be relayed far more quickly by the Royal Signals mobile Y-Special Wireless Sections and battalion intelligence officers, one of whom, Bill Williams, recalled:

> Despite the amazing speed with which we received Ultra, it was of course usually out of date. This did not mean we were not glad of its arrival for at best it showed that we were wrong, usually it enabled us to tidy up loose ends, and at least we tumbled into bed with a smug confirmation. In a planning period between battles its value was more obvious and one had the opportunity to study it in relation to context so much better than during a fast moving battle such as desert warfare produced.[39]

Wireless in the vastness of the desert was the only effective mode of communication, but wireless messages are always subject to intercept. Bertie Buck's Jews from Palestine provided specialist skills. Most were German in origin and understood only too well the real nature of the enemy they faced. The Germans had their own Y Dienst (Y Service) and the formidable Captain Seebohm, whose unit proved highly successful.

The extent of Seebohm's effectiveness was only realized after his unit had been overrun during the attack by 26th Australian Brigade at Tell el Eisa in July 1942. The captain was a casualty and the raiders discovered how extensive the slackness of Allied procedures actually was. As a consequence the drills were significantly tightened. If the Axis effort was thereby dented, Rommel still had a significant source from the US diplomatic codes, which had been broken and regularly included data on Allied plans and dispositions, the 'Black Code'.

Reverses following on from the apparent success of *Crusader* were exacerbated, as Bletchley historians confirm, by 'a serious misreading of a decrypt from the Italian C38m cipher'. Hut 3 could not really assist the British in mitigating the defeat at Gazala or, perhaps worse, the surrender of Tobruk. This was one which Churchill felt most keenly as 'a bitter moment. Defeat is one thing; disgrace is another'.

Until this time it had taken Bletchley about a week to crack Chaffinch, but from the end of May, the ace code-breakers were able to cut this to a day. Other key codes 'Phoenix' and 'Thrush' were also broken. Similar inroads were made against the Luftwaffe. 'Primrose', employed by the supply formation and 'Scorpion', the ground/air link, were both broken. Scorpion was a godsend: as close and constant touch with units in the field was necessary for supply, German signallers unwittingly provided a blueprint for any unfolding battle.

On the ground 8th Army was increasing the total of mobile Y formations, whilst the intelligence corps and RAF code-breakers were getting fully into their stride.[40] None of these developments could combine to save the Auk, but Montgomery was the beneficiary of high level traffic between Rommel and Hitler, sent via Kesselring (as the latter was Luftwaffe). The Red cipher, long mastered by Bletchley, was employed. Monty had already predicted the likelihood of the Alam el Halfa battle, but the intercepts clearly underscored his analysis.

By now the array of air force, navy and army codes penetrated by Bletchley was providing a regular assessment of supply, of available AFVs (Armoured Fighting Vehicles) and the dialogue of senior officers. The relationship between Rommel and Kesselring was evidently strained. Even the most cynical of old sweats, Bill Williams, had cause to be impressed: 'he [Montgomery] told them with remarkable assurance how the enemy was going to be defeated. The enemy attack was delayed and the usual jokes were made about the "crystal-gazers".'

A day or two later everything happened according to plan.[41] Ultra was dispelling the fog of war.

In some ways, the Desert War provided the coming of age for the Bletchley Park code-breakers, as intelligence officer Ralph Bennett explains:

> Until Alam Halfa, we had always been hoping for proper recognition of our product … Now the recognition was a fact and we had to go on deserving it. I had left as one of a group of enthusiastic amateurs. I returned to a professional organisation with standards and an acknowledged reputation to maintain.[42]

By the time of *Agreement*, the Allies were getting ahead in the intelligence and ciphers game. What would let them down, and what to some extent remains controversial, was the apparent total lack of secrecy surrounding planning and preparation for the mission.

Fitzroy Maclean was not the only one hearing rumours. J. J. Fallon, a Royal Marine, recalled 'friends telling me their destination; it was equally common knowledge in the cafes and bars together with the clubs frequented by servicemen'.[43] On 2 September, Lieutenant Colonel Unwin had dispatched a corporal of his 11th Battalion from Haifa to the combined training centre at Kabret to pick up some kit. Later that same day, the wretched NCO was overhead gabbling in the NAAFI (Navy, Army and Air Force Institute). He had recounted details of a supply convoy he passed, talked about the gear he had transported and where it was going. He confided that a big 'op' was imminent involving destroyers and hundreds of marines. He speculated this was an outflanking expedition aimed at Halfaya and more.[44] He soon found himself in very serious bother, but the damage may have been done.

'Loose talk cost lives' – an always true wartime saying, and yet to what extent loose talk compromised the operation is very hard to judge. Gossip generally doesn't leave traces in any archives. Marines were warned not to appear on deck in their battledress while the destroyers were berthed at Alexandria. This was probably too little and far too late.[45] Stirling emphatically denied any leak emanating from his SAS, Guy Prendergast would have been equally vehement on behalf of LRDG, and both would very probably have been right. Those at the sharp end know their lives depend on secrecy. It's those behind who are never at risk who might blab.

Stirling was adamant that the problem was to be found in the clubs and bars of Cairo. David Lloyd Owen warned Haselden that the bazaars were buzzing and the latter agreed, though he was hopeful the Axis would not have picked up sufficiently on the chatter. Rear Admiral L. E. H. Maund, serving with combined operations, was more specific in his allegations. He asserted that security within LRDG HQ at Kufra was lax and details of the mission were being openly discussed there, and that the presence of SIG personnel in German gear was common knowledge.[46]

At the other end of the operational zone, talk at Haifa focused on the marines. Gossip breeds rumour, which leads to speculation and debate, practically as good as a signed copy of the operational orders for any lurking Axis agents. Moving the entire contingent, men, ships and supplies to Kabret, which could be effectively sealed off, was considered and then rejected. A New Zealand officer stationed at the divisional base outside of Cairo was apparently heard openly discussing the operation.[47]

There was an element of comic opera when laundry-men bringing the men's shirts back aboard the ships were demanding immediate settlement 'as you go to Tobruk'! This was hardly calming. Did the

Axis in fact know? This is uncertain. There is some anecdotal evidence suggesting a heightened awareness, but no specific proof that security in Tobruk was beefed up to any extent. Surely if the enemy did know, then Haselden's party would never have passed through the wire unchallenged, as they were to do. The Operational History is emphatic that there is no evidence of Axis foreknowledge, and nothing of the actual events suggests they were in any way primed.

Nonetheless, this was potentially very bad. Despite the Allies' capacity for successful eavesdropping and accurate reporting, knowledge of the actual garrison strength at Tobruk was very thin indeed, and based, as it appeared, mainly upon wishful thinking. It was estimated that the Italians might have a weak brigade with perhaps a battalion of Germans. Optimistically, it was suggested that most of these would be bivouacked some way above and outside the town. Nor was it considered likely the Axis possessed sufficient MT (motor transport) to bring their men in.

If information on troop strengths was scanty, assessments of attack aircraft available both from the Luftwaffe and Regia Aeronautica were far more accurate. Intelligence suggested the latter could deploy some 30 Macchi 200 fighters from El Adem and Tobruk aerodromes and two dozen torpedo bombers at Derna, with some Ju 88s and Me110s. Another 30 Ju 87 Stukas could be scrambled from Sidi Barrani and be on target within the hour.

Within a couple of hours' flying time, the Germans could fill the skies with planes from Crete and other airfields, an offensive total of some 130 aircraft.[48] The raiders would be at high risk during daylight, even if they could take and mount the port's complement of AA guns. The marines had been blandly assured that the RAF had the matter in hand. There was no detail on this and Air Marshal Tedder's* objections

---

* Arthur Tedder, 1st Baron Tedder (1890–1967), commanded the RAF in the Middle East.

to the whole scheme were based on the lack of Allied fighter cover. This planning gap was to produce fearful consequences.

What would be of considerable value to the mission was up to date aerial reconnaissance. If the planners could get their hands on a full photographic survey in 1:16.800 scale this would reveal the extent of any new defences, new dumps and camps, enhanced transport and railway links, and, as a useful bonus, would corroborate (or show the lack of) the accuracy of current maps. This intelligence would be a tremendous boon, and Brigadier George Davy entreated the RAF to oblige via their Photographic Reconnaissance Unit (PRU) on 30 August. His request came with a health warning in that increased air traffic over the port might alert the enemy. In any event the PRU was too busy to comply: as the commanding officer put it, 'the existing operational commitments of PRU aircraft can barely be met with present resources ... I cannot place the demand for special photography of the Tobruk area on the highest priority from any given date.'[49]

This was not helpful, but such a recce might not have provided much useful information anyway. The photos would have enabled the planners, and therefore the participants, to build up a better picture, but it appears unlikely this would have had an impact on the final outcome. Training and preparation were in the event inadequate, the landing boats were totally unsuitable and the entire scheme hopelessly over-reliant on a series of disconnected elements coming together.

Unwin's marines would deploy an HQ section with communications detachment, A, B and C companies of the 11th, an MG (machine gun) platoon, mortar platoon, attached gunners, sappers and medics. All would wear light desert kit with commando boots and carry bare rations and water. This was ideal fighting gear, and having everyone

---

He was not an admirer of Montgomery.

dressed the same would reduce the risk of 'blue on blue' incidents. Additional stores of ammunition (100,000 rounds of .303, 100 3-inch mortar rounds, 200lb of gun-cotton slabs with 50 primers) were to be off-loaded on No. 4 jetty by late morning.

Before a single marine was able to come ashore, the landing beach would be marked by an SBS detachment using Folbots. Lieutenant Kirby was in charge of the canoeists who, with their boats, would be carried on the submarine *Taku*. They would ship out from the sub at 0130 hours and *Taku* would signal the destroyers at 0200 hours that the SBS team was safely ashore. Once on the beach at Mersa Mreira, Kirby would set up the landing lights: one would be placed on the eastern flank of the cove entrance, the other half way down the passage on the same side. Two long flashes would be sent out every two minutes from NE to NW from 0245 hours and keep flashing till the landing boats were safely in. A red light meant all clear; white spelled danger.[50]

Both destroyers would disembark their marines in the small lighters, strings of which would be pulled by the motorized launches. Marines were to be ashore at Mersa Mreira by 0330 hours, sorted, formed and moving on their objectives within 45 minutes. It was A Company's job to secure the outer, west-facing perimeter. C Company would move against the coastal gun positions at Mengar Shansak, taking these and German AA guns alongside. Having neutralized these they would probe westwards, rolling up the outer batteries till they had reached the No. 4 jetty. This would allow the sappers to begin their work of destruction. The mortars would go with C Company, but could be retrieved by battalion HQ to attack enemy positions wherever they needed battering.

While A and B companies were thus gainfully employed, B Company would head straight for the town centre, sweeping up AA positions en route. This done, they'd look to the ravaging of the MT workshops and facilities. Once the Argylls were put ashore on the eastern flank from Force C's MTBs, they would reinforce the western perimeter. C Company of the marines would redeploy in support, leaving three full companies to hold the rim. B Company of the marines would support the Scots but, at the same time, were tasked to effect the liaison with Haselden's Force B. The demarcation line between the seaborne units and Force B would be the road that linked the hospital to the western extremity of the quays.[51] Essentially, the regular infantry, beefed up by the Fusiliers' MG platoon, would secure the area whilst the specialists continued blowing things up.

Part of the intended booty comprised the numerous SFs or Siebel Ferries;* squat, square and ungainly, these workaday lighters were ideal for the movement of supplies from ship to shore. They each carried their own light AA guns and it was hoped to net at least ten of them. Those that could be cut out were to be dispatched eastwards, and those that couldn't were to be sunk to the bottom of the harbour. Once the blowing up was finished, Force B would send up a multi-coloured flare, a signal for the British ships and MTBs to enter the port, confirmed by radio. Casualties would either be shipped out to the destroyers by captured ferry or, if too badly wounded, handed over to the Italian hospital. By 1900 hours the entire force was to be up and away.

With their initial, vital mission complete, the SBS team would pitch in with the marines targeting the harbour and cutting out the German lighters. *Taku*, having launched her cargo, would steam clear at top cruising speed and stand to some 40 miles offshore. Once the port itself was secure, this would be the trigger for the two destroyers to enter.

---

* Siebel Ferries (Siebelfähre) were shallow-draft catamaran-style landing craft used by the Wehrmacht during the war. They served in a range of roles as transports, flak ships, gunboats etc. They had originally been developed for deployment in Operation *Sea Lion* (http://en.wikipedia.org/wiki/Siebel_ferry, retrieved 21 April 2015).

Both *Sikh* and *Zulu* had been cannily camouflaged to look like Italian craft. Once they got into the harbour, they would list over to one side and pump oil, accompanied by ample outpourings of black smoke; the guns would be depressed and upper decks kept clear.

The purpose of all this mummery would be to give the impression the destroyers were already crippled and out of action. This, it was fervently hoped, would be sufficient to persuade any nosey Stukas that they weren't viable or hostile targets.[52] Some would argue Allied fighter cover might have served rather better. This was all both very complicated and inter-dependent. And this was just Force A. The marines could not accomplish their part without the other two main elements fulfilling theirs.

John Haselden, often viewed as the prophet of Operation *Agreement*, would lead Force B. This was the stuff of Henty. The unit would attack from the landward side after an epic desert crossing. The colonel's friend and admirer David Lloyd Owen, with Y1 Patrol of the LRDG, would guide 83 commandos from D Squadron Special Service Group, commanded by Major Colin Campbell of the London Scottish. The raiders, with added detachments of gunners, sappers and signallers, would be crammed into eight 3-tonners. LRDG would rely on their tested and more nimble Chevrolets. Lieutenant Poynton, the RA (Royal Artillery) officer, had a tough assignment; he and his very modest squad were expected to man the captured guns while Lieutenant Barlow would look to AA defence. Bill Barlow had in fact served during the siege of Tobruk, so possessed considerable personal knowledge, likely to be an invaluable asset.

The SBS contributed Lieutenant T. B. Langton, an ex-Irish Guards officer, who as well as being adjutant had the vital task of signalling to Force C, the MTB-borne detachment offshore, that the vital cove had been secured. Without this confirmation they could not land.

Lieutenant Harrison commanded the sappers, charged as ever with the blowing up of things, and Lieutenant Trollope led the signals section. The team also fielded a lone representative of the RAF, Pilot Officer Aubrey L. Scott, responsible for liaison.

Bertie Buck with Lieutenant David Russell of the Scots Guards was in charge of the tiny SIG squad.[53] As they had previously at Derna, the SIG troopers would pose as German guards, the commandos their POWs. This ruse, it was hoped, would get them through the perimeter wire. If they were closely challenged, the SIG would be close enough to the sentries to ensure they caused no further difficulties. Russell, like Buck, was a fluent German speaker.

Peter Smith, incorrectly, lists two further British officers, a Captain Bray and Lieutenant Lanark. These men did not in fact exist. Gordon Landsborough in his 1956 classic Tobruk Commando assigns these names to Buck and Russell. At the time of Smith's writing, certain War Office restrictions still applied[54] and the use of these noms de guerre was a necessary literary fiction. Likewise, Landsborough lists the four other ranks as Corporal Weizmann (real name Opprower*), privates Wilenski (probably Goldstein), Berg (30777 Private J. Rohr or Roer) and Steiner (10716 Corporal Hillman 1 SAS). There was also a Private Rosenzweig.[55]

The SIG behaved, spoke and were equipped as Germans; their love letters, carefully written, were also in German. Opprower called his fictitious girlfriend Lizbeth Kunz, in fact an ardent Nazi and near neighbour of his before he fled the Fatherland.[56] Buck tested his men

---

* Opprower was a German Jew who'd escaped the Nazis at 16 after his father had been murdered by them. In Palestine he'd volunteered to join the British Army, but, dissatisfied with the mundane duties he'd been assigned, he made his way to Egypt and volunteered for something more exciting. He had to go AWOL on three occasions before somebody finally took notice; see Sugarman, p. 166.

relentlessly. Their cover stories had to stand up, though none could be in any doubt as to their likely fate if they fell into Axis hands. After the previous debacle, the Germans were aware of the unit's existence. As a bonus, Buck did entertain hopes, in Stanley Moss/Patrick Lee Fermor style, of seizing a German general who had a billet in the town!

This was the reason Buck took only one other officer and five soldiers with him. The bluff really needed around a dozen to look totally convincing. Operation *Agreement* did not succeed, but the SIG did. Their role in the mission was absolutely critical. If the bluff failed, if Force B had to fight their way in, the whole plan would be unravelling from the start. As a sub-unit, they kept themselves apart; the commandos frankly preferred this. Since the earlier betrayal, the whole unit was looked on with suspicion.[57] Haselden had his own pet project once inside the wire, which would involve releasing the thousands of Allied POWs who it was believed were being held in large holding areas ('cages') inside the defences. Popski was cynical from the start, or perhaps this was providential hindsight; success, as they say, has a thousand fathers, but failure is always an orphan!

So much for land and sea: what of operations in the skies? The RAF was due to appear overhead at 2130 hours on D1 and the raid would continue to 0330 hours on D2, though no flares would be dropped after 0100 hours. It would be massive, one of the biggest of the Desert War. The northern flank would get the heaviest pounding, and even once the raid was ended a number of planes would stay in the air above the harbour until 0500 hours to keep the AA guns and radar fully diverted. It was hoped, as mentioned, that the fury of the bombardment would drown the noisy approach of Force C's MTBs.

Another job for Force B's signaller was to set up a marker at Mersa Umm Es Sciausc. This was a very large triangle with sides 20 yards long, lit by three glim lamps with the signal 'OK' being flashed from an Aldis. Once this was sighted, the planes would return their acknowledgement 'TOC' and then transmit the codeword for success, 'Nigger' (this was considered an acceptable term at the time), to Captain Micklethwait.[58] The RAF also hoped to bomb other Axis airfields along the coast and drop a few bombs on Crete for good measure (Crete was subsequently taken off the hit-list as a target too far, given the resources available).

Admiral Harwood, whose reduced fleet bore the lion's share of eventual losses, described the operation as 'a desperate gamble'. He acquiesced because he felt he had no choice, yet one feels his predecessor, the brilliant Admiral Cunningham, would have rejected the whole business. Operation *Agreement*, like other strategic failures grew and acquired an irresistible forward momentum all of its own. Wise counsels were not sought or heeded. Subsequent, equally ill-judged intervention in the Dodecanese in 1943 was another example of hasty and inadequate planning, as was, most clearly, the Arnhem disaster the following year.

Yet not all were necessarily caught up in the unbridled enthusiasm for *Agreement*. On 29 August, the joint planners published a very sober assessment of the likely consequences, not of failure but of success. The overall effect on the Axis's maintenance position if the capacity of Benghazi was curtailed would be minimal unless Tobruk was effectively neutralized. Raids carried out in the Jebel Akhdar would have little beneficial effect, as the enemy had moved the bulk of his operations and supply eastwards. Substantial reserves had been accumulated both inside Tobruk and to the east, enough for up to a fortnight if normal traffic and supply through the port, measured daily, matched consumption. Assuming that the harbour could not be effectively blockaded and thus denied to the enemy, it would be unlikely to remain out of use for any more than a week and any lighters lost could be replaced. At best, then, the operation, if it achieved its objectives, would inconvenience the Axis for a very short time only and oblige them to live off their stores.[59] In the light of so downbeat an assessment, the overall worth of the operation was questionable from the outset. Derring-do is laudable and boosts morale, but only if it produces tangible results.

Somewhere amid the windswept Libyan sands
In stygian darkness, frozen to the bone,
His great-coat swathed about his limbs,
This Christmas eve a soldier stands alone.

For three years now he has not seen his wife,
Three years of blood and sweat and toil and pain
Three Christmas eves have seen him far from home
Perhaps one day will bring him back again.

For him, no crackers, no comic hats, no party games
No Santa Claus to shake the kiddies' hands
No Christmas cards for him, no family feast,
His company, the barren empty sands.

As midnight comes, it brings the next on guard
A muttered word, their conversations cease
The corporal, next relief, all three turn around
A star blinks out; it is like a star of peace.

Leslie Davies, *Christmas at Agheila*

CHAPTER SIX

ACROSS THE SEA AND THE SANDS

David Lloyd Owen, who would lead the LRDG element, was a close personal friend of John Haselden, for whom he also had a great deal of respect. Lloyd Owen also admired Shan Hackett,* who was part of the planning effort and tasked with keeping the infinitely more volatile Stirling suitably in check. Haselden was uneasy at the way in which his proposal for attacking the enemy at Tobruk had grown into such a massive operation. Both Stirling, for all his gung-ho tendencies, and Guy Prendergast, commanding LRDG, shared these fears. Part of Haselden's original idea was for his commandos to free the large numbers of Allied POWs believed to be kept in compounds, though

---

* General Sir John Winthrop Hackett GCB, CBE, DSO and Bar, MC (1910–97) was an Australian-born British soldier. He served in the Arnhem battle and was also a painter, university administrator and author, and in later life a respected and sought-after commentator.

intelligence on numbers was pretty thin. It would be the job of Lloyd Owen's Y1 Patrol* to guide Force B – Haselden's men, plus the SIG squad and supporting detachments – overland to Tobruk.

This was the genius of the original idea, which had never envisaged a more conventional amphibious approach. Haselden believed, correctly, that the Axis would never imagine a raiding force could come in from the landward side over so many empty miles of desert. Tobruk was a port, and ports get attacked from the sea. The essence was a blend of total surprise and the unexpected. With a limited set of objectives, this might just have worked, and the commandos could have no better pathfinders than the LRDG.

Bagnold's brainchild had grown into one of the most efficient Special Forces units ever created. Selection was rigorous. Even David Lloyd Owen himself, who would end up running the whole show, came perilously close to being rejected on his first patrol, recalling that 'Guy [Prendergast] was never the sort of person to beat about the bush and he made it quite clear that Eric [Wilson] had not reported very favourably of me.'[1] Happily, Guy Prendergast took a longer view. The unit came to embody that spirit of derring-do, combined with astonishing proficiency, which the Axis could never dream of matching. In the grim, leaden days of 1940–41, LRDG vastly boosted Allied morale, providing echoes of Thomas Doughty, Richard Francis Burton and T. E. Lawrence.

Patrol members would never have won any commendations for spit and polish. Most had joined to escape just such subservience to routine. On a patrol, the men might go without washing or shaving for days, burnt by the relentless, omnipresent sun, scoured by harsh corrosive winds, coated in cloying layers of dust thrown up by the vehicles. Patrols

---

* Y is for Yeomanry Patrol, of which LRDG at this stage deployed two.

were a team effort; officers, NCOs and men were all equally important cogs in a very small and tight machine. Each depended on the other. Informality was a badge of efficiency, not slackness.

Very few Allied units can have featured a more eclectic and mongrel military attire. Obviously, patrols were drawn from several continents and brought their own kit with them. Some of this was vintage Great War issue. Headgear was varied in the extreme, from colonial-style pith helmets to the distinctive Arab *keffiyeh,* held in place by the traditional band or *agal.* This gave wearers a suitably Beau Geste look and was ideal for protection against dust, but was rather less suited to the range of mundane tasks that made up a large portion of the desert raider's daily life, namely kit and vehicle maintenance, chores which had not affected the Bedouin. Woollen cap comforters and latterly black RTR berets became more commonplace.[2]

Conditions in the desert varied radically from day to night, from stifling, almost crushing, heat to stark, penetrating cold. Standard battledress with heavy serge greatcoats alternated with KD (khaki drill) shirts and shorts with personal gear carried in '37 Pattern canvas webbing. Peculiar to the desert was the kapok-lined Tropal coat. This was a very heavy and stiff item of kit that was unsuitable when moving but very warm for static or sentry work. Leather sandals or *chaplis* – much easier for moving over soft sand – often replaced standard infantry boots.[3] The South Africans had introduced a lightweight durable form of footwear, descended from their Voortrekker ancestors' design, the 'desert boot' – latterly and enduringly turned into a fashion item by shoemakers Clarks.

A team of staff officers and planners who had immediate responsibility for the conduct of *Agreement* and the lesser spoiling raids (of which more later), included such elevated figures as the commander-in-chief himself, the senior RAF officer, together with Brigadier Davy the DMO and Guy Prendergast. Force B would concentrate at Kufra for the long, hard slog up to Tobruk. Lloyd Owen was due to arrive at the oasis, LRDG HQ, bringing the commandos in from the distant Delta, by 31 August.[4]

Kufra Oasis is around 40 miles in length and less than half that in width, nestling in a bowl of shallow hills. There are four separate lakes lying in the bowl with the settlement of El Tag built on its northern rim, a dun-coloured riot of earth brick buildings, seemingly 'as old as time'. Bill Kennedy Shaw describes it:

> From the high wireless masts in the Italian fort at El Tag, built over the ruins of the Senussi 'zawiya' [religious centre], you could see the whole oasis – thousands of date palms, thinly scattered on the upper slopes and thicker around the salt marches; the mosque and market places at El Giof; the two sapphire-blue lakes as salt as the Dead Sea, though you could dig a well of sweet water five yards from the margin; tiny patches of cultivation, laboriously irrigated by donkey-hauled leather buckets from shallow wells.[5]

After the oasis had fallen to Free French forces ranging out of Chad and the years of Italian supremacy had been brought to an end, the place was garrisoned mainly by French colonial troops lacking any heavy weapons or substantive infrastructure. When LRDG first came to occupy Kufra and its aerodrome,[6] Bill Kennedy Shaw described the lush, sprawling oasis as 'the secret of the Sahara', even with its ancient romance stripped bare by arrogant Italian conquerors. Before then, the great Senussi warlord Mohammed el Mahdi es Senussi had brought his people to the pinnacle of their local power, and that magic still resonated. LRDG, for all its workaday pragmatism, still had at its core its individual unit talismans, those remarkable pre-war romantics like Kennedy Shaw who had fallen under the spell of the desert. Kufra was the fairytale oasis, quite vast, isolated from the rest of mankind by fathomless distances of arid, heat-blasted sands and bare, burnished rock.

Still, it was not so remote as all that, and Lloyd Owen, after he'd guided the commandos in, became instantly worried over the amount of loose talk, considering that far too many of those who were to take part in these raids were talking too much about the chances. He himself had heard rumours spilling from the bars and cafes of Cairo long before he was first briefed by Haselden. 'I was very suspicious that security had been blown, and I told John Haselden of my fears when he arrived at Kufra.'[7] There was little at this stage that could be done; everyone could be told to keep quiet but any damage would already have happened. It was an inauspicious beginning and Tobruk still lay some 800 miles distant.

The adventure had begun in a more relaxed mode, in mid August. The LRDG element had mustered at Abbassieh Barracks outside Cairo in holiday mood, having completed their previous mission and free from the dangerous tedium of road watch.* Troopers were free to enjoy the sybaritic lures of the ancient metropolis before returning to the war. Despite the need for rapid movement and the LRDG's traditional reliance on unarmoured transport, the force was to be blessed (or encumbered) by two Stuart light tanks or 'Honeys' as they were called.

Named after the hard-riding Confederate raider of the Civil War, this was a fast and versatile vehicle, armed with one 37mm cannon and numerous machine guns. They'd first appeared in North Africa

---

* Road watch was a form of traffic census, tallying Axis transport on the principal arterial roads. It was utterly tedious but difficult and dangerous, and a staple of LRDG work.

in time for the *Crusader* battles with mixed results; they were handy in reconnaissance but outmoded and outgunned in tank-to-tank encounters. Light or not, tanks were not suited to LRDG-style operations and would at best be an encumbrance. By happy accident, they contrived to collide early on the march and were gratefully written off.[8]

Commandos, if considered irregular by more conventionally minded officers, were still very much part of the regular army. Smartness was expected. They had no real experience of desert warfare and even less of the informal ways of LRDG, whose cavalier appearance raised more than a few eyebrows. The commandos were elite, yet these bearded ruffians were even more elite, Homeric and omnipotent. Lloyd Owen's men were normally based at Faiyum Oasis, a fertile basin scooped out of the desert just south and west of Cairo, watered by a branch of the Nile. It was here on 24 August they first glimpsed their charges, emerging from a shimmering, dust-shrouded haze and crammed aboard a small convoy of eight 3-tonners.

Major Colin Campbell of the London Scottish was in charge, a tall impressive kilted officer, not yet afflicted by the dysentery that would progressively sap his energies. The commandos themselves were drawn from 1st Special Service Squadron, the rump of Middle East Commando: 38 NCOs and men with seven officers. They were all volunteers, as were the various specialists. Somewhat out of place were the RAF liaison officer Pilot Officer Aubrey L. Scott and a pair of landlocked sailors, whose job would be to guide Force C in from the sea to the landing cove. Nobody knew their destination at this point, unless the wags in Cairo had already told them!

Combined, the two units appeared ill-matched. The LRDG lived in the desert; it had become their natural habitat. They had developed and adapted to meet its challenges, its extremes and its demands, those demands that so hostile and unforgiving an environment naturally imposed. Physical toughness and stamina were essential, and went without saying. That much they shared with the commandos, yet Campbell's men did not know the desert; they had not yet seen its sparkling, life-enhancing dawn or the deep gilded calm of sunset. They were fit, trained and proud, but still unready.

After a brew, without which no British Army operation can possibly be undertaken, the joined up convoy moved off. The two components were not a good fit. LRDG vehicles, like their owners, were part of the desert, stripped and bristling, laden gun buses that boasted firepower far greater than any other conventional soft-skinned patrol. The trucks lumbered after these trail hounds and soon fell behind. Away from the Delta, the late summer's heat still radiated. The commandos, perched above their mountains of stowed kit, were uncomfortable and exposed, but the discomfort they felt here was only a pale shadow of that which they might expect once they left the security of the cultivated land.

Early on the road, one truck skidded over and down an embankment, cargo spilling from its ruptured bowels. Miraculously no one was hurt. As an officer had been driving the general view was what else could be expected? 'Ruperts' (officers) were not to be trusted with serious matters like driving.[9] Crowding among the remaining seven vehicles became even more acute. Bowling along the floor of the Nile Valley, mile by mile, being progressively swallowed by the vast African continent, the force covered 200 miles that first hot day. Scott also managed to come a cropper, much to the amusement of his army colleagues whose only words of consolation were that it was a far less dramatic fall than coming down in a plane!

For that night they were all billeted in a cotton mill in the small Egyptian town of El Minya. Their host was none other than John Haselden, who had a great stake in the country. Officers dined in his elegant villa while ice-cold beer refreshed the weary, dust-caked warriors. After the Spartan rigours of the day, it was a very relaxed evening. Lloyd Owen and the other officers enjoyed a convivial dinner, starched linen and gleaming silverware an imperial twilight away from the harsh realities of industrial war.

The food bettered NAAFI standards by a significant margin, and liveried servants kept glasses topped. European women, bright as fireflies, lent a touch of glamour and perhaps a hint of flirtation. An orchestra played, and their host, clearly a man of wealth and taste, beamed and entertained, his eye attentive. It was wonderful theatre, a night to remember. Nobody could foretell the future. Remarkably few knew this man was the inspiration behind the whole scheme or guessed what the final cost would be.

Next morning they piled southwards again, along the course of the timeless Nile, as far south as Asyut. The dirt road was no autobahn but when the LRDG vehicles peeled off, away from the road into the waiting vastness, the going got much worse. As the ride grew rougher, so the sun climbed higher. Exposed and choked by the inevitable dust cloud, the commandos began to get their first real taste, in the most literal sense, of what they'd taken on. This was just the beginning. Kufra was hundreds of miles to the west, Tobruk far, far distant.

And this wasn't the worst. El Dakhla Oasis lay 200 miles south-west and there was a track of sorts, an ancient camel route that had been used for centuries, although historical connections were probably not uppermost in the men's minds as the convoy shuddered and jolted. The LRDG, sure as thoroughbreds on the home straight, knew the way, even when the ill-defined track seemed swallowed up by the shifting sands. The army drivers, however, were new to this type of treacherous, sliding and altogether unforgiving terrain. The overladen trucks frequently got bogged down and their sweating human cargo

British gunners at Tobruk manning a captured 149mm gun take a break for a game of darts, 1 September 1941. (IWM E 5113)

Unloading lighters in Tobruk Harbour. (IWM E 8433)

The first German vehicles to enter Tobruk park in the main square after its fall. (IWM MH 5856)

Major 'Jock' Haselden (1903–42). (IWM HU 16530)

The SIG: Dov Cohen, Rosenzweig and Maurice Tiefenbrunner. (Jewish Military Museum)

The SIG: Tiefenbrunner, Corporal Drory/Drori, Goldstein & Rohr. (Jewish Military Museum)

LRDG crew shelter in the lee of their Chevrolet truck. (IWM HU 24964)

G Patrol vehicles ready to leave Siwa Oasis. (IWM HU 16614)

Captain David Lloyd Owen
(1917–2001). (IWM HU 25299)

LRDG personnel pose in a doorway (Cecil Beaton).
(IWM CBM 2220)

Member of the LRDG patrol at ease
(Cecil Beaton). (IWM CBM 1214)

An LRDG trooper poses with a Vickers 'K'
machine gun. (IWM E 12410)

LRDG truck halted for a midday meal. (IWM HU 71344)

LRDG Patrol at breakfast. (IWM E 12406)

Two LRDG troopers on Road Watch duty. (IWM E 12434)

Members of Y Patrol reading mail (Cecil Beaton). (IWM CBM 2219)

Three LRDG Chevrolets traverse the desert. (IWM E 12385)

An LRDG truck negotiates a sand dune. (IWM E 2298)

A heavily laden Chevrolet. (IWM E 12373)

Close-up of a Chevrolet showing its armament. (IWM E 123800)

Head and shoulders portrait of an LRDG trooper (Cecil Beaton). (IWM CBM 1212)

Personnel from Y Patrol. (IWM HU 25277)

LRDG troopers camouflage a vehicle. (IWM E 12403)

David Stirling with an SAS Patrol. (IWM HU 69650)

A heavily armed SAS/LRDG Jeep, armed with a .50in Browning heavy machine gun up front and a Vickers 'K' gun at the rear. (IWM NA 676)

Commandos riding on the back of a truck during Operation *Agreement*. (IWM HU 3718)

A group of eleven NCOs and men. (IWM HU 3707)

Trucks halt at Gilf Kebir – the officer with the binoculars is most probably David Lloyd Owen. (IWM HU 3715)

A group of seven commando officers who took part in Operation *Agreement*. (IWM HU 3708)

Commandos heading over the desert towards Kufra. (IWM HU 3716)

Camouflaged truck in a laager. (IWM HU 3710)

An officer chatting with other ranks. (IWM HU 3711)

Men swimming in the salt lake at Kufra. (IWM HU 3714)

Group of 46 officers and men of 1st Special Service Squadron. (IWM HU 3709)

Men digging out a stranded truck. (IWM HU 3712)

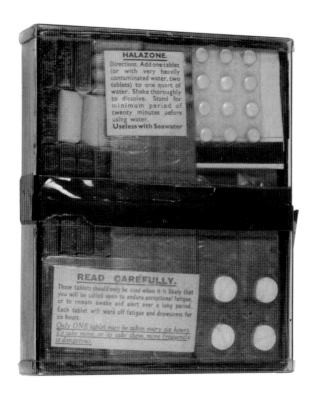

An LRDG survival kit (as carried by David Lloyd Owen). (IWM EQU 12209)

Admiral Harwood taking pictures of wrecked Axis shipping in Benghazi Harbour. (IWM A 14228)

HMS *Sikh*, a Tribal class destroyer that entered service in 1938 and was sunk after the raid on Tobruk. (IWM A 8931)

HMS *Zulu*, another Tribal class destroyer, also entered service in 1938 and was sunk after valiantly attempting to save HMS *Sikh*. (IWM A 6376)

HMS *Coventry* with *Dulverton* and *Beaufort*. (IWM HU 89668)

A motor torpedo boat (MTB) at speed. (IWM A 56)

MTBs in line astern showing the crew and deck armament on a lead boat. (IWM A 60)

A Fairmile Motor Launch. (IWM A 15790)

A near miss. (IWM A 41620)

HMS *Coventry* ablaze on 14 September, after being dive-bombed and sustaining four direct hits. (IWM HU 89667)

Bombs exploding over Tobruk as part of the air attack on 13th/14th September 1942. (IWM CM 2990)

was required to dig and heave and shove the sand channels beneath stubborn, spinning wheels.

Dakhla Oasis is one of the seven in Egypt's western desert, 50 miles broad east to west and a third of that in depth, an outpost of the pharaohs since 2,500 BC. Although British archaeologists had begun to uncover its treasures since the beginning of the twentieth century, much of this heritage was still untouched during the war. It is not one community but several, scattered along the chain of sub-oases: mud-walled, silent settlements, dun-coloured and labyrinthine, ancient and enigmatic.

Cool waters were welcome bliss, but their lavish feasting from the night before was not to be repeated as they ate Maconochie's stew and bully beef. Moving out and still heading south-west, they faced the crushing, unpredictable jolting over rock-strewn wadis or a mad rush, scaling the great breakers of sand dunes, risking a disastrous slip over knife-edged ridges. Movement and momentum were critical to continued progress. Heat engulfed them and dust enveloped them: the devil could take the hindmost.

These 'balaklavering' rushes were a case of every truck for itself. If you got bogged down, you were on your own and it was time to dismount, unload and get digging, seared by the merciless sun. Major Campbell, who had now clearly contracted dysentery, was in a worse state than most; such unrelenting hardship pure hell for anyone exhibiting symptoms of illness. The LRDG were past masters at this game of course, past masters at anything to do with deserts generally. As the professionals halted every hour to let the amateurs straggle in, everyone's sense of humour began to evaporate as surely as the water boiled in radiators. At last they passed the brooding russet bulk of the Gilf Kebir, southern marker for the impenetrable waste of the Great Sand Sea, bigger than the whole of Ireland.[10]

Happily, this obstacle was now behind them and the way to Kufra was clear, along the old caravan trail joining the oasis to Wadi Halfa and distant Khartoum. Almost clear anyway, since there was an alarum as the dust of another column churned in the distance. The accepted drill was that, in the event of colliding with enemy forces, which this far south would probably be Italian Auto-Saharan patrols, LRDG would form a well 'tooled-up' defensive screen while the commandos would barrel on straight for Kufra. In this case, the interlopers turned out to be friendly SAS en route.

By the time they came into Kufra, they'd covered just under a thousand miles in 8 days.[11] It was now 31 August and they'd have six days in Kufra, a surreal environment for those not accustomed to it. Many of the larger buildings were inherited from their Italian builders, with wonderful shade and cool, limpid waters. For the officers, there was much business to be done.

Stirling and his SAS leaders were later flown into Kufra aboard Hudsons while Buck, Russell and the SIG squad were delivered by Bombay aircraft. From the start the SIG were different, apart. Their uniforms, weapons and drill were very distinctively German and, as remarked, they were distrusted on account of the earlier debacle: where there was one turncoat, there could be more. Tensions between British and Jews in Palestine did not make for instant bonding. These were allies not friends. Haselden, the ringmaster, duly arrived on 4 September and convened a general officers' briefing.

Like Montgomery, Haselden radiated confidence. Even in its adapted form, this operation was still his child. A man of extraordinary courage and that much abused term, charisma, he possessed the gift of carrying all before him, as though the effort of will could influence reality. The briefing, if high on aspiration, was rather low on realism. Haselden was convinced the port's defenders would comprise nothing more formidable than low-grade Italian units. He was equally adamant that 4,000 Allied POWs were incarcerated inside the perimeter, with four times as many corralled in camps south of Benghazi.[12] Much of this was wishful thinking rather than tactical insight.

Again, similarly to Monty, Haselden had the ability to cascade his enthusiasm through all ranks. His briefings were the first chance the men would have to really understand their target and the full and ambitious scale of the operation. There were no dissenters, despite the distances, the manifold dangers, uncertainties and staggering odds. They were all up for it. The really cunning part of Haselden's plan was the use of the SIGs. Buck's men, perfect in the role, would pose as DAK while the commandos would appear as their quiescent captives, looking suitably dejected. The fact they'd be crammed in Allied transport, re-branded with Afrika Korps insignia, was immaterial as the Axis had a large stock of captured vehicles. This ruse would get them up to the wire. It might get them through. If the guards grew suddenly suspicious, then they'd be swiftly and very surely silenced.

This time at Kufra was a chance for officers and men to get to know each other. It is something of a cliché, but those bonds of comradeship would be the threads that could make all the difference on so complex and risky a mission. The four main groups, however, LRDG, SAS, commandos and SIG, tended to keep apart, especially SIG – nobody wanted anything to do with them. Besides, their aloofness was a necessary part of the drama they were to enact. Campbell, slightly older and a strict disciplinarian, thought of as 'old school' but a superb soldier and much respected, was now increasingly debilitated by his dysentery, which would continue to plague him throughout. His second-in-command, Lieutenant Graham Taylor, had seen service with the New Zealand patrols of LRDG and was cast in that informally aggressive and forceful mould. Lieutenant Michael Duffy had also served a desert apprenticeship.

Two other officers, lieutenants Ronald Murphy and Mike Roberts, came from the famous Royal Northumberland Fusiliers, working as machine gunners for the duration of the war. Roberts also had responsibility for MT overall, a vital and demanding role. Desert warfare was all about mobility; no vehicles, no war. Campbell wasn't the only one sporting tartan, as Lieutenant Hugh Davidson Sillito was with the Argyll and Sutherland Highlanders. 2nd Lieutenant Bill MacDonald, a Kiwi who had fought in the Spanish Civil War, had been battling fascism for rather longer than most. Tom Langton, also a lieutenant, was a tall, lanky officer from the Irish Guards; for want of other duties, he became adjutant. He was a former rowing blue with a history of surviving risky operations behind him.[13]

Lieutenant George Harrison RE (Royal Engineers) led his detachment of eight sappers, who duly brought their impressive dowry of explosive devices and substances with them. The Royal Engineers have always excelled in the art of both building installations and blowing them up. 'Trolly', or Lieutenant H. H. Trollope,[14] commanded the signallers. Unlike many of his fellow officers, Trolly did not like the desert and did his best to minimize its extremes.

'Old' John Poynton was a gunner, possibly in his thirties at this time, thus a geriatric compared to his youthful comrades. He and four artillerymen were from coastal defence. Poynton had taken care to conceal the fact he had a barely healed left arm, broken only a few weeks earlier in Cyprus.[15] Another gunner was Lieutenant Bill Barlow. He wasn't christened William but Hugh and for whatever reason disliked that name. He did like the desert though; he had earlier seen service at Tobruk during the siege and had fought throughout the North African War. Medical care would be provided by Canadian Captain John 'Gibby' Gibson RAMC. His appointment would prove a very sound choice.

Squadron Sergeant-Major Swinburn from the Leicesters was the senior NCO and a very big man indeed. Very much the epitome of the stiff-backed professional, he commanded instant respect. Sergeant Evans came from the Welsh Guards, Jock Walsh from the Black Watch, Paddy O'Neil, unsurprisingly an Irishman, from Tipperary and the armourer Sergeant Alford RAOC out of the south-west of England. Included in the ranks were one rugby international and a Clark Gable lookalike!

For the best part of a week, the force stayed beneath the shady palms of the ancient oasis, merely the most recent band of desert warriors to drink from its wells. Kufra remained timeless. Even the Italians, setting their reviled stamp, however briefly, on the necks of those they'd conquered, had made little real impact. And now they were gone, and their performance in the war didn't suggest they'd be coming back any time soon. Hasleden's arrival on the 4th had been the trigger to dispel any incipient stir-craziness that was beginning to develop. He was in overall command and came highly recommended by LRDG. His cheerful enthusiasm and calm confidence were inspirational. After hardly any tidings except for defeat, they were going to take the fight directly to the enemy and hit him just where he thought he was safest. Lloyd Owen was not alone in his profound admiration of the man:

I shall never forget that keen, bright look on every face as John unfolded a large map of Tobruk in front of them and they began to murmur to each other in speculation as he, in his genial, vague way, explained the risks he demanded and convinced them of the sincerity of his confidence. Till that time few of us had had the chance of knowing John well, but from that moment everyone had the utmost confidence in his leadership and the party loved him to a man.[16]

If Haselden had any doubts, he kept these to himself. John Poynton certainly had doubts. He and his four gunners were to hold the captured coastal guns. This was plainly nonsensical and he said so. Originally, he was to have had 26 soldiers but all except the remaining quartet had been diverted elsewhere. In theory these would now come in with Force C, from the sea. Clearly, this was or should have been a worry. No doubt it was, but nothing was changed nor could have been at this stage. It was a case of make do and mend. More reassuringly, the mechanics and armourers were constantly at work on the utilities of war.

Buck and his team were busy with their artwork, giving the 3-tonners an Axis makeover. The SIG were thorough. Each door carried the distinctive sign of the black palm tree backed by a swastika. Written over every bonnet was the symbol *Beutezeichen* – 'booty', and even the necessary divisional marker, ER 372, was added, a nice touch and a very credible detail. That last evening, everyone enjoyed a good supper, perhaps not up to the standard of Haselden's fare, but still memorable, washed down with grog and easy camaraderie. They all knew this was their Rubicon – there was no going back.

Ahead of them lay over 700 miles of the worst kind of desert conditions, with the great enemy fortress their final destination. Lloyd Owen and Y1 had to traverse this vast wilderness navigating through the Zighen Gap, then pass through two belts of sand sea. He'd slide them through the next gap, avoiding the Kalansho Sand Sea while giving enemy-held Jalo a respectable berth. LRDG were more than tour guides. Whilst reconnaissance and intelligence-gathering remained their prime function, they did enjoy attacking the enemy. The commandos wouldn't be the only ones going through the wire. Lloyd Owen's patrol was to attack and destroy an RDF (Radio Direction Finding) station inside the perimeter, pausing just to gather valuable loot stolen to order for GHQ. This accomplished, they'd come back in again to attack any

Axis planes they might find. That was before they forayed in yet again to free the POWs. LRDG excelled at this brand of mayhem, and it was considered much more fun than road watch.

Haselden was happy to leave route-planning to Lloyd Owen. Life for the desert raider was very far from representations depicted in action movies or the boys'-own style of graphic comics beloved of this author's generation. It was gruelling, unceasing, uncomfortable, monotonous, frequently unhealthy and occasionally very dangerous. Hitler's infamous Commando Order wasn't issued until October 1942, however, and LRDG units in the desert at this time, unlike some that came later, were not affected.

To add to the normal discomforts, sandstorms could blow up seemingly from nowhere and blot out the world in a frenzied, abrasive shroud. A hot, enervating *qibli* (humid wind) whispered distractingly from the deep, empty expanses of the desert, sapping energy and draining the will to continue. Libya also hosted any amount of local wildlife that was apt to do harm: there was a whole cornucopia of insect varieties, harbingers of many ills, poisonous snakes and scorpions, unwelcome and very dangerous bedfellows. Oases or Bedouin encampments were havens for innumerable and voracious plagues of flies. Desert sores and the spectre of *cafard* lurked in the shadows.

Patrols had to be largely self-sufficient and every item of equipment, every drop of fuel and water was measured. As the vehicles moved out, a lighter command car probed ahead, choosing routes and keeping a trained eye open for unwelcome visitors. Flags were used for communicating changes of plan or alterations to route. Trucks would always attempt to remain within eyesight of each other. Behind the command vehicle came the radio truck (which couldn't operate its wireless on the move), then the rest of the patrol in three troops, each having a trio of trucks, travelling as widely dispersed as the ground would permit. As a rule, the heavily laden mechanic's or fitter's vehicle drove with the rear troop, ready to attend stragglers or breakdowns. It was the second-in-command's job to act as rear-end Charlie.

Somebody was always on the lookout for prowling Axis planes. Patrols threw out great plumes and swathes of dust, unavoidable and very visible. It was often possible for the LRDG to simply brazen it out by masquerading as 'friendlies' when the unfriendly were overhead. If enemy aircraft were sighted and looked set to attack, the alarm was raised by sounding trucks' horns and then the patrol would halt, scattering the vehicles over a wide area with at least 100 yards between each.

Clever dispersal using natural cover, augmented with camouflage, would often do the trick. If the hunters proved persistent and aggressive, the patrol would disperse at speed. Only one truck could be strafed at any one time and the driver would 'jink' and swerve to confuse the fighter's aim, speeding off after a lightning turn at 90 degrees to the angle of the attacker's run. Over hard going the vehicles could crack along at a fair rate, perhaps as fast as 50mph, which made them a very tricky target.[17]

Such adrenalin-pumping moments were mercifully rare. The trooper's day started early, before first light, as the cook toiled over an open fire to get a brew and breakfast on. Though LRDG generally fared better than their regular army comrades, water was strictly rationed to 6 pints per man per day. The first of these was served as a mug of hot tea, Tommy's universal benison. He might also begin his day with porridge, bacon fried from the tin and biscuits with marge or jam. Working off excess calories was never likely to be a problem.

There was nothing to be gained by moving off before the sun had climbed to at least 20 degrees above the horizon, sufficient to activate a sun-compass. Everyone packed stores and kit and vehicles, gear and weapons had to be checked. Guns, constantly getting fouled by blown sand, would have been stripped and cleaned the night before; a blockage could easily become a death sentence. This was the time for the wireless officer to radio HQ and for the commander to brief all troopers on the intended day's travel plus RVs in case of dispersal. On sensitive ground or near the coastal littoral, all traces of the overnight camp would be systematically eliminated. Attention to detail was the measure of survival.[18]

As the sun climbed, filling the noon sky and with the heat building to a furnace, a halt was called. Navigation using the sun compass and driving generally became near impossible. The blinding white glare flattened the ground, hiding a multitude of evils, unseen dips or wadis. Men lolled beneath the shelter of their trucks, whose metal was so hot it seemed it must surely melt. A cold, sparse meal of cheese and biscuits was eaten, with another precious pint of warm water, barely enough to replace sweat. The signaller would be busy with his midday call. Heat was everywhere, a molten universe whose colour was drowned out by the harsh, unyielding, unwavering light: no dark, no contrast, no shadow. As the afternoon began to wane, and the heat moved from unbearable to just manageable, the patrol would move off.

As dusk approached, a suitable camping ground had to be identified. This needed easy concealment and all-round defence with good fields of fire. Like a wagon train, the vehicles laagered around the hub of the communications truck, circled and parked for a fast getaway should any inconsiderate foe appear to disrupt a night's well-earned rest. Though the patrol carried its daily sustenance on board the vehicles, rations might be supplemented by fresh game. Gazelle were sighted from time to time and a decent shot could boost the pot.

By dusk, the trooper's working day was still far from over. As cavalry looked after their mounts, so the LRDG cosseted their vehicles. The ground was murderously hard on the trucks. Jerry-cans (so called as these were a pre-war German steel design that held 4.4 gallons or 20 litres of fuel) were used for re-fuelling. Oil and hydraulics were checked, as were tyre pressures and, if necessary, adjusted. Stores were counted, loads sorted. There was no scope for waste or sloppiness.

The ubiquitous jerry-can was a gift from Rommel, far superior in robustness and design to the 2-gallon British tin. The design made the container easier to lift and to store. A fit man could carry one in each hand in the open, and, while heavy when full, it was easy enough to fill from. Transferring fuel from 2-gallon British tins to the larger German jerry-can in an enclosed space got everybody high on fumes. American-type cans, copied from the Axis model, were found to be much inferior in design. Finally, Britain started producing her own, exact copies this time, and these were very successful, though they didn't begin to arrive in theatre until early 1943. Some two million of them were produced.[19]

Then it was time for an evening brew, over an open fire built with used packing cases, a primus or an improvised stove. The evening meal was served hot and the daily tot of grog given out. This was the social highlight of the day and could be swilled neat or diluted in tea to suit. The Rhodesians created a cocktail variant, mixing the raw spirit with Rose's Lime Juice, the 'sundowner' or 'anti-*qibli*' pick-me-up.

Men bedded down in pits shovelled from soft sand, nastily reminiscent of shallow graves. Those on sentry duty stayed awake, as would the wireless officer and navigator. He had to finish up his dead reckoning, which was checked by an understudy. He'd then use his theodolite for an astrofix, again checked by his junior, so an exact location for the camp could be determined and agreed. Only with this level of scrupulous care could the LRDG hope to function. Bill Kennedy Shaw relates how the theodolite was used: 'before the war I had spent many desert nights sitting for hours cramped on an empty petrol tin before the car's headlights, working out the elaborate formula which ended, if all went well, in a latitude and longitude'. By 1940, this process was being made easier by advances in the science of aviation. Obviously, in a moving plane, a lengthy calculation is pretty hopeless as the plane has already moved on a considerable distance. Pilots had come to rely on books of tables, which drastically cut back on the time needed to work out a 'fix'. This greatly eased the burden on LRDG navigators.[20]

For Lloyd Owen the tricky part of this long haul up to the coast would be passing the enemy garrison at Jalo. He aimed to slip between them and the encroaching sand sea during the night. Italian planes, based at the oasis, carried out regular daily sweeps both morning and evening. He aimed to be clear in darkness and lie up at Hatiet Etla, some 90 miles south of Tobruk. Lloyd Owen wanted to get there by the 10th – Haselden was rightly anxious not to cut the timing too fine and to ensure men, weapons and kit were fully ready.

Jim Patch, the navigator, had volunteered for the LRDG originally as a gunner. For a short spell portee-mounted guns had accompanied patrols.[21] These had proved more of an encumbrance and the idea was soon dropped. Jim then learnt the secret arts of navigation. For LRDG, the patrol navigator was a key player. Many have likened the Western Desert to an ocean. If so, then it was the British who were the sailors and LRDG the real pathfinders. Maps were either primitive or non-existent. The exploration undertaken before the war by Bagnold and Clayton was, naturally, invaluable, not just because of the topography charted but on account of the specialist kit that they created. This wasn't confined to the simple genius of the condenser (a device for recycling the steam given off by vehicle radiators, thus saving water); Bagnold had also developed the sun-compass.

Without going into details of exactly how the sun-compass worked, the principle can be briefly described as keeping the shadow from the sun of a vertical needle (which projected from the centre of a small circular table graduated into 360 degrees) on to the appropriate reading in order to maintain the direction required. If one was forced off this bearing it was still possible to read the direction in which the truck was then travelling. There were problems connected with the sun's azimuth at various times of day and seasons of the year, but these too were overcome by the inventive genius of Bagnold.[22]

On a day-to-day basis the patrol commander, at break of day, would decide upon the direction of travel and set his compass accordingly. The navigator, riding in the second truck behind the commanding officer, would adopt the same setting. The compass itself was fixed between driver and front passenger so the former could steer to match his bearing. At the same time the navigator would take a speedometer reading and, should there be any deviation from the right bearing, he'd note the speedometer reading and the fresh bearing. As a basic form of dead-reckoning, this proved very robust, especially if augmented by the use of the theodolite to take an astrofix at night.

Jim Patch was now navigating for Y1 and the commandos. Although the latter were beginning to get the hang of the desert, they were still the amateurs. This didn't always sit well with Jim.

The journey continued through broken country with many hills and wadis. Every time we stopped and I marked our progress on the map, one of the commando officers would come over to me and want to look at the map and then take bearings on the different features shown on it in order to check our position. I had to keep pointing out that it was LRDG practice to rely far more on the navigator's dead reckoning than on bearings taken on anything marked on an Italian map. Taking a lot of fancy bearings might have been all very well at the OCTU

[Officer Cadet Training Unit] but it was a waste of time and indeed, dangerous in the situation in which we found ourselves.[23]

Given the vast distances traversed by patrols, being away from any kind of base for weeks on end, good, reliable communications were an absolute essential. The raiders had to be able to transmit the intelligence they'd gathered and receive orders in return. British wartime radios have not enjoyed a good press, but the No. 11 set more than proved itself under desert conditions.* Though not initially intended to reach out over long distances, the No. 11 managed to operate at an extreme range of 1,400 miles. Sky-wave signalling† and key operating were used exclusively.

Security was obviously paramount. The Axis were good listeners and a single slip could spell disaster. Frequencies and call signs were varied twice daily. The sets were powered by two 6-volt batteries, one from the vehicle carrying the set and another with the radio itself, both charged by the truck generator. For distances of up to 500 miles, a straightforward 6-foot rod aerial would do the job, but for transmission over that distance a Windom aerial‡ was needed. As a rule, each patrol had three timed slots in a day when they could radio in – morning, noon and evening. Due to the nature of the kit and the need to erect an aerial, transmission couldn't be managed on the move. It took time

---

* The No. 11 Set comprised a radio transceiver featuring a single tuning unit and was designed in 1938 to replace the 1933 No. 1 Wireless Set. Originally intended to be used in tanks for short to medium range communications, it nonetheless served LRDG well.

† Sky-wave refers to the propagation of radio waves reflected or refracted back toward Earth from the ionosphere, an electrically charged layer of the upper atmosphere. Since it is not limited by the curvature of the Earth, sky-wave propagation can be used to communicate beyond the horizon, at intercontinental distances. http://en.wikipedia.org/wiki/Skywave, retrieved 22 January 2014.

‡ Technically this refers to an off-centre-fed bi-pole antenna fed by symmetrical open ladder line and co-axial cable via a balun: http://hamwaves.com/cl-ocfd/history.html, retrieved 22 January 2014.

too to encipher and/or decipher the messages. As a result, the midday slot was usually avoided.

Of course, the equipment was only as good as the operator, and veterans like Lloyd Owen have nothing but praise for the wireless operators who served with them. These men were the patrol's lifeline, the umbilical cord that linked them to a distant HQ. The radio-man carried a heavy burden, as his hours were long and he needed technical skills to keep his set operational. The nearest repair shop was probably a thousand miles away.

Hatiet Etla was a good lying-up place with plenty of scrub around to camouflage the vehicles, seven commando 3-tonners and five LRDG trucks. There was time for drill and last minute rehearsal, Lloyd Owen remembered: 'Ken Tinckler, who spoke German, acted the German guard who became suspicious and called out to the guard commander. The dispirited British prisoners at once leapt to life, produced weapons, wiped out the guard and drove off. I was impressed'.[24]

On the morning of 13 September the combined force moved off, driving to within about 40 miles of the wire. This was a sobering march. Ahead lay the enemy, secure in his fortified lair. Surprise and guile were the commandos' only advantages, steeled by courage and resolution. All of the officers must have been wondering if the operation had indeed been blown, compromised by all that loose talk and whether they would be in fact be running smack into an ambush.

Soon it would be time to part. Haselden's men were to bowl boldly down the main road, relying on their cover, with Buck, Russell and the SIG playing their allotted roles. Lloyd Owen would pass through the perimeter two hours after the commandos, LRDG taking on any opposition in their path. Two trucks would be parked up to provide a rearguard and the rest of Y1 would hit the RDF station, blending vandalism with larceny. They'd then fall back to the perimeter and set up as a blocking force. At dawn, they'd attack again, this time seeking out enemy aircraft. Once the attack was over, Y1 would come out via the eastern gate and hold this for the rest of the day until they were ordered back inside yet again, this time to free POWs and herd their charges to the shoreline where the navy would take them off.[25]

For a 20-man patrol, lightly armed, this was a very busy schedule, and with the inestimable blessing of hindsight, illustrates everything that was wrong with planning Operation *Agreement*. For the LRDG, any one of these objectives would have been sufficient. For so small a force, surprise was their only trump. Once that was played, the only thing to do was to get out fast. LRDG were to return across the desert to Kufra and, having thoroughly stirred the hornet's nest, every Axis plane that could fly would be on their tail. Kennedy Shaw recalls:

> So, on the evening of the 13th the force moved once again towards Tobruk. We were all rather quiet and at the occasional halts conversation was a little forced. With clouds of dust rising high in the air from the ploughed up desert which had been the scene of so much bitter fighting.[26]

Their approach ran through the old *Crusader* battlefields of dismal repute. At El Duda the skeletal detritus of war surrounded them, a surreal, lunar landscape of industrialized destruction; twisted, broken barrels of abandoned guns pointing in mute supplication to an empty sky and the scorched and blackened shells of burnt-out tanks. On the far horizon there was movement, dust of other vehicles. They had caught up with the war. Kennedy Shaw described the moment of parting as follows:

> I stopped my truck and backed it below the horizon where I stood with John. We waited a few moments and the evening was growing cold. Then he turned and wished us all the best of luck. As his force drove past

they waved goodbye and we felt these men had a cold courage which filled us with admiration, and then, all of a sudden, we began to feel kindly towards those who had bored us a bit on the way up. For a few minutes we stood and watched them go, feeling bare and huge on this naked, scrubby waste of dusty earth.[27]

***

While LRDG and the commandos had been eating their final meal at Hatiet Etla, the amphibious forces A, C, D and E were in motion. The two Tribal Class destroyers had sailed from Haifa, having loaded the cumbersome dumb lighters and their powered tugs. Both *Sikh* and *Zulu* would transport three boats with engines and six without, so each launch would pull two hulls. The tugs were 25 feet long and mounted a V8 engine, cannibalized from other craft. The towed boats were shorter, around 14 feet long and crudely thrown together with green, unseasoned timber, roughly nailed and caulked with a layer of canvas. Each of these unwieldy craft had to accommodate a full platoon of marines plus their gear, and had to be capable of being launched over the ships' sides. In training, simulated landings had been rehearsed, but using only the powered boats. The key, critical task of towing the dumb lighters in was never practised. So the marines would be going in blind aboard jerry-built boats.[28]

11th battalion of the Marines had embarked at 2100 hours on Friday 11 September, departing Haifa nine hours later. They got to Alexandria at 2000 hours on the 12th where the men were given small compasses and issued with silk maps to be kept hidden in their epaulettes. They'd be fighting in tropical kit, KD shirts and shorts with rubber-soled boots and minimal gear. They sailed from Alexandria at 0500 hours on that fateful Saturday; four hours later they were informed of their mission.

An hour after that, their escort, Force D, caught up with them, HMS *Coventry* and her accompanying Hunt Class destroyers. They were on their way and it seemed the God of War was smiling as they enjoyed a perfect passage of halcyon sailing with not a hostile plane in the skies. By 1900 hours, as late summer's light began to fade, they were gearing up and testing their weapons. As darkness fell, both *Sikh* and *Zulu* parted company with their escort, first steering west and then south. Tobruk was now ahead.[29]

Both destroyers were larger vessels, yet neither was designed as a troop transport, so every inch of space was crammed with marines and their kit. Most carried the bolt action Lee Enfield Mark III or IV rifle, the famous Lee bolt and 10-round magazine capacity that had generated such fearsome firepower in 1914 that German officers became convinced their opponents were each using an automatic weapon. They also carried .45 calibre American Thompson sub-machine guns, the 'Tommy gun' of pre-war gangster films. Alongside these, they had home-made 9mm Stens, a backstairs compromise of wartime expediency hurried into production after the disasters of 1940 when the German MP 38s and MP 40s so effectively boosted the Wehrmacht's available firepower. They also fielded Brens, carted plenty of Mills grenades and officers carried .38 Webley revolvers, junior brothers of the .45 model issued during the previous war.

It is often said that war is around nine parts tedium and one part action. This is very true of amphibious operations. The British Royal Navy knows its business very well indeed, as it should, since it has been doing it for hundreds of years. The two destroyer crews were all old hands and worked together like cogs in a well-lubricated machine. For the marines, cramped, hot and in some cases apprehensive, there was little to do except perhaps play cards, doss down as well as possible for some sleep, grouse generally – the soldier's enduring prerogative – and think, although perhaps not too much.

One of very few non-combatants embedded with the marines was Captain Earle Graham from the Army Film and Photo Unit. He had joined the Desert War before the end of 1941 and had experienced life under siege in Tobruk. He'd even done a stint filming LRDG engaged in their favourite chore of road watching. He recalled: 'Sergeant Crapper and I were to go with the second wave and I decided we should go separately so as to get the widest coverage'.[30] Graham, who was to have a very lively adventure, here refers to another telling weakness in the plan. The boats, as well as being bad, were insufficient in number to take all the attacking marines in a single lift; two would be needed. None of this boded well.

Not only big ships were to be involved. Force C would be hauled by little boats – two flotillas of motor torpedo boats and three motor launches, all sailing from Alexandria. Onto these sleek craft would be crammed the Argylls and a RNF (Royal Northumberland Fusiliers) platoon with machine-guns, plus the supporting detachments of sappers, gunners and others. The trio of launches would be Fairmile Bs, some 112 feet in length with a displacement of 85 tons and powered by twin 650bhp petrol engines, capable of 20 knots. They'd originally been built as submarine hunters armed with depth charges but had been deployed for the earlier St Nazaire raid as commando transports, where their lightweight construction had proved a serious flaw. One of them, ML (motor launch) 353, had been built in Thomas Cook's Cairo yard, more used to turning out Nile pleasure craft.[31]

The MTBs were from a British design but built by the Electric Boat Company at their Bayonne Plant in New Jersey. 'Optional' extras included power-operated .50 calibre turrets and a 20mm Oerlikon cannon. These highly effective guns were produced by the Swiss company of the same name and based upon an earlier German model. The 77 feet 'Elcos', as they were known, were fitted with British torpedo tubes, self-sealing fuel tanks and additional bridge armour. As ever, the imperative for protection and firepower came at a cost of decreased performance, but the boats could still hammer along at an impressive 40 knots.[32]

All in all, these were excellent craft. They were sound, fast, highly manoeuvrable and a pleasure to sail. What they were not was troop transports. At best they were cramped, cluttered and often very damp. With a party of regular soldiers with all their gear aboard, and, in the case of the Fusiliers, carrying machine guns, conditions would become seriously disagreeable. Lieutenant Denis Jermain was commanding officer of 15th MTB Flotilla and senior in the 10th Flotilla was Lieutenant Bobby Allan RNVR (Royal Naval Volunteer Reserve). Denis Jermain, like a number of MTB officers was young, only 24; Charles Coles, in charge of MTB 262 of 10th Flotilla, was a year younger. The small boats offered a means of rapid promotion for this youthful generation. As both flotillas were now to be combined, there was the thorny question of who should command overall.

Jermain had very considerable experience, and handling small craft was a far cry from steering their grander brethren. Bobby Allan, however, was senior and listed for promotion to lieutenant-commander. Their lords and masters decided the best solution was to bring in a suitably qualified commanding officer. They chose Commander J. F. Blackburn DSO, RN. He knew the target, having previously commanded HMS *Ladybird,* who despite her genteel-sounding name was a venerable gunboat that had seen and done much service during the Tobruk siege. She'd carried out troop ferrying and amphibious operations until she was finally bombed and sunk in Tobruk harbour on 12 May 1941. She was one of the few naval losses 8th Army paused to mourn.[33]

Despite these seemingly spot-on credentials, Blackburn had never commanded small boats. These were a far cry from the lumbering 600-ton *Ladybird* with her 6-inch guns and top speed of 7 knots! Jermain might be young, but he understood completely the capabilities and limitations of the MTBs. Blackburn was clearly a first-class fighting sailor, but he equally clearly did not. Jermain was effectively shut out of the planning process and his considerable store of knowledge on mounting small-boat coastal operations went unused.

His fellow boat skippers had already heard from him how he'd go about locating the cove at Mersa Umm Es Sciausc, but his superiors did not take on board his ideas for storing the additional fuel that would be required for such a long passage. He wanted bespoke deck-mounted long-range tanks. Jermain had form with these from his days patrolling home waters. This was a sound and tested method, but vetoed for *Agreement* on grounds of too much cost. Fuel would instead be stored in deck-stowed flimsies. These leaked badly and no enemy pilot could have asked for a more inflammable target.[34]

The MTB crews did train, however. Each loaded with 10 soldiers, the MTBs practised running into the shore. This proved a grand spectator sport for all the louche denizens of the Alexandria Yacht Club, including members of the Egyptian Royal Family. A greater security hazard would be hard to conceive since 'Alex' was a cosmopolitan entrepot, bursting with dubious characters, any of whom could be and some doubtless who were reporting to Axis paymasters.

Commander Blackburn did not participate in these exercises. Jermain and the other officers no longer sat in on meetings. The commander hailed Charles Cole on MTB 262 from the jetty, enjoyed his subordinate's traditional hospitality, toured the boat and departed. That was pretty much it. When the boat commanders were finally summoned for a briefing by the Staff Officer Operations (SOO), some were not backward in criticizing the plan. Particularly outspoken was a New Zealander, Lieutenant Mabee. He didn't mince words and was warned his temerity would jeopardize his place on the raid. As a keen angler, the SOO did suggest the boats be repainted to match the natural hue of sea bass, a very tricky fish to land. More practical assistance came in the form of fly button compasses and silk escape maps, just in case they had to find their way back overland.[35]

In fact, both Jermain and Coles had already spent time in Tobruk harbour, having been there on 21 June, the day it fell to the DAK. Naval

HQ had blithely dismissed Jermain's warnings despite the fact he'd been looking directly at the advancing Germans swinging down from the escarpment. Charles Cole's boat was immobilized as he strove to change a busted propeller. They had had a very close shave. And as an indication of how lax security in Alex was, the astonished sailors found a gaggle of local suppliers crowding Mahroussa jetty and insisting on payment of all outstanding invoices. They were clearly aware of the planned departure, as were the labourers engaged in refuelling. This was not reassuring.

The MTB and launch flotilla sailed out from Alex in fine style at 1800 hours on the 12th, a glorious evening, their foaming wake soon leaving the ancient metropolis behind. Coles had been expecting suitably piratical commandos, bristling and soot-blackened, but instead he had impeccably turned out Highlanders, *proper* soldiers as he was informed; the Argylls acknowledge no superior.[36] Clear of the harbour, they fanned out into two columns. Bobby Allan, newly promoted to lieutenant commander, led seven boats from 10th Flotilla. Commander Blackburn took station with Denis Jermain on board MTB 309 with the other eight boats of 15th Flotilla in line astern. An early loss occurred when MTB 268 had to return to port having developed engine trouble, moving her human cargo across to one of the Fairmiles. Now there were 18 boats in all.

Like the destroyers, the boats enjoyed a troublefree if somewhat cramped passage, their decks already cluttered with fuel cans and full to the gunwales with men and kit. But the weather was wonderfully balmy and no enemy disturbed their progress. It is 360 nautical miles from Alexandria to Tobruk and it was heading towards evening when the flotilla began its approach. Over the wine-dark sea they'd cruised at a very sedate 7 knots, far slower than the thoroughbred engines were accustomed to gallop.

It was now that Commander Blackburn's lack of familiarity with small boats led to a catastrophic error, the first of several to blight Operation *Agreement*. At 2200 hours he gave the order to increase speed for the run in to 24 knots. There was nothing amiss in this, but Jermain relayed the instruction with signals requiring the boats to notch up their speed in lifts, five knots at a time. This was standard practice, enabling engines to build up their revs incrementally and allowing skippers to hold formation as their craft surged ahead. Blackburn seems to have been impatient with this and demanded speeds be increased forthwith.

Jermain reluctantly complied and, in the black night, boats quickly lost cohesion and drifted apart into small groups. No single craft was now guiding the flotilla into the cove at Mersa Umm Es Sciausc. Overhead, the bombers droned; the inferno they were creating on land lit up the ravaged harbour with great rolling, thunderous crashes and sheets of bright flame spiralling into the night sky, but the dark coastline on either flank stayed impenetrable.

***

As the commandos in their trucks barrelled across the last ragged fringe of open desert towards the coast road, LRDG watched them go with a mixture of admiration and apprehension. Lloyd Owen had decided he'd move Y1 a bit closer to the perimeter, make a brew, grab some hot food and then move off. As they followed the great, billowing cloud of dust that marked Haselden's passage, they saw the equally unmistakable haze from an enemy patrol moving along a parallel course. Kennedy Shaw recalled that 'the setting sun was low in the west and we had that advantage when I gave the order to drive fast in open formation towards the enemy'.[37]

Patrol trucks bristled with weapons. Whatever was needed for the fight had to be with the troopers as they took on an enemy. There would be no supporting fire from aircraft, armour or artillery. For desert raiders, being able to dispose massive firepower in an instant conferred an immediate and enormous advantage, likely to be decisive. Convoys of Axis vehicles could very quickly be deterred from resistance by a few well-directed nonlethal bursts. Those which were made of sterner stuff would receive the full deluge. This wasn't buccaneering, it was rather a micro-version of industrial warfare. In such sharp sudden encounters, he who shot first with accuracy and weight of fire would decimate his opponents and shred their vehicles.

The standard British medium machine gun, the redoubtable Vickers in .303 calibre, was mounted alongside the heavier .5 calibre weapon. Browning equivalents were also popular. A variant of the conventional .303 was the gas-operated Vickers K. These were essentially intended for use on aircraft and when mounted in pairs could deliver a tremendous volume of sustained fire.

Swift as terriers, the raiders raced to intercept. Lloyd Owen crouched over one of their machine guns, hunched up against the anticipated crack and whine of enemy bullets: he felt that the radiator in front seemed very large and vulnerable. There was no fusillade as the Italians were totally surprised and disorientated, never imagining they'd encounter the Allies so far behind their own lines: Kennedy Shaw remembered that some fell to the ground in tears and screamed about their homes and families.[38] If this was the measure of the opposition, then Haselden's predictions were spot on. They weren't here to take prisoners, who were cursorily questioned and then seem either to have escaped or become casualties; it was time for food. The trouble was, they couldn't raise the commandos and a lack of communications began to feed the worms of doubt.

It was a moonless night as the LRDG moved off towards the wire, driving in line astern. The distance was around 15 miles and Lloyd Owen aimed to reach the outposts at 1000 hours. First they had to scale the escarpment, Sidi Rezegh of evil fame. This necessitated clearing rocks and half-building an accessible track. Once again Kennedy Shaw describes the scene: 'at the bottom we halted and heard the first sorties of the bombers roaring overhead and then the rumble of bombs over the next horizon'.[39]

It had begun.

Above the earth, on searchlight-silvered wings, rides death
In his most awful form – the hand of war;
And from the earth in shuddering cry goes up –
Sirens – whistles – bells warn the world
That death rides out with crosses on his wings.

Sergeant F. Cremer, RAMC, *Untitled*, September 1942

CHAPTER SEVEN

THE 'DESPERATE GAMBLE'

It was time for the Air Force to do its bit. Australian soldiers, grumbling through the Greek disaster, had labelled the RAF 'rare as fairies'. Whilst unfair, this was understandable in the circumstances, but by the late summer of 1942, the precious, vital balance in the skies above the desert had begun to tilt in the Allies' favour.

The Desert Air Force (DAF), variously known as Air HQ Western Desert, the Western Desert Air Force and First Tactical Air Force, performed a vital role during the Desert War. Formed in 1941 to provide close air support to 8th Army, the DAF comprised squadrons drawn from the Royal Air Force, its South African and Australian counterparts, and latterly the USAAF. Prior to the formation of a united air arm, RAF Middle East Command, then under Air Chief Marshal Sir William Mitchell, was responsible for a quartet of regional areas: Egypt, Malta, Iraq and Aden. When war broke out in the Mediterranean theatre, the

RAF, now under Air Vice-Marshal Sir Arthur Longmore, had some 29 squadrons with no more than 300 machines spread over this vast canvas.

In Egypt, Air Commodore Raymond Collishaw could deploy nine squadrons, whose primary tasks revolved mostly around support and aerial reconnaissance with the odd dogfight against planes of Mussolini's Regia Aeronautica. Three squadrons were equipped with Gladiators,* largely outdated, one with Lysanders† and several squadrons had the medium bombers Blenheims‡ and Bombays.§ Despite the disparity in numbers, the RAF, soon augmented by Hawker Hurricanes,¶ began to gain an ascendancy through aggressive tactics and a certain sleight of hand to convince the Italians they were facing rather more squadrons than was the case.

Re-supply of aircraft was a major difficulty and this involved the long flight via Takoradi on West Africa's Gold Coast. By the end of November 1941 the RAF had received two Hurricane and two Wellington bomber squadrons. Consequently air support for Operation *Compass*, if stretched, was adequate. However urgent the demands of the Desert War, the RAF here tended to be the poor

---

* The Gloster Gladiator was the RAF's last operational biplane. Obsolete by 1940, it nonetheless did good service, famously in the defence of Malta. Gladiators flew many sorties during the Desert War; on 17 August 1940 they destroyed eight Italian bombers for no loss.

† The Westland Lysander, famed for its role in SOE (Special Operations Executive) operations, was a highly versatile liaison aircraft that could land and take off on remarkably short strips.

‡ The Bristol Blenheim, a medium bomber, was later converted to long-range fighter and night-fighter duties.

§ The Bristol Bombay medium bomber was obsolete by 1940. It had a fixed undercarriage, could carry a bomb payload or 24 troops, and was used by Colonel David Stirling's fledgling SAS as a transport.

¶ The Hawker Hurricane, staple fighter aircraft of the RAF in 1940, was powered by the legendary Rolls-Royce 'Merlin' engine and produced in large numbers. It was a modernized variant of the earlier Hawker Fury biplane and was outclassed by the BF109 E and F.

relation and usually received those machines not required for or suited to defence of Britain.

At the end of July 1941 Collishaw handed over to Air Vice-Marshal Coningham. However, by the end of the year the whole of Middle East Air Command came under the aegis of Air Marshal Arthur Tedder, destined to be one of Montgomery's most bitter opponents. Three wings were deployed in the skies over North Africa: 258 and 269 wings covered the front, with 262 Wing held in reserve over the Nile Delta. As the direct threat to the homeland receded, more and newer machines were sent to the Mediterranean, including more Hurricanes and the Douglas Boston medium bomber.* A further useful addition was the P-40 Tomahawk/Kittyhawk.†

Throughout 1942, the DAF provided long-range interdiction and tactical support to 8th Army, though its fighters were significantly outclassed by the German Messerschmitt BF109 E and F variants,‡ which inflicted heavy losses even if their Italian counterparts were outdated and outclassed by the DAF's machines. It was not until August, with the arrival of Spitfires, that the strategic balance in air to air combat shifted in the Allies' favour.

In part, this was due to a shift in tactical doctrines, utilizing the Luftwaffe concept of close army co-operation through the deployment of forward air controllers, which was the DAF's answer to the gunners' Forward Observation Officer. The DAF then began to deploy 'cab-ranks' of fighter-bombers, waiting to be directed onto specific targets.

---

* Boston-Douglas A20/DB-7 Havoc, an attack medium bomber.
† The Curtiss P40 fighter and ground attack aircraft was outdated by 1940 in the fighter role. Its lack of a two-stage supercharger meant it could not attain the altitude necessary to take on the BF109, but it was extremely successful in ground attack.
‡ Designed by Willy Messerschmitt in the 1930s, an advanced metal monocoque frame and superb performance made the BF109 the staple of the Luftwaffe, although latterly this role was shared with the Focke-Wulf FW190. Over 30,000 were produced.

By this means the DAF won control of the desert skies and provided significant and highly effective tactical support to the 8th Army during the Second battle of El Alamein, the pursuit and the Tunisian campaign.

The DAF contained many pilots from German occupied territories; No. 112 Squadron mainly comprised Polish airmen. The Polish Fighting Team ('Skalski's Circus') was attached to No. 145 Squadron. From July 1942, the US Army Middle East Air Force (USAMEAF), under Major-General Lewis H. Brereton, attached USAAF fliers from 57th Fighter Group and 12th Bombardment Group to DAF formations. Initially these personnel were classified as 'observers', as technically US servicemen were only permitted to serve in American units.[*] Nonetheless, from mid-September, squadrons of US P-40 Warhawks and B-25 bombers[†] were officially attached to DAF formations. By the end of the Second battle of El Alamein, USAMEAF was re-constituted as 9th Air Force.

Unquestionably the most famous and successful Axis air formation engaged in the Desert War was Jagdgeschwader 27 'Afrika' (JG27). I Gruppe was first deployed to support Rommel in the Gazala battle in April 1941, led by Captain 'Edu' Neumann. On 19 April, JG27 claimed its first four combat 'kills', and more would soon follow. German fighter formations, prizing the 'Red Baron' spirit of competitive aces, flew their superior BF109 Es ('Emils') and latterly the F or 'Friedrich' types (technically and often qualitatively superior machines), with great skill. II Gruppe arrived in theatre in September and then III Gruppe was sent from the Eastern Front in November. Now synonymous with DAK, on 24 March 1942 JG27 claimed its thousandth victim, a Boston bomber.

---

[*] The Arnold-Portal-Towers Agreement was a joint UK/USA undertaking regarding deployment of air forces entered into by General Arnold and Air Chief Marshal Sir Arthur Portal in June 1942.

[†] The North American B-25 Mitchell medium bomber was named for US aviation pioneer Billy Mitchell. These aircraft were successfully deployed in a number of theatres.

The Bombay carrying General Gott was a 'celebrity' kill on 7 August. Though highly effective against inferior Allied fighters, JG27 did not score many successes against bombers. There is a suggestion that the fighter aces were more concerned with adding to their tally than with strategic intervention. By the time of the Second battle of El Alamein more and better Allied fighters, in the shape of Spitfires, were beginning to have an effect. A trio of German aces swiftly fell and, in December 1942, the remnants of JG27 were withdrawn from theatre. The tide had irrevocably turned.

In the first wave over Tobruk on the night of Operation *Agreement* were Wellingtons and Blenheims from 201 and 205 groups. They were tasked firstly to provide cover for the assault troops, secondly to form a diversion against enemy radar and thirdly they were to spy the 'success' signals from the troops and transmit the messages back to HQ. Lastly, they were to undertake reconnaissance for naval forces both going to and returning from the raid.[1]

This was precisely the reverse of the concept for *Waylay*, which had reserved air support for the extraction phase. In hindsight, this was undoubtedly the preferable option. Air raids, whilst dramatic and terrifying, achieved very little in terms of tactical gains. Tobruk had been systematically bombed by both sides, yet, scarred and defaced, most buildings were still standing remarkably intact. An air raid would thoroughly alert the defenders and risked forfeiting the essential ingredient of surprise. Something in the order of a hundred RAF planes would target Tobruk that night, including five Boeing B-17 Flying Fortresses, led by Major Max Fennell and contributed by the 7th Bombardment Group of the USAAF.*

---

* The Boeing B-17 was a UH four-engined heavy bomber destined to play a significant role in the Second World War, especially in the strategic bombing of Germany. Developed in the late 1930s, it was still in service 30 years later.

David Jefferson quotes from a memoir of the bombing raid compiled by Staff Sergeant Wilbur (Bill) Mayhew, who served aboard one of the B-17s that had taken off from Lydda in Palestine. The US bombers, great shining monsters, would fly in at varying altitudes so as to minimize the risk of mid-air collision. Mayhew's aircraft was first in the bombing zone. He saw their role as keeping the AA and port gunners fully occupied so they would not detect Force A coming in.

> There was a 50 per cent overcast, and the reflections on these clouds of anti-aircraft fire, bombs bursting on the ground, and shells falling from naval vessels [in this he was clearly mistaken as there was no naval bombardment at this stage] a few miles offshore made this an eerie scene for us.[2]

Mayhew recalls a Wellington ('Wimpy') caught like a fly in the web of piercing searchlights, barking guns hungrily following the beams. The tornado of fire engulfed the unlucky bomber, and in a few seconds the plane exploded. Another Wellington was dispatched moments later as the Fortress began her bombing run. 'The line of tracers coming up ... looked like they were headed directly for my turret. It was very unnerving to watch the slow approach of that line of steel coming directly at me.'[3] The Fortresses were in fact flying at far higher altitude than the older Wellingtons, effectively above the reach of the guns. This wasn't apparent to Bill Mayhew and his fellow fliers, who expected to be hit at any second.

Then it was bombs away 'and a few moments later there was a terrific explosion on the ground directly beneath us. He [the bomb aimer] had hit an ammunition dump. I could read a magazine in my turret'.[4] After some 40 minutes over their drop zone the aircraft turned and headed for home. They could be forgiven for imagining they had dealt the defenders some very palpable wounds. It was around midnight now and both Tribal Class destroyers had swerved south to commence their run in towards the landing beach.

In terms of actual results, all that the air raid achieved was to bring the Axis defenders onto full alert. Italian *braggadocio* would later seek to claim credit for the successful outcome. In fact, as was usually the case, it was the German defenders who deserved any plaudits (which Rommel freely bestowed in the aftermath). Their after action report noted that despite seven hours of continuous air attack, damage was minor and casualties few.[5] DAK high command ensured its various detachments were all on the *qui vive* and primed units, encamped in the desert, to be ready to move. German reports suggested some 600 bombs had fallen for the loss of seven 'kills'.

By 2300 hours, Major-General Otto Deindl, in charge of the Koruck Security Battalion based a few miles west of the fortress, had been fully warned of the air raid. The Bavarian general was a dedicated career soldier and visiting senior officer, who now ranked highest amongst DAK personnel. He had several detachments of guard/police units under his hand, field and military police with two companies of the Guard Battalion Afrika (Wachbataillon Afrika), plus a pioneer formation over 700 strong.[6] His next in command, Major Hardt, had responsibility for all of the logistics personnel attached to the base, perhaps some 1,450 men in total.

The Luftwaffe could field over 300 effectives and Major Hartman, commanding the AA defences, could dispose of as many as four dozen of the dreaded 'eighty-eights' and an abundance of highly effective 20mm cannon. These guns, as was normal with the Germans, were Luftwaffe rather than Army. There was also a diminutive naval presence. Within the port itself the Kriegsmarine had a flotilla of minesweepers and the armed lighters. DAK could probably deploy some 3,000 assorted personnel as an initial reaction force, far heftier than Haselden and the planners had blithely forecast. These men were now on full alert, manning their guns, the rest ready to move as required; and this was only the German contingent.

Anticipating that an attack might occur, the codeword was '*Landealarm*' and Major Hardt assumed command of all fortifications north of the town and harbour. He'd have the main coastal highway at his back for reinforcement and re-supply. There is no evidence to suggest that the DAK had been put on alert prior to the RAF raid. This would clearly suggest that Rommel had not received any intelligence concerning the proposed amphibious attack. Lapses in security, lamentable and inexcusable as these were, did not determine failure or pre-doom the assault.

Then there were the Italians. Mussolini's new legions have not enjoyed a good reputation and 8th Army did not rate them. This was partially unfair. Well led, the Italians could fight as bravely as any, although as a rule their officers treated the men very badly. General Giannantoni was away sick that month and his deputy Colonel Battaglia was left to hold the fort. The Italian defence was predicated on the basis of an independent plan, which implies the Germans didn't trust them sufficiently to merit collaboration. Il Duce's navy was able to contribute Rear Admiral Lombardi, who, like Deindl, was visiting. In fact, he was senior officer overall and had at least one reliable unit, a company strength formation of marines from the San Marco Battalion commanded by Lieutenant Colotto. They had even carried out a modest yet successful raid of their own on 29 August.[*]

Italian gunners also manned the northern coastal batteries at Fort Peronne and those guarding the southern approaches at Mersa Biad.

---

[*] A select squad from this unit had been put ashore behind Allied lines and had successfully sabotaged rail links between Alexandria and the front at El Alamein, a neat surgical strike: see Smith, p. 91.

Although manned, these were still being upgraded and extended, but could nonetheless boast of strong blockhouses and supporting trench systems. As with the Germans, there were security police, supply and support types, plus three destroyers in the harbour.[7] A crack Bersaglieri* battalion was in readiness as close as Bardia (although it took no part in the battle). Allied estimates had woefully and optimistically miscalculated, guessing as Smith continues 'there may be the equivalent of one Italian Infantry brigade in the area and in addition up to 1,000 German troops at a staging camp some fifteen miles to the east. It is believed to be unlikely that there will be sufficient transport available to enable them to take immediate counter measures.'[8]

The briefing concluded with a bland warning that 'accurate dispositions of enemy forces in the area are unknown'. Had the true strength and readiness of the opposition been known, it seems unlikely Operation *Agreement* would have been allowed to proceed. Already the air raid had failed to damage the defences and had merely served as a wake-up call. The Axis forces were now very much alert.

After parting from their LRDG shepherds, Haselden's commandos, in four 3-tonners each holding 30 soldiers,† drove straight for the wire. One vehicle, in approved LRDG manner, was left behind with its distributor cap removed and concealed as a last ditch insurance and getaway. Haselden, as Martin Sugarman points out, had not fixed a specific RV point with Lloyd Owen in the event of the survivors having to try and get out by land. This was a telling omission.[9] They now had about 4 miles to go. Buck drove the first vehicle, with each

---

* Bersaglieri were elite Italian light infantry and sharpshooters, formed originally in 1836. They were marked by their distinctive headgear.

† Normally, the prisoners would be sandwiched 40 to a vehicle, but the commandos needed room for their concealed weapons and gear (see Sugarman, p. 167).

of the others driven by one of the SIG. They carried fake passes and papers, good enough for casual scrutiny. Anyone who decided to peer too hard might find his life expectancy dramatically curtailed.

About to hit the main highway, they saw two German trucks barrelling straight at them. They simply ignored these newcomers and were ignored in turn; so far so good. Next up, in the dying light, was a Storch or other light plane, which circled then went on. Once onto the hard tarmac, the first they'd been on since leaving the Nile Valley, they simply merged with the flow. Nobody took any notice. Why would they? Such convoys were a common sight and the Axis had more Allied vehicles nearly than the Allies. At the fence Buck, ever the consummate actor, leaned languidly out to show his papers, but the bored Italian sentries just waved them through. The bluff had worked. Their great, long gruelling journey through the vast expanse of desert had not been wasted. Haselden was right. The SIGs were sublime, even bandying casual insults, in best Afrika Korps mode, with their allies.[10]

Once inside, they drove on unchallenged except for a minor road rage incident when passing a German convoy heading in the opposite direction. One vehicle, likely a staff car, struck a glancing blow off the bumper of the middle commando truck. Private Opprower thought the car belonged to a senior officer. Wisely none of the disguised raiders stopped, but angry voices followed them into the gathering darkness. The incident was doubtless written off to the usual hazards of a busy military highway, but soon after the raiders discovered they had an attentive escort of three motorcycles – most likely military police. After what seemed like an eternity as their shadows buzzed around, the bikes, apparently satisfied, sped off.[11]

It was now nearly 2100 hours, practically full dark. What looked like a cliff edge loomed ahead menacingly. Haselden casually confirmed, 'that's the bomb-proof oil storage depot we must destroy later tonight'.[12] All around lay the tented camps of the enemy. They prowled unnoticed. The sheer dazzling bravado of the bluff was their talisman. The enemy did not credit that the British could undertake such a feat. The ruse was brilliant and had succeeded beyond reasonable expectation. Buck and his team played their roles to perfection. Getting out, of course, by whatever means, might not be so easy.

Buck was leading the way, seeking the junction that would access the track leading down towards the target zone and landing cove. It was where it should have been, but someone had very inconsiderately thrown a substantial fence across. An anxious halt ensued as Buck disappeared into the night, groping for some way through. The delay only lasted a few moments but to the tense commandos, fingers close to gun-butts, it must have seemed a lot longer. There was a second track further down that was clear. Off they went.

For quarter of an hour, they bumped along the sandy track with the busy sweep of the highway behind and above and the scent and murmur of the sea coming closer. The next sentry was German; he was swiftly dealt with and his weapon brought in as a trophy. Five hundred yards further on, the small convoy halted. Men got out, easing stiff limbs and breathing the clear night air of a balmy late summer's night, with the buzz of insects chorusing around. Nearby they could plainly see the angular, silent outlines of the coastal command centre, their first target. They got kitted up for battle as the air raid began, the sweeping cones of light searching the skies as bombs fell on Tobruk.

Campbell was to lead a detachment eastwards from the landing cove and take out two gun emplacements on that flank, then push further east and repeat the process with more enemy guns at a place dubbed 'Brighton Rest Camp'. This lay 2 miles or more away and there'd be no rest for anybody that night. The major was very weak by this time, drained by his debilitating condition. At the last moment, Haselden detailed Tom Langton to accompany his group as a backup. This was sound in one respect, but dangerous in another. Langton's primary role was to signal to the MTBs during their crucial approach to Mersa Umm Es Sciausc. Failure here would be catastrophic and, with hindsight, sending Tom Langton off on a separate mission east in the treacherous, uncertain dark was disastrous.[13]

Ahead of them lay the Mediterranean, a fine glow from the water lending a kind of dim silhouette to the broken, ragged ground around. Light from search beams poked at the heavens, and commands to mustering AA crews rang clear across sharp night air. The hornets' nest was stirring. The Axis hadn't twigged that the commandos were in their inner sanctum, but the British bombers were blasting away any overall surprise. For students of precise timekeeping, the commandos were on target almost to the minute, having covered the best part of 2,000 miles of the most hostile terrain on earth, a great deal of this under the noses of the Axis.

Pilot Officer Scott, perhaps wishing he was with his comrades massed overhead, was feeling his way forwards, clutching his Aldis lamp. Lieutenant Trollope and his communications team were setting up. Graham Taylor was establishing a blocking force to secure the western approach. Haselden, Buck, Russell and the SIGs targeted a nearby structure and walked unopposed through the door. The drowsy garrison, sweat-grimed, somnolent and probably very bored, was rudely awoken. There was no resistance, only shock and panic. In fairness, the front line was 300 miles away to the east, so the raiders were completely unexpected. No shots were fired. Haselden brusquely interrogated the twitching captives, at least one of whom was subsequently 'shot while trying to escape' (in fact bayoneted), but they had probably little useful to tell.

The 'Italian House', as the raiders labelled the building, was probably some coastal villa, left stranded amongst the panoply of war. The captured NCO informed the Allies that there were perhaps 50 or so gunners spread across the various emplacements. He knew and was happy to reveal the location of the command post. Overhead the blazing hurricane of the bombing raid provoked a sharp retort from the AA batteries, which stabbed flame and fury into the sky. They still hadn't been discovered.

Haselden commandeered the villa as his command post, Captain Gibson was soon setting up a first aid station, while Trollope lugged over his signals kit using one of the trucks. This would now be the nerve centre of this crucial phase of the plan. All in all, at this preliminary stage things seemed to be going well. The bombers were providing cover and distraction; the commandos had successfully established their penetration without giving notice. Graham Taylor now led a silent, purposeful and bristling line towards the town. It was almost like a night exercise. Taylor was flanked by his 'minders', a London Scottish NCO and two squaddies, Mackay and Allardyce.[14] The other section leaders, Sillito, MacDonald and Barlow were strung out left and right; Poynton and his gunners kept pace on the left flank.

Noise from the air raid ebbed and flowed like the tide. They met with no challenges. These young men, each armed with his weapon of choice, were the cream of the 8th Army, seasoned by the desert winds and focused entirely on the job in hand. They seemed immortal, Olympian, led by an officer they admired and respected and whose own resolute brand of confidence had inspired them. He had taken a huge gamble in embarking upon this desperate, far-flung mission and yet until now had succeeded almost beyond hope. Nothing could or would stop them.

It seems to have been at this point that the captured Italian NCO made a run for it. He'd been hog-tied to a commando NCO but somehow slipped free and took his chances. Sergeant-Major Swinburn nailed him with his bayonet. Private McCall suddenly went down in a burst of friendly fire – 'blue on blue' in the modern idiom. Everyone froze, but there was no repeat and Lieutenant Taylor was already at the sandbagged redoubt of one of the gun emplacements. There was a very nervous moment as the Taylor, Webley revolver at the ready, crept through the narrow entrance, briefly and infuriatingly snagging on camouflage netting. Nobody was home; the guns and two searchlights were unmanned.[15]

Another smaller position loomed ahead. Again Graham Taylor led the way and now his luck ran out. The defenders here were present, ready and awake. Taylor was shot and wounded. He was dragged clear and a shower of grenades killed the Italians within. Still conscious, the injured Taylor was left in a nearby, unoccupied hut. He was fit enough to hope he might pick up some handy booty, but the Italians had left only a single Chianti bottle and that was empty.[16] David Sillito took command and the sweep continued. The crump of falling bombs had masked the sound of gunfire and grenades.

More enemy bunkers loomed, the defenders still blissfully cocooned in their bunks. Death was swift, sudden and terrible, inflicted by more shattering grenades with a full accompaniment of automatic fire. Sillito now did his own kicking in the door routine with the largest of these attacks taking out an entire platoon of shocked Italians. John Poynton, using a captured German Mauser,[17] cleared other positions on the west flank of the headland.

Lieutenant MacDonald discovered underground shelters, his men bombing each gallery as panicked Italians spilled into the night. None paused to pick up a rifle. They just bolted, scattering like rabbits in front of the hunters. No prisoners were taken. The commandos had gained the ground they needed and the harbour installations were now ahead of them. They were masters of the small peninsula. All they had to do was hold it. Informed of his victory, the wounded but still very much conscious Taylor instructed Swinburn, the Geordie sergeant, to send up the success signal. His watch told him it was midnight. All points west were now secured, but what of Campbell's detachment to the east?

After the brief sound and fury of the attack, a lull descended. Graham Taylor was helped back to the RAP (regimental aid post) at the villa where Gibson found the bullet had nicked one lung. He was amongst half a dozen casualties; the rest seemed to have been hit, in the confusion, by 'friendly' fire. Buck with Russell and the SIGs had been off on a private foray of their own, taking out several enemy MG and AA positions. Their job was then to act as an additional blocking force against any early attempt to recapture the peninsula.[18] They'd cleared all their initial objectives, but the gunners proved more resolute and the SIGs had to fight off four counter-attacks. They were only a handful, but they held onto their gains, using grenades rolled down the barrels to disable the enemy guns.[19]

John Poynton and his team, Lance-Bombardier Stanton and gunners Fairbairn, MacFarlane and Schyberg, were holding on, but, like Buck's SIGs, were gradually coming under increasing pressure. He did think of attempting to bring at least one gun into action, but on closer examination they all proved to be ageing, sightless and ammunition-less. As gunners without guns they became infantry. Haselden couldn't spare any reinforcements as he had none to offer. An hour had passed with no sign from Campbell. The MTBs and destroyers would now be close. The RAF had stopped dropping flares. If success could not be signalled unequivocally by 0200 hours, the raid would be called off and his men would be stranded, their only hope being an overland break-out with all enemy forces in hot pursuit.

Major Campbell had worries of his own. As his men moved forward, encountering a wadi or defile, they also discovered the area was mined. This had not been anticipated; getting through proved to be something of a trial. The sappers carefully cleared a path. This was both dangerous and hugely time consuming, and time was a commodity they did not possess. It was nearly midnight as the commandos filtered through the gapped lane. Progress eased as they cleared the minefield, but then a rifle banged off to their front, causing another halt. Mike Roberts was ordered to take a section on and flush out the enemy, driving them back onto the guns like woodcock. Seeing the two red streamers signalling success flare up from the west behind them underlined the urgency.

Tom Langton sought and received permission to recce the beach. It was deserted, with just the rush of waves filling the cove and no sign of enemy presence. This at least was reassuring. Langton and Mike Roberts both got back to Campbell at the same time. Neither had in fact sighted any opposition, but time was running out faster than the swiftest tide. On Langton's advice, they moved eastwards hugging the coast, one flank covered by the open sea. Each section proceeded almost independently, seeking out targets of opportunity. Roberts was the first to brush an enemy pillbox and charged in, Tommy gun blazing. Next, they came across a communications post and this was cleared in classic commando style.[20]

Mike Duffy's section had located the main gun emplacements but found them unoccupied. Isolated pockets remained and were systematically being cleared. Their deadline loomed very close indeed. They'd advanced perhaps a mile or so. Langton rightly worried about his need to get back to the cove fast and asked if he could send up the success signal from this flank. Campbell acquiesced and up went the flares. Both east and west of Mersa Umm Es Sciausc were now in Allied hands. It was 0115 hours and the raid was on.

By the time Haselden got the coded message 'Nigger' transmitted and it was received and decoded it was almost 0200 hours, and tension at GHQ was palpable. It seemed now that the commandos had achieved their immediate objectives and secured the landing cove. Regardless of what followed, this was one hell of an achievement.

Tom Langton set off to reach the cove in time to signal the MTBs. Campbell's commandos reformed and continued their eastward march in search of the alluringly named Brighton Rest Camp. However, Langton had stashed his Aldis lamp back at the villa, Haselden's command post. The original time frame would have allowed for the detour back to retrieve it. Present realities did not. The only compromise was his torch, far less powerful and throwing a white rather than red beam. At least Pilot Officer Scott was in place on the west headland, his Aldis flashing out as prescribed. Langton, improvising with his torch, followed suit from the east. The signalling had been due to commence by 0130 hours; three long flashes every two minutes on a north-east and easterly bearing.[21] There was no sign of the MTBs. Without reinforcements, the bridgehead must become an untenable salient.

For all the commandos had achieved, things could still go horribly wrong, as was now about to become clear.

***

The submarine HMS *Taku* had risen stealthily from the sea at 2300 hours, some 10½ miles north of the port.[22] The water might be inky black but the coastline was illuminated by the best efforts of the RAF and USAAF as they rained destruction on Tobruk. From the sea this looked pretty spectacular, with the bloom of exploding bombs, flaring crescendo of flames erupting in gouts of bright, voracious fire, sweeping cones of light criss-crossing as searchlights sought out targets for the frantic, hammering AA guns. It must have looked as though nothing could hope to survive.

Helpfully, the muzzle flashes clearly indicated Mersa el Mreira, where the marines were to go ashore.

Lieutenant-Commander Hopkins had surfaced so far out both to charge his boat's batteries and to give the SBS team onboard a chance to ease cramped limbs and get the circulation going before their flimsy craft were launched. Lieutenant Kirby, the senior 'Folbotist', thought the weather favourable, and the sub began her run towards the shore just after midnight. By 0100 hours it was time to get the canoes into the water. This would be tricky as *Taku* was a sleek underwater predator, not a landing craft. SBS and their kayaks* emerged from the torpedo loading hatches with their assisting crew members. The wind was coming from the north-west, the boat riding down from the breeze to allow the raiders to assemble their kit in the lee of the gun platform. The jackstay provided a useful, not to say vital, grip.[23]

They might be few, but the SBS team had a pivotal role to play. It was their job to get ashore in the right place ahead of the main amphibious assault and mark out the landing beach. A blind attack is a doomed attack. There had been time for rehearsal, however, as the four-man SBS squad had joined the sub before *Taku* sailed from Port Said. For four days they'd endured the claustrophobic world of the submariner. By Second World War standards, *Taku* was pretty much state of the art. She was a T Class boat, able to stay out for 42 days, and whilst lighter in the water packed more punch than her predecessors. There still wasn't a lot of room, however.

The SBS had used her to attack Benghazi, planting limpet mines *Cockleshell Heroes* style against Axis shipping, at least one of which had

---

* These were probably made by Granta. Anyone interested in more information could refer to Quentin Rees' *The Cockleshell Canoes: British Military Canoes of World War Two* (Amberley, Stroud, 2008) or the website http://www.brunel.ac.uk/~acsrrrm/kayak/.

gone down. A month before, Roger Courtney, an SBS pioneer with CSM (Company Sergeant-Major) George Barnes had relied on her when they blitzed Axis positions at Mersa Brega.[24] This time around she wouldn't be needing torpedoes; she was a taxi rather than a raider. At 1530 hours on 13 August, Hopkins had received a signal direct from the top instructing him to report on conditions at the landing beach by 0130 hours next morning. If all looked feasible, then the codeword was 'Mallard'. If the commandos might expect to get ashore but be unable to withdraw, then the word was 'Puffin'. If all looked impossible then it was 'Shag'. Some might see this as appropriate to the whole operation.[25]

At the start of the recce on 13 August, all seemed to go well. Raiders and sailors had practised the cumbersome drill of assembling the canoes and sorting the port kayak was completed in less than two minutes. This was impressive, as unfortunately was the inconsiderate wave that broke over *Taku's* hull. It swept SBS, sailors, boats and kit clear over the side and into the water. All personnel were dragged clear, but the canoes were not. Happily, no comments by those present have been recorded. There was nothing for it now but to drag out the sub's rubber dinghy. This was too big to be pumped up inside the hull, so had to be inflated on the spume-ridden deck. Soon, the hand pump followed the rest of the lost kit into the unfathomable sea.[26]

Lieutenant Kirby decided to call it a day. All attempts to get off the sub were now frustrated by the waves, the sea much choppier than anticipated. One of the other commandos, Captain Horton, a gunner, volunteered to swim for it if the sub would close to within a mile of shore. Hopkins wasn't having any of it. He reasoned that the amount of light onshore would expose his ship unacceptably and that Horton, while game, had already had a pounding when he went overboard first time. He couldn't hope to make the distance, burdened with all his signalling gear. At 0134 hours *Taku* moved off, and Hopkins sent an emergency signal '0134 hours Mallard – Beach unmarked'.[27]

This was the codeword informing that a landing could be made, and this signal doomed 11th Battalion and both destroyers. Crucially, as David Jefferson points out, Hopkins did not know what type of assault craft were being deployed. He assumed 'any power driven boat would be perfectly capable of competing with the swell'.[28] No doubt he was quite correct in this assumption, but what he had neither seen nor been briefed on was the type of jerry-built, flat-bottomed packing cases the marines would be trying to use, most of which had no engines. Had he been aware of this, then it is equally certain he would have advised very differently.

Hopkins' report went up the chain of command. His immediate superior, Captain 1st Submarine Flotilla, was supportive, reporting:

> It is clear from the narrative that every effort was made to land personnel for 'Operation Agreement' but the weather was too bad. Having had nine men in the sea on a dark night within three miles of Tobruk, the commanding officer was correct in abandoning any further attempts to land them.[29]

This appears to be a powerful argument, but we can wonder how differently Hopkins might have reacted had he been fully briefed. This was not his fault or that of the SBS; it was a failure of planning and co-ordination.

Admiral Harwood, at the top of the ladder of command, concurred and, when forwarding his report to the Admiralty mildly observed that 'it was unfortunate that that the attempt to land the beach-marking party... was defeated by the swell'.[30] Hopkins later referred to his boat's role as having been 'minor'.[31] It wasn't; it was crucial. Whilst understandable in the circumstances, this failure to get the landing party ashore was to sow yet more seeds of tragedy.

Having parted company with their escorts at 2100 hours on 13 September, *Sikh* and *Zulu* raced across the sea towards Tobruk and despite their weighty cargo, still managing a speed of 24 knots. Overhead, the bombers droned. At 0100 hours, Force D swung around to the east again, deception complete, bumping their own speed up to 22 knots.[32] The crucial time was 0200 hours on the 14th. If nothing had been heard by then it must mean the whole operation had been aborted and the recovery plan had to be put into effect.

As it was, the signal was very late in coming, with only five minutes to spare. As the two Tribal Class destroyers commenced their run in, still 70 miles from Tobruk, the RAF/USAAF obligingly lit up the horizon with their efforts. At a distance, these appeared very impressive, although whilst obviously terrifying for the defenders, the actual damage being inflicted was minimal and was achieved at the telling cost of losing surprise. This is the raider's talisman; once it is lost the mission is almost by definition a write-off.

David Jefferson is convinced the Axis had prior knowledge of the raid based on the shocking lack of security. Whilst this knowledge would not be surprising, Peter Smith is equally adamant that they did not, and this author agrees with him. He quotes interviews with Hans-Otto Behrendt, stationed with DAK's Intelligence Section G2 based at Sidi Abd-El-Rahman. Behrendt confirms that Tobruk was not that high on Rommel's radar at this time and no special alerts were in place: 'Tobruk seemed to be far away, and since this affair presented no immediate danger, it did not call for special attention.'[33] Rommel's personal interpreter, when interviewed in the mid-1980s, couldn't even remember the raid.[34] The actual wake-up call was delivered by the RAF and their USAAF colleagues. At 0230 hours on the 14th a note in the German war diary confirms, in very bland terms, a heavy air aid, followed by landings. There is no suggestion these were in any way anticipated.

At 1100 hours on the 13th Major-General Deindl was alerted at his HQ, 12½ miles west of the town.[35] His informant, Oberst Liehr, commanding the Guard Battalion Afrika, warned that such a heavy air raid might well be the curtain-raiser for amphibious operations, and he suggested a heightened state of alert, Operation *Landealarm*. This sage advice was heeded and Hauptmann Schultz-Ingenohl was given responsibility for responding to any attack. Needless to add, the Italians were largely ignored. Although General Deindl was on paper massively outranked by Admiral Lombardi, Schultz-Ingenohl reported back to the German officer instead.[36] The defence of Tobruk was to be mainly a German affair, whatever their largely despised allies might later claim.

Just before Deindl was alerted, Luftwaffe AA gunners under Oberleutnant Grelli reported possible landings at 2245 hours. Belatedly, they were reinforced by Italian troops and wheeled their handy 20mm guns directly to the harbour area. Quite what or who had been sighted remains unclear, as there was no actual Allied activity offshore at that point and Haselden's commandos still seem to have been undetected. By 0020 hours, Schultz-Ingenohl was receiving messages from his subordinate Leutnant Petzel* that enemy were coming ashore 2 miles east of the town. There was no hint of panic here. The alarm had been raised, and reinforcements would be arriving soon.

Deindl reacted promptly, ordering his subordinate to hold on and hold out till he could come up with help. All units within the fortress were now placed on alert. Schutz-Ingenohl was also instructed to call

---

* From 5th Company, 686th Supply Battalion: see Smith, p. 147.

out a reserve battalion, the 909th Supply, to establish a block from the Gazala position to the main road, and that the unit's HQ section should be ready to act on further orders. The net was already closing and not a single British soldier had come ashore. Axis fixation on amphibious assault continued to blind them to the reality that the perimeter was already breached but from the landward side. The Germans considered an attack from the land was clearly too fantastical, so they looked out to sea while Haselden's men were clearing the Italian guns.

By 0030 hours, the alarm had been sent out and DAK units, with typical clockwork precision, were filtering into their combat stations. Patrols were sent out regularly but all they had to report initially was wild and pointless fusillading by their panicked Italian allies, which constituted a far greater menace than any British raider, of whom there appeared to be no sign.[37] What did become clear when the two destroyers were finally sighted and engaged between 0200 and 0300 hours was that the Italians had in fact vacated many of their supposed forward positions. Oberleutnant Rosenstiel, a sector commander, failed to detect any sign of Italian troops. Hauptman Rippich reported from his zone that the sole representatives of Mussolini's army were a single artillery piece and one MG post at Fort Peronne.

Like a well-oiled machine, the DAK moved fully to action stations. At 0210 hours, Deindl contacted Oberst Liehr of Guard Battalion Afrika, warning of a landing at Tobruk and ordering that his battle-group should muster at Kilometer Post 19, leaving only covering forces behind to watch the coast. One motorized company was to head straight for the muster point and then drive along the main highway and into Tobruk.[38] At this time Deindl, despite his prompt and careful moves, had no real idea as to the level or intensity of the threat his soldiers were facing. Part of the wider German response was to make ready a hefty force of sufficient weight to knock any Allied interlopers back into the sea. The plain reality is, given this, that even had all landings gone swimmingly, the men coming ashore would soon have been facing impossible odds.

Part of the slackness of the overall Allied planning was that no serious consideration appears to have been given either to the strength of the riposte or the relative ease and speed with which it could have been delivered. Haselden's original, modest proposal had been predicated on the basis that resistance would be both Italian and weak. Insofar as Force B on the eastern flank was concerned, this had turned out to be correct. To apply the same reasoning to the far larger raid now under way, however, was foolhardy in the extreme. Even with the blessing of hindsight, it is entirely logical to assume the enemy would put measures in place to safeguard so vital an asset. Had the weight of these forces been perceived, then surely the raid would have been stillborn. *Agreement* was the hybrid result of a hopeful compromise, neither the subtle stiletto thrust of Haselden's original idea nor weighty enough to grab the fortress and hold it.

Deindl could call upon three DAK formations: 580th Reconnaissance Battalion, ordered up to Mersa Matruh, 3rd Reconnaissance Battalion, on standby, and Battle Group Everth, comprising a single Panzer Grenadier battalion plus one light artillery unit.[39] This was effectively a full brigade that could be added to the number of defenders in the port. Against this the attackers had a battalion of marines, supporting infantry and specialist units, less than a company of commandos and no heavy weapons. It was never a viable contest.

During the early hours, these Axis defenders were building a clearer picture of events. Oberst Hardt reported to Sonderfuhrer Dr Geiger*

---

* Sonderfuhrer is a non-military specialist who is assigned a role normally in a staff or intelligence function: see http://www.wehrmacht-awards.com/uniforms_firearms/uniforms/shoulder_boards/Sonderfuhrer, retrieved 23rd May 2015.

that the 'English' had landed 2 miles to the east at Mersa Umm Es Sciausc. Mistakenly, he assumed the commandos' penetration had come from the sea; the Axis still hadn't realized the approach was overland. Hardt recognized that the Italian positions had been overrun, which doesn't seem to have come as much of a surprise. Hardt's command post was just north and east of the town, overlooking the harbour.[40]

By 0330 hours Hardt was able to confirm that the coastal defences were all manned and ready; even the Italians were at their guns. The coast itself lay some 800 metres distant. He was notified that enemy ships (the two Tribal Class destroyers) had been sighted under a mile offshore and were being engaged by artillery and searchlights, whose piercing beams now held them fast. Hardt grabbed a mixed platoon of DAK and Luftwaffe, commandeered a truck and a single car and then drove towards the sound of the guns. Artillery and small arms fire was crackling in the early morning air. Most of this appeared to be coming from the west. He is quoted by Smith as saying 'on the way I requested a meeting with the Italians' officer who I only knew as the man in charge of their coastal artillery. I must place on record that I found them over nervous and without any discipline'.[41]

So much for their allies. Hardt and his score of Germans spread themselves amongst these doubtless very nervous defenders to give order and backbone to the defence. He knew that the smooth cogs of the DAK machine were alert and in motion, so they just had to hang on. He could easily see the two British warships trading shots with the coast guns. He probably didn't realize just what a hopelessly unequal contest this was.

As Haselden's men cleared the eastern flank, the marines and specialists aboard *Sikh* and *Zulu* made ready. They were fully dressed for battle in light tropical kit but burdened and gleaming with weaponry: rifles, Tommy guns, Brens, grenades, demolition charges, the stuff of death and destruction. 'First Flight on equipment' was the call. This was the moment, the test; the sharp end of all their training and preparation.

No. 7 Platoon of A Company were pathfinders, their task being to surge ashore, seize and secure the beachhead. The tugs and dumb lighters, questionable at best, were also insufficient to get everybody ashore in one lift. Thus 7 Platoon would be followed ashore by C Company under Major Wood, with Lieutenant Myers of the RA and 30 volunteers from 261 Heavy Anti-Aircraft Battery plus assorted specialists, sappers, signals and medics. A slightly unorthodox trio of naval safebreakers, able seamen Brown, Gray and Kay; safebreakers were primarily recruited from civilians, generally locksmiths. Their job was obviously to break into enemy safes, seeking intelligence and presumably whatever might arouse their interest.[42] Lieutenant-Colonel Unwin would be aboard the spearhead, a powered launch that was also temporary home to a naval lieutenant from *Sikh* and would carry communications equipment.

The full complement numbered around 150 and was designated as Force A, the next wave being Force B. They were to come ashore with three motor boats, each towing two barges. The regular and comforting thrum of ships' engines stopped at 0310 hours. Both vessels were around 2½ miles from the shoreline. Nobody was aware of SBS's failure to mark the beaches or the dire consequences this would engender. Men began moving as 'boat stations' was piped. Getting the lighters off and into the water in the pitched, rolling darkness proved problematic. The coast ahead was black dark, a sharp contrast to the seething inferno of the town beyond.

It is often said, and may sound trite, that when things begin to go wrong, they go wrong without end. In this instance, such gloom was fully justified. Even as the leading starboard-side launch was being let down into the water, one of the falls gave way and had to be fixed, which was a nasty, sweating, cursing, blindfold job. It was also time-consuming, and time was scarce. It was supposed to take 20 minutes to get boats and men underway. In practice, it took twice that and it wasn't until very nearly 0400 hours that the first lift moved off. Both destroyers now turned away, heading westwards at 15 knots. They were soon lost to view.[43] The only way for the bobbing, rolling launches, their ungainly, flat hulls wallowing, was forwards towards the shore.

Dawn was not far off. The first intimations of day were streaking the horizon, but progress was agonizingly slow. They'd dodged one sweeping searchlight beam, but another caught them less than half way in and the enemy guns pounced. The inelegant, slow barges were a gunner's dream. There was no covering fire. Surprise was their only shield, and that had been thrown aside by the fury of the air raid. Men and boats were hit. The closer they edged the worse it got. A choppy sea, deep water and a rock-littered beach didn't help. Previously, they had not rehearsed the critical process of towing. Ropes parted and in at least one case immediately fouled the powered boat's propeller.

Corporal Leslie Joseph Andrews leapt overboard to clear the blockage and struggled for an hour under increasing fire. Daylight was another enemy. He got the job done but missed the landings. For many, this would prove a fortuitous accident.[44] All was confusion. Boats were limping along and some sinking. The numbers of dead and wounded were increasing. Enemy fire was accurate and relentless. 'Tug' Wilson, a rating from *Sikh*, was with the marines. He recalls that much of the enemy 'hate' was directed at the destroyers as they pulled away out of range. Some boats were certainly hit, but his greatest test came as they closed on the beach and their lighter was ripped open like a flimsy can by the rocks:

We began sinking almost at once and we went out over the side into waist-deep water; deep, cold water and in the complete darkness, as well. Then there were rocks on the beach itself, when, according to the operation, it should have been a plain, sandy beach! But there it was, here were these rocks which should not have been there and, of course, this instantly made us realise we had been landed in the wrong place.[45]

And indeed they had. They were nowhere near Mersa el Meira, but several miles west at Mersa el Auda and Mersa el Crim, right beneath the muzzles of the coastal guns with Hauptmann Rippich's HQ just inland. They were a long way from their objectives. All thought of surprise was lost; instead, they were facing very determined and well dug-in opposition, and it would soon be broad daylight.

Here was a marine's worst nightmare; fully exposed by a relentless rising sun, totally disorientated, enemy fire coming in thick and fast and accurate. Men were going down all around, the boats shearing like matchwood on the rocks, half still foundering in the swell. They were overboard and up to their waists or even shoulders, the weight of their kit a curse that dragged them under, sodden, their movements seeming cloying and agonizingly slow with each dragging footstep a marathon. There was no air cover, no supporting bombardment. Men didn't know just where they were, except that it wasn't where they were supposed to be. The enemy, however, knew just where they were.

At 0414 hours both destroyers turned again and swept back in. Their task was to gather in all the returning lighters and get the second lift on board. The navy was blissfully unaware of the chaos towards the beaches. A number of boats were holed and sinking; men were struggling in the swell, a good deal of their kit lost as they floundered in heavy water. The tugs had constantly stop-started as ropes snapped and jammed their propellers. The barges were a nightmare to tow, hopelessly heavy and unwieldy, crammed to the brim with laden marines. Commander White on board *Zulu* did manage to establish radio contact with the hapless Unwin, unwitting ringmaster of this dismal circus. His was the leading launch, except it wasn't leading, as it had broken down and was being shepherded by another. Everybody hoped everything else was going well. It wasn't.

This time the warships came in much closer, to within a mile. The decision, whilst always risky, was a logical response to the gathering confusion. The closer the ships got, the sooner they'd gather in their erring boats and could get the second wave ashore. This had to be the right thing to do. Again with hindsight, we can see this was catastrophic, for it brought the destroyers almost under the muzzles of the guns and any contest would be short-lived given the crushing weight of firepower the shore batteries could deploy. They were already in action and the rising sun would be their herald.

Lights were seen, bright white light coming from the direction of Mersa El Meira where they should all have been, but whoever was doing this it wasn't the SBS. Colonel Unwin and his useless launch were located and he was brought aboard *Sikh*. Much had gone wrong already and more was to follow, much more and much worse.

Barely was the flotilla of landing craft clear of the destroyers' bows than B1's tow broke. This took time to repair. Unwin was aboard A1's motorized launch. Her tow was next to go, fouling the propeller. Efforts to untangle the mess failed and the colonel transferred to C1. Doing so in haste, entirely understandably, he unfortunately left the radio behind.

As he was in A1, Lieutenant Ramseyer judged it impossible to clear the propeller and instructed his passengers to take to their paddles. They applied themselves with gusto, but, for the reasons explained, this proved largely ineffective. Massively loaded with men and kit, lumbering and sluggish, the dismal craft simply wallowed. It was half an hour since they left the ships and the boats were going nowhere quickly. The enemy searchlight played over them every half minute and their guns were seeking the range.

It was at this point that Unwin decided to return to *Sikh* and confer with Captain Micklethwait. It seems likely the marines' officer had decided to abandon the whole show. In the circumstances this would be entirely right. All element of surprise had gone, the Axis had his tiny flotilla fully in their sights, dawn was creeping closer, the beach was unmarked and difficulties with the boats were multiplying. The decision was sound, but how could it be implemented? Radio contact had failed and the craft were heading towards a hostile shore. The captain was rightly concerned about risks to his ship, which were mounting by the minute, and may have expressed these fears in very robust sailor's terms. His fears were about to be fully justified.

Meanwhile Ramseyer, still wallowing, had slipped the tow to A3 so each could proceed towards the shore independently, if indeed progress could be achieved. Behind them, reduced to mere spectators, the destroyers' guns roared in reply to the enemy's, great stabbing strikes of fire, flashing in the growing light. At one point *Sikh* got between A1 and the coast and the lieutenant took the chance to bundle his no doubt disgruntled passengers back up her shining sides. Most got off, but he and a couple of others, Corporal Auld and Marine Price, were left stranded as the ship moved clear. As they bobbed towards the unwelcoming shore, they could see enemy on the beach. Gamely, they opened up with rifles, provoking a furious fusillade in reply. They continued drifting onto the murderous rocks, stumbled ashore and were immediately captured.

The same thing occurred to many others. The second boat, A3, made it to the beach, but Sergeant Alford and his entire platoon were captured. Corporal Andrews finally cleared A1's fouled gear, by which time the tactical position had completely changed. From that point on he would be the rescuer, taking men from the water as *Sikh* finally lost her gallant fight. As Unwin was transferring to C1 he had yelled across to Major Jack Hedley, who was leading his flock from B1, to take the boats in and establish a beachhead. This seems somewhat at variance with the suggestion he was getting ready to dump the whole show. The three craft plugged towards the shore. With around 300 yards to go, a storm of enemy fire erupted. They crawled nearer, taking both hits and losses. B1 was holed and began to settle. The survivors had to swim for it and both lighters ended up on the rocks.

Lance-Sergeant Bert Warren was one of those who did get ashore. He and the rest were greeted with intense fire, which kept them immobile for a good quarter of an hour before they could filter around to the left. Somewhat bizarrely there was a large, pavilion–like tent on the beach, which turned out to be the German medical post. A no doubt surprised group of 14 prisoners was mustered. Major Hedley and his platoon had managed to struggle ashore from their sinking launch, grasping for a foothold or a toehold as enemy shells and tracer lit up the dawn. They were 3 miles too far west and the beach they were on was dangerously exposed.

Another slowly weaving strand of craft trying to get in was V tow, who'd disembarked from *Zulu*. Sitting ducks, they were badly shot up. Men were lost and more drowned as V3 crashed against the unforgiving rocks. U tow had a circular and frustrating journey, never reaching land. They had stood clear to allow B to get in, then made for the sound of surf further west, then veered back towards the first beach but saw no one. Next, they decided to chug back towards *Zulu*, but she was already drawing off.

Completely on their own now, they decided to try and motor eastwards 80 miles to the RV at Mersa Shegga where they could hope, after four days, to team up with some of their MTBs. This was a very faint chance. Moving agonizingly slowly like a shoal of half-stranded whales, they were quickly picked up by Axis planes in daylight and very soon surrounded by naval craft. They all went into the swelling Axis bag.[46]

Yet another of *Zulu's* spawn, W had set off ahead of its siblings U and V, heading for what they wrongly took to be a landing light. Predictably, things went wrong. W2 was disabled when the tow rope yanked her flimsy bows apart. Her laden passengers then had to be re-distributed amongst the remaining two already burdened craft. On they chugged until their progress was suddenly and rudely halted by one of the harbour booms. The navy officer supervizing the tow was knocked out by random shrapnel. Lieutenant Clarke RN, in overall charge, realized they were very much where they ought not to be and turned to the coxswain to reset the course. He didn't know where they were either, so there was nothing for it but to retrace their weary, wobbly passage back to the destroyer for fresh bearings.

More tribulations ensued as the rear barge, W3, foundered. Surgeon-Lieutenant Sugars RNVR, 11th Battalion's MO, led the survivors in a desperate swim for the shore, jettisoning most of their cumbersome kit. After an exhausting half hour in the water, they fetched up by the German beach hospital. They were very soon made prisoners.[47] Only W1 was still floating by then, and it fell into the same course as V tow, with precisely the same result. Both of these had been lost and not a single blow delivered against the enemy.

With so many of the players still incarcerated, the subsequent enquiry could not question Unwin as to how he'd arrived at his decision to call the operation off, which was unquestionably the right one, but it was critical to establish how he proposed to do so. A major contributing factor to the total confusion was the distribution of the No. 18 radio sets. Lack of any viable communications had made a very difficult job totally impossible. In total 350 men had climbed into the boats, only 70 of whom made it onto the beach, and the wrong beach at that.

They were still marines, however, and were still eager to take the fight to the enemy. Major Hedley was in charge and the survivors clawed and battled their way off the sand. In the wild fury of the fight, it may have been the case that the beach hospital was attacked with grenades. This is questionable, but the enemy certainly appeared to think so and fought back with equal savagery. The odds were pretty hopeless, as the coast was a hornet's nest of Axis troops, now fully stirred. Hedley knocked out an MG post and put his marksman's skills to good effect with his .38 revolver.[48] By 0900 hours he, with those still on their feet, had taken temporary refuge in caves. They had many who had been wounded, ammunition was running short, many rifles had jammed in the wet sand and, although they had one radio still functioning, they couldn't raise any friendly contact. Their situation was critical.

Operation *Agreement* was unravelling fast. Haselden's commandos had established a narrow salient in the east and Jack Hedley's band of survivors were clinging on in the west. Most of the marines, however, had never seen the beach. There was no possibility of getting a second wave ashore. To even attempt this would have been suicidal. Both destroyers were vulnerably exposed to the full weight of enemy shore batteries and already taking hits. Their very survival was now at stake. Any expectation the raid might achieve its objectives was now history; it was just a question of saving as many as possible. The Germans now had the initiative and they weren't likely to let go.

Over six months later in April 1943, aboard that venerable warhorse HMS *Canopus*, Major-General E. C. Weston convened a court of enquiry investigating causes of failure.[49] Many who might have been witnesses had become casualties and many more were still POWs. One witness who was on hand was Lieutenant Leslie Frank Ramseyer RNVR, who'd served on *Sikh* and went in on the first of the first lift's tows – A2.

The lieutenant's testimony offers a searching and critical insight into what did go wrong. He firstly argued that the landing craft were inadequate, which can hardly be disputed. He confirms that the tows parted on four occasions. Sea conditions were partly responsible, but the clumsy design of the lighters was a major contributing factor. The awkward craft did not glide smoothly through the waters but jerked forward in response to the swell. Inevitably, this put tremendous pressure on the ropes (2½-inch manilas). Similar problems had occurred in training, but were remedied simply by extending the tow. When the powered craft broke down, marines attempted to row. Again, these arduous efforts were defeated by bad design; the freeboard of the lighters was too high to allow for efficient use of paddles.[50]

These high sides also meant the boats were exposed to the foibles of any wind that might be blowing, which neatly frustrated anyone's best endeavours to keep on a straight course. The boats were too blunt and unwieldy, the sides were too high, oars would have been far more effective than paddles and a proper towing device should have been fitted. Lieutenant Ramseyer's own boat was wrecked on the rocks and he himself captured. He was firmly of the belief the Axis knew all about the raid beforehand, though this remains questionable. He does comment that the air raid served only to alert the defenders.[51] It seems now quite clear that this was a major error.

Ramseyer concludes that the failure to mark the correct landing beach was crucial. It is possible the lights seen further west that may have led the marines so drastically adrift were accidental, perhaps torches from a shore patrol or lights from a German field hospital. The overall picture that emerged would have veered towards farce had it not led or contributed to tragedy.

'Greater love hath no man',
We turned our eyes away
To where the sunshine on the hills
Claimed glory for the day.

'Than this that he should give',
Our thoughts cast far away
To red-gold hair, soft creamy skin
And sunlight in the bay.

'Should give for his friend his life',
Our memories floated wide
And wandered in some distant vale
To the lapping of the tide.

'Amen', the chaplain's voice soft fell
We bowed our heads to pray,
'Oh God, it cannot be, this price
So soon be ours to pay'.

E. Yates, *Parade Service on Deck*

CHAPTER EIGHT

DEFEAT

David Lloyd Owen was a worried man. The first, long and arduous part of his strenuous mission had been accomplished with commendable élan and pinpoint accuracy, but once inside the wire, Haselden's men were alone in the lion's cage. For LRDG, it was now a waiting game. The troopers enjoyed, by desert standards, a lavish evening meal – after all, nobody quite knew when they might consume another and the next 24 hours promised to be very busy. What increasingly began to gnaw at Lloyd Owen was the lack of contact. As night deepened and the radio remained obstinately silent, his worries multiplied: 'I remember tripping over the stays of the aerial in the dark as I kept walking anxiously between the fore and the harassed wireless operator'.[1]

It was a dark, moonless night as the LRDG, fortified by a generous dram, set about their nefarious business. As they motored over the stripped desert some 15 miles from the port, they had to negotiate the evil escarpment of Sidi Rezegh. This was difficult and painstakingly slow. Overhead the bombers droned; it was about 2200 hours. In the night, they reached a concrete pillbox, part of the Axis outer cordon. Lloyd Owen told his driver to hit the gas pedal and they spurred by, but the trucks behind opened fire with rippling bursts of automatic fire, shockingly loud, and the lightning flash from flaming muzzles burst the stillness.

Getting the convoy back together after this brief fury of alarm wasn't easy and it took time. Worse, the one truck that was missing held all the communications.[2] This was disquieting, but soon the crew showed up minus the vehicle, which had stalled and failed to start again. A near-farcical episode ensued, as Lloyd Owen with ten troopers searched for the lost truck. Verey lights were risky but necessary in the pitch dark. Their first find turned out to be nothing more exciting than an abandoned water cart. The LRDG vehicle was finally located, but it stood uncomfortably close to the enemy bunker. Sergeant Hutchins dealt with the defenders, soon silenced, while Lloyd Owen prepared to blow up the truck. Happily, this proved unnecessary as the engine turned and fired: it turned out that two back tyres were blown and had to be replaced.

Time was haemorrhaging fast. They needed to be through the perimeter and attacking the RDF post by midnight. The RAF was providing an impressive sound and light performance, illuminating the way ahead and drowning out engine noise. The raiders pressed on, not meeting any opposition. Soon they were on the main road, expecting, as they barrelled along without lights, to be challenged at any moment. They weren't. There was no manned checkpoint as Lloyd Owen had feared, only abandoned steam rollers and barrels marking the defended zone. 'There was no sound and I hoped and I hoped that this was the perimeter deserted. So I walked along it, plaintively shouting 'Rosalia' which I knew to be the enemy's password.'[3]

As it turned out, this wasn't the real boundary and it was now after 0100 hours. Lloyd Owen decided to lie up where they were and attack at dawn, knocking out the RDF station before falling upon the aerodromes. Still no radio contact with Haselden. If he couldn't be contacted, he could certainly be heard; the staccato crescendo of battle sounded loud and clear, rising and swelling as the commandos stormed their targets. The racket swelled the boom of big guns offshore and jagged flashes of light seared through the darkness. The LRDG troopers, seasoned hands at all this, took the opportunity to sleep.[4]

They didn't get much rest, as headlights approaching gave notice the enemy was stirring. Lloyd Owen boldly blocked the highway, Tommy gun at the ready, while an ambush party lurked in readiness. It was only one car and a few deterrent bursts proved enough to persuade the driver to halt and get his hands up. This was just as well, as Lloyd Owen found his own personal weapon had jammed. The officer from the crop of prisoners spoke some English and suggested he was in fact fleeing the battle rather than seeking to join it.[5] His car was rolled off the road.

What the hell was going on? Lloyd Owen could plainly see the naval battle was continuing. Dawn was fast gathering and by now the port should have been in Allied hands and the ships moving in. The choice was stark, and as commanding officer only he could make it. Either they kept going and attacked their assigned target, albeit somewhat later than planned, or they could withdraw, get clear and try to establish communications with HQ and hopefully Haselden's commandos. Kennedy Shaw recelled that 'reluctantly but with a disappointed relief we retraced our steps of the previous night. We moved fast in the increasing daylight and watched the enemy sentries pacing idly in the cold, grey dawn and others lighting fires for their early cup of tea'.[6]

It was the right call, given what was happening elsewhere; to press on would have been bound to lead to disaster. They headed back to Sidi

Rezegh to the empty airfield there for another attempt at establishing communications and deepening angst for Lloyd Owen, wracked by guilt he'd left his comrades and his friend in the lurch. Kennedy Shaw explains that 'the sun was rising higher and we had to move again further away to lie up in safety; so we drove fast for twenty miles, only stopping once when we saw a German aircraft flying at about fifty feet across our path.'[7] Despite being so close, the Axis plane apparently detected nothing and flew on. The LRDG couldn't know this, but their luck was holding. Only when a link to HQ was finally achieved, later that morning, with the patrol well bedded down in good cover, did they learn of the navy's failure. Lloyd Owen had made a difficult and courageous decision. It was also the right one. Nobody had any news of Haselden.

At Mersa Umm Es Sciausc, Tommy Langton had employed his torch as a poor substitute for the Aldis lamp frustratingly left behind at the Italian house. He could see Pilot Officer Scott's signal from the other side of the bay quite clearly. Langton now noticed he'd also lost his watch in the flurry of action.[8] His efforts did not go unrewarded, as he recalled: 'After a short while, I saw two MTBs come in; after that, however, no more appeared'.[9] What should he do, keep signalling or get down to the beach?

He wedged his torch and left the beam on. No sooner had he covered a couple of hundred yards than he saw a light out to sea, apparently signalling. Now he dashed frantically back to his own and re-commenced flashing. Nothing happened. This was a lonely and uncertain business, adrift from the fighting but knowing that his role was absolutely vital. He set off again, only to find his rucksack and SMG (sub-machine gun) had been filched from where he'd stowed them.[10] This was inconvenient as he ran into a couple of the enemy. Having only his .38 revolver, he battered one with the butt and this seemed to discourage them!

Finally on the beach, he found the pair of MTBs that had come in, busily unloading the Northumberland Fusiliers detachment with their machine guns. This was much-needed support, adding significantly to the commandos' firepower. Still, the newcomers were only of slender strength: just No. 14 platoon, led by the stalwart Sergeant Miller, with Corporal Wilson, lance-corporals Ridley and Watt, fusiliers Harbottle, MacDonald, Shields and two brothers called Leslie.[11]

Tommy Langton raced back to his torch and started signalling again. By now the hornets' nest was thoroughly stirred, and searchlights were quartering the skies and coastline. A battle was obviously raging westwards. Tantalizingly, the lights showed up the rest of Blackburn's flotilla, still searching for the cove, but Langton could also see trouble: 'the MTBs got caught in the searchlights and I could see their wake and tracer bouncing off one of them.'[12] Langton reckoned, rightly, that there was now very little chance of the boats getting safely into the cove. Dawn was fast approaching, grey light filtering out the darkness. He returned again to the beach where only one grounded MTB remained. There was nobody in sight. He made his way back to Haselden's command post as the gunfire around was getting steadily louder.

With the action begun and the two wings of the commando operation moving in divergent directions, Haselden couldn't really exercise much direct command, trusting as he must to his subordinates. He had the wireless truck brought close up to the CP (command post). Not a great deal happened and the colonel, increasingly anxious, sent Lieutenant Russell of the SIG down to the cove to investigate. Like Langton, he heard the swelling hurricane of fire and witnessed the two MTBs that made it nosing in. One, as mentioned, ran aground and the other, having unloaded, moved off before dawn.[13] A threat was approaching, however. Undetected, as night gradually gave way, a substantive mixed German–Italian force had infiltrated around the wings of the commandos' divergent assaults to launch an attack on Haselden's CP. The defenders, no more than a couple of weak platoons, fought back and a firefight for the Italian house erupted. Meanwhile, over to the west, *Sikh* and *Zulu* were fighting for their lives.

As intimations of dawn streaked the sky, those German shore batteries found their range. The destroyers came in close to rescue marines, but swiftly found themselves the target of choice. As Peter Smith points out,[14] these ships were built for agility and were not heavily armoured. David Jefferson refers to the experiences of Trevor Lewis, chief engineer on board *Sikh*, who recounts a very robust exchange between Unwin and Micklethwait, the latter clearly blaming the former for the danger his ship now faced.[15] Lewis recalls that the destroyer was captured in a searchlight beam at around 0500 hours. An early salvo from the feared 88s struck the gear room, destroying the forced lubricating pumps, after switchboard, fire and bilge pumps. The starboard main engine seized straightaway, though the port turbine kept going for another ten minutes.[16] Next, more rounds hit the steering gear and immobilized it completely. The rudder was jammed and *Sikh* became a sitting duck.

The Royal Navy did not give in lightly, however, and the crippled vessel returned fire from all guns. The onset of full daylight was lit by the flash of her muzzles and the heavy crack of the German artillery raking her. Destroyers depend on speed and are not built to withstand bombardment like dreadnoughts or fat-bottomed monitors. The odds were hopeless from the outset. *Sikh* was armed with QF (quick firing) two-pounder 40mm auto-cannon, known as pompoms. These were excellent weapons, but as one of the ship's gunners, S. G. MacDonald, explained, the pompoms were out-ranged by the redoubtable 88s and, in any event, could not be depressed sufficiently to engage ground level targets.[17]

The 88s were clearly visible when firing in the dark but it would be hopeless to try and engage them other than by sight and guess. They would be reasonable targets for guesswork, for the original shore fire was from batteries to the north-east of the ship's position, and it seems to me that the Germans brought the 88s to come close to the ship's beam where we would be a very easy target, I assume. After all it was pretty portable, besides being a potent weapon.[18]

The next salvo struck A gun and it went up in flames as its ammunition exploded. A body of the marines who had been pushed forward onto the mess-deck suffered dreadful casualties with many men hideously mutilated, as one witness recalled: 'they were screaming from terrible burns, with their skin from neck to fingernails trailing behind them. Some leapt over the side in their agony'.[19] The gleaming ship that had brought them here was transformed from sleek and neatly trimmed into a vision of the inferno. Scorched, bent and twisted metal contorted the once-pristine decks, and black-fringed flames and the stench of burning oil competed with the sweet sickliness of roasting flesh.

When Trevor Lewis reported the engine damage to Micklethwait, the captain ordered 'half ahead with both engines'. This was a desperate expedient, but getting beyond the range of those mighty 88s was all that mattered. However, both engines then seized up. Below decks was a horror story: 'dropping down the gear room hatch, it became obvious that nothing could be done; the port and starboard fuel pumps had been smashed by the force of the explosion, the compartment was four to five feet deep in oil and water, and both the leading stoker and stoker who had been on watch appeared to be dead'.[20]

With the ship going round in uncontrollable circles and taking such heavy and destructive fire, there was no prospect of gathering in any of the lighters. The crews of both X and Y guns were amongst those trying to get the launches and dumb lighters to the beach. In order to return fire, the gunner officer with a quartet of ratings made his way aft to bring X gun to bear. Trevor Lewis remembered that X gun, manned by chief gunner's mate Harry Seymour, was the only one still firing.[21] Lewis, with one of his fellow engineers, struggled to bring a small auxiliary oil pump into action to ease the screaming, tortured engines.

Other engineers were attempting to fix some form of manual steering mechanism. The ship's turbines, that steady, omnipresent hum and the beating heart of the destroyer, soon shuddered to a grinding, tormented halt. Heat in the engine room swiftly soared to unbearable temperatures, the fans having failed. All through his ship's final agonies, the captain was a pillar of calm, as survivors kept up the hopelessly unequal fight to the bitter end.[22]

Zulu was attempting to get alongside and fix a tow. It was now 0545 hours.[23] Getting the line aboard was achingly slow. Shells bracketed both ships. *Zulu* was soon taking hits as well. It seemed as though the full fury of the Axis was blasting from the shoreline. Now, however, daylight was their ally, allowing the line to be secured and the crippled *Sikh* to be dragged clear. Another salvo burst, however, and *Zulu* took a direct hit, which ripped out the bollard, snapped the line and inflicted casualties.[24] It was 0625 hours.

Major R. W. Sankey RM was aboard *Zulu* and was a witness to the two destroyers' desperate struggle:

> About the third salvo from the coast defence battery, 'Sikh' signalled that she was hit and disabled ... We moved slowly along the coast just off the landing beach, the coast defence battery still firing. 'Sikh' opened up and 'Zulu' followed suit. Range was then 2,000 yards. Star shells were put over 'Sikh' and also at times 'Zulu'. Other coast defence guns had joined in, mortar fire was heard and we could see

tracer being fired by the Royal Marines ashore, also heavy firing at the harbour entrance.[25]

Sankey records that it was around 0530 hours that his ship abandoned her attempts to sweep up the lost sheep in their useless lighters and focus on aiding *Sikh*. A trio of searchlights now had her fixed like a fly in their web, however. The major ordered all the marines on board to come forward and assist in getting the tow across. *Sikh* was still moving in the water at around three to four knots, which frustrated the first attempt: 'a number of coast defence light and heavy batteries were firing at 'Sikh' and 'Zulu', also light and heavy anti-aircraft guns, pompoms and in one case a machine gun post'.[26]

The shell that shattered the bollard and tow wire also killed Captain Ellis of the marines, as well as wounding numerous sailors and other marines. The ships were being hit relentlessly. *Zulu* was rocked by another direct hit just abaft the foremast. More men died, and ammunition, stored on the crammed decks, was set off by the blast. Corporal Murphy, Lance Corporal Campbell and Marine McFarlane wrestled with the blazing boxes and chucked them overboard. Both ships continued to take hits.

Zulu was game for another try, but her own survival was now at stake. It could only be a matter of time before she too was crippled. Micklethwait ordered Commander White to steam clear and *Zulu* sped off after laying down more smoke. The doomed *Sikh* was completely alone. There could be no escape. Trevor Lewis recounted that even at the last X gun was still banging away bravely. A few Axis planes screamed by overhead, but were more intent on chasing the destroyer that appeared to be escaping. *Sikh* was going nowhere. As Commander White recalled, for the men onboard *Zulu*, this was a very dark moment:

At the time, I myself had decided that this most dreadful decision was the right one and I was quite sure that 'Zulu' would not have avoided severe damage if I had again closed into a mile of the coast. Courageous signals were received from the 'Sikh' as we left her to her fate and she was last seen firing with her forward guns and being repeatedly hit.[27]

It was just after 0730 hours that Micklethwait gave the order to abandon ship, the hardest command for any skipper. His destroyer had a tremendous record of service and it must have been doubly galling that she should be lost in an action so hopelessly one-sided and for which she was so ill-suited. Trevor Lewis thought the shelling had stopped as the stricken vessel began to wallow. He and a mate decided to salvage what they could of their own gear from the mess before they went over the side. The place was a shambles, yet he found some cherished photos of his family and, providentially, a small bottle of rum, spiritual solace in more ways than one. And then they went over into the bright blue Mediterranean and swam clear. Both Unwin and Micklethwait were assisting men into the waves ensuring everyone got off before they jumped.

They were not alone in the water, but turned back to see the captain ceremoniously haul down her tattered ensign from both the fore and aft masts before he too went into the sea. As would be expected, he was the last man to leave. Despite this honour in defeat, it was a sad time, as Micklethwait explained:[28]

It was not long before the end came for 'Sikh' as she heeled over to starboard and finally sank. We were left feeling alone in the world, shocked, afraid yet still struggling to survive. It is a solemn, heartbreaking experience to see the ship you have loved going to the bottom.[29]

Left hanging onto a Carley float, Lewis and the other survivors were eventually pulled clear by the Germans along with the wounded, dying and dead. All were treated with decency, with brandy and cigarettes provided. Those who could stand were marched into a military barracks/HQ, where Micklethwait addressed them. Officers and men were then led away for interrogation. There was one last stir of excitement as some of the POWs recognized the stocky senior German officer who strode past them – the Desert Fox himself!

Lewis had to argue to keep his snapshots. His Italian inquisitor was all for contemptuously binning them, but his German counterpart intervened on the seaman's behalf – war without hate indeed.[30] The interrogators were keen to know how Haselden's men of Force B had got ashore; they had still not realized they'd come overland. This certainly supports the idea that the Germans in Tobruk at least had no specific prior intelligence on the raid.

***

It was no better on the beach. The chaos of getting ashore, being on the wrong beach and the opposition far stronger and much readier than expected meant success was impossible from the outset. Nor was withdrawal an option. There were no available boats and the destroyers were in imminent peril. Major Hedley was now senior officer. A former ranker, his was an unenviable role. The only expedient he could come up with was to get off this accursed, fire-swept sand and up onto the high ground ahead, knock out any guns and hope to establish some sort of viable bridgehead for the second wave to come ashore, if indeed, there was a second wave.

Their very thin foothold by the shoreline was constantly being raked and highlighted by merciless light from flares. Dawn would soon leave them fully exposed. All he could do was to get the men organized and moving. Lieutenant C. M. P. Powell leading 7th Platoon of A Company had already started. There was only one way to go and that was inland. Retreat would have been preferable but there was nowhere to retreat to. Evacuation would have been best, but there was no prospect of that either.[31] Sergeant Povall was of like mind and drove his men forward with bayonets fixed, hacking through Axis MG posts and slit trenches, driving inland and sniping relentlessly. Marine Foley, reduced to only his bayonet, used this to great effect, laying waste to a German MG position armed with nothing else.[32] SNAFU it might be, but the marines were far from cowed.

A narrow wadi led up from the shore. This afforded some cover but not much; the attackers were still under sustained and heavy fire. They swarmed up, taking on enemy positions with great élan. Daring and momentum carried them on and onto higher ground. Next, they encountered an Italian encampment whose inhabitants clearly wanted nothing to do with these wild-eyed raiders up from the sea. They surrendered and were sent stumbling down to present themselves as captives to the few still holding on at the beach itself.

'Tug' Wilson was one of those guarding what remained of the boats.

I felt a bit lonely after the marines vanished and the shooting started. I can recall one or more of the landing boats' crews nearby being smashed up [they were under prolonged mortar bombardment] because we were spread out so much. There was some comfort in the fact that I had the stripped Lewis machine gun out of the boat which kept me busy. Trouble was the blasted thing kept jamming.[33]

They captured several Italians, including a group who seemed to come down to the shore from inland, probably those rounded up by the marines as they attacked. As Tug notes, 'they were not prisoners for long'.

Major Hedley was also driving forwards away from the deadly beach. He took on and took out a truck-mounted MG with a Mills bomb. A noted shot with a pistol, he neatly gunned down five Italian defenders with a single shot apiece. A revolver only holds six rounds, however, and the gallant major soon found there were many more Italians than he had bullets. Corporal Hunt, despite a life-threatening wound, managed to polish off an NCO threatening Hedley and both survived. This occurred just in time, as even the courageous corporal was about to temporarily succumb to his wounds.[34] Lieutenant Powell, advancing to the right of Major Hedley's group, continued his storming assault.

As dawn crept in, they'd got to the head of the sheltering wadi. The view at first light wasn't encouraging. Ahead, the bare ground continued to rise, devoid of cover yet well covered by enemy guns. There was nothing for it but to go on and to take on the defenders with suppressing fire while groups of marines crept forward to knock out the MGs. They succeeded and got to the top of the ridge. Hedley had all of 17 men with him. Happily on that unhappy morning, there was a sole, solid building ahead, which provided temporary respite as the officers pondered what to do next.

Their options were limited and all equally unattractive. Any respite was temporary. Going back to the beach was suicidal and pushing on was pointless as they'd just be moving deeper into enemy territory. It was plain no reinforcements were coming, but Axis planes came out like the dawn chorus. Movement in daylight was going to be impossible. Staying put wasn't much of an option either. Dodging from what cover there was, the group crept forward again up another sheltering wadi, which revealed a series of caves at its head. These would make good lying-up places until darkness offered some chance of escaping eastwards along the coast. The radio at least was still functioning, but nobody was picking up.

Despite the supreme courage of the marines, the game was pretty much up. Hedley had hoped to remain undetected until dark, but the Axis had quickly worked out where they must be lying up and were soon converging in overwhelming force. The marines smashed their radio and came out with hands raised. It must have been a very galling moment after so much blood had been sacrificed.*

Tug Wilson and a handful of raiders were still pinned down on the beach. Their own capture was imminent:

> When it became dawn, the Germans knew we were behind the rocks and were firing mortars at us from an escarpment on the right. And the German officer, when it became dawn, demanded our surrender. He told us to stand up. The marines had gone on and had by then all been captured; we were the only ones left on the beach at this time who had not been captured. This German officer stood up and told us to stand up and hold our arms, rifles etc in the air, right up in the air, then throw the weapons down. He spoke very good English.[35]

There were only a few survivors left on the beach and Tug's first thought was for his feet. Having fought since landing in soaked boots and socks, he asked his German captor if he could change into the dry, spare pair in his pack. Permission was granted and, dry shod, Tug was marched into Tobruk. Despondently, he noticed that, despite the intensity of the bombing, there was surprisingly and frustratingly very little evidence of actual damage. Everyone was assembled in a compound and subjected to preliminary interrogation. This was quite unnerving, and when a group of less than a dozen of them was selected and told to stand aside,

---

* Hedley and Powell were awarded the DSO (Distinguished Service Order) and Povall and Hunt were given Conspicuous Gallantry Medals, with the DSM (Distinguished Service Medal) for Corporal Andrews and Marine Foley.

most thought they were about to be shot. In one sense they were, but only through the lens of a camera. This was a photo opportunity for the DAK. Tall and strong looking POWs had been chosen for the shoot, presumably to magnify the glorious nature of the successful defence.[36] At least they got fed.

***

From 'the other side of the hill' the Axis view was considerably rosier. By 0430 hours Oberleutnant Soldt, 1st Company, Guard Battalion was able to report from the muster point at Kilometer Post 19 that his men were on the move, as ordered, and they were just west of the port. Further orders, received ten minutes or so later from Schultz-Ingenohl, clearly indicated there was no cause for undue haste.[37] Major Hardt on the coast now had a grandstand view in the breaking dawn and watched with satisfaction as the two destroyers were relentlessly pounded by the shore guns.

He moved his squad closer to the beach to ensure a solid hold. He records that *Sikh* went down at around 0900 hours. He further reported 'four or five destroyers and also a cruiser and a torpedo-boat off the coast, about 10 kilometres from the shore'.[38] Clearly he was wrong here; possibly he was referring to Blackburn's flotilla. It's also possible, as Peter Smith points out, that the return of the two destroyers led Axis defenders to calculate there were more warships than was in fact the case.

It was at 0500 hours that Anti-aircraft Group Tobruk's 3rd Company, 914th Battalion opened up on the MTBs trying to get into Mersa Umm Es Sciausc. For the tiny craft this was bad enough, but the German firepower was soon boosted by the 20mm cannon of their comrades in 4th Company. The 20mm was a formidable weapon and the fragile hulls of British MTBs were not designed to take such a battering. A scratch flotilla of armed Italian lighters, 17 all told, had been deployed around the harbour mouth. Il Duce's navy could throw in the cruiser *Dandolo* with her 4-inch guns and supporting fire from three Italian destroyers.[39] What possible chance did Blackburn's slim flotilla have, now the enemy was fully alert and spoiling for a fight?

Major General Deindl had every confidence in the capacity of his men (although he largely ignored the Italians) to defend Tobruk. His only worry was that his units, spread out as they were, could be assaulted in turn by strong landing parties. This was what he needed the Guard Battalion for. He needn't have worried, however. By 0550 hours he was informed by 3rd Company that they were en route to protect the vital radio station (this was of course the LRDG objective). Major Hardt's messages from the western flank were encouraging. At 0545 hours, he confirmed that two destroyers were on fire and flak was chopping up the landing craft.[40] Hauptmann Nitzki, commanding 88mm Flak Battery 1/60, was directing his fire on *Sikh* – it would have been obvious to the Axis officers onshore that his was an increasingly one-sided fight.

As the regular updates came in to Deindl, it became increasingly clear that his defences were more than holding up. The adjutant of Koruck Battalion at Staff HQ in Tobruk affirmed that DAK and Luftwaffe formations were moving seamlessly into position. Whilst it is always easier to plan for the defence than to attack, the precision and effectiveness of the German planning has to be contrasted with the blind optimism of the Allies' raid. By 0600 hours reports from the watchers above the marines' beach could confirm that the landing craft, or what was left of them, were withdrawing and, half an hour later, that the Allied ships were moving off to the east.[41] The defence had held and the attackers had been seen off. From the Axis perspective, it was a pretty satisfactory night's work.

By 0700 hours, Rippich, in overall charge of the more northerly, western flank, could confirm his men had taken 70 prisoners for very modest losses, around eight men killed, another eight badly wounded and under a dozen minor injuries.[42] It would seem overall that DAK losses were around 30 dead all told.[43] For the British, it could still get worse, however. German soldiers from 2nd Company, 532nd Battalion came across a beached launch or lighter where they found a complete set of plans, orders and even a readymade address to the local Arab population! This was astonishing booty, and may well be the source of the idea the Germans were fully aware of the whole enterprise from the start. From an Allied perspective, it was yet another reprehensible failure of security.[44]

Admiral Cocchia swiftly claimed the honours in finding these orders, actually the work of an Italian signal rating named Zinni. The Axis junior partners would go on to claim much of the credit for the successful repulse of Operation *Agreement*. Peter Smith relates how Captain Micklethwait and other POWs were greeted by their Italian interrogator with the sneering quip – 'you were two hours late, why?'[45] Small wonder so many survivors felt they'd been rumbled from the start.

Haselden's men were still in the game, but the net was tightening. Surprise, audacity, dash and courage had won possession of their piece of hostile North Africa, but a bridgehead without a bridge was likely to become a trap. And it was. Aside from the Fusiliers and their two Vickers guns, there had been no reinforcement. The enemy was awake and recovering from any initial shock. They had thought to fight low-grade Italians, but instead were battling high-grade Germans. The two arms of the commando deployment were flung out east and west, forming a fragile salient. Their HQ was under attack. There was no hope of LRDG getting close enough from inland to open up an escape route. From his westerly vantage, John Poynton watched with a gunner's eye as the shore defences swung into action against Blackburn's MTBs.

Searchlights probed like bright scalpels, paring back the layers of dark, with the small, vulnerable craft shown up as they dodged and swerved. Each beam of light was followed by a hail of shells, bright fireflies of tracer swooping along the cones. Still the little ships didn't give up. There would be no successes for the Royal Navy that night, but that wouldn't be for lack of will, effort or endurance. The MTBs kept coming back but the weight of fire drove them off. Only dawn brought an end to this one-sided game.

Meanwhile, what was happening to Campbell? His continuing *chevauchée* eastwards aiming for Mersa Biad had resulted in several hours' silence. Haselden sent David Sillito to find out. The ground was, as before, difficult, with enemy posts still manned and the possibility of mines everywhere. Sillito found himself facing the business end of a 20mm Breda, a very nasty sensation until Sergeant Swinburn shot the gunner first.[46]

In fact, Campbell's party had found no rest at 'Brighton' camp. Quite the reverse, as the enemy were ready and alert, their defences fully manned. A storm of fire greeted the commandos as they attempted to infiltrate the network of bunkers and pillboxes. These were providing interlocking fields of fire with support laid on by the bigger guns north of the port. Campbell was wounded, and while some damage was inflicted by grenades chucked down air vents, there was never a prospect of further success. The two lieutenants, Roberts and Murphy, helped the injured major get clear. They fell back towards HQ.

The search had to be called off anyway as dawn broke, by which time Campbell's survivors were struggling back. On his own return journey, Sillito ran into Tommy Langton, who confirmed there was no point in further signalling as the rest of the MTBs could never now hope to get into the cove undetected. Worse, he'd stumbled across an enemy position they'd all missed first time around. Langton, with Private Glynn, now set off, mounting their attempt to find Campbell. As night retreated, dawn showed just how many enemy outposts had been missed; the hornets' nest was buzzing. Shells from guns across the harbour were now falling into the narrow salient. It was a Wagnerian dawn with fountains of earth, rock and dust kicked up by the impact, lethal shards of stone skimming like shrapnel.

Of the SIGs, Weizmann (Opprower) and Wilenski (Goldstein) were hanging on to the positions they'd won earlier as they had received no fresh orders. As dawn surfaced, Berg appeared and passed on new instructions from Buck, who told them to ditch all their Axis kit, papers included, get into British gear and destroy the remaining vehicles. It would soon be every man for himself, and being taken in DAK uniform was a guaranteed passport to Buchenwald.[47] Berg moved on and the other two set about using spare fuel to ignite one truck. Inside a handy cave, they stripped completely. Free of incriminating evidence but also naked, they had to find British battledress. Needless to say, there was no fresh supply in the vicinity, so they were forced, with great distaste, to rob the dead.[48] Corpses were not in short supply.

Both Buck and Russell appeared. The pair had been off trying to sow mischief in other quarters, though quite what and where has never been defined. Possibly they'd been looking for the supposed POWs, trying to capture the high-ranking Axis officer mentioned previously, or undertaking a spot of breaking and entering to relieve the enemy of his pay chest.[49] None of that mattered now. The situation was critical and could only get worse. It was obvious that, as the commandos originally stormed the Italian house, a number of the garrison entrenched nearby or bolting from the building had got clear and raised the alarm. They'd now been able to guide several Axis companies directly onto Haselden's

HQ, around which the unequal battle was raging. Full dawn meant certain annihilation for the defenders, hopelessly outgunned and running low on ammunition.

It was nearly 0600 hours (authorities vary). Haselden couldn't wait for news of Campbell, so sent word for him to destroy all enemy installations he controlled and then try and filter out his survivors through the net before it closed completely. This was unnecessary advice, as this was exactly what he was already trying to do. Around the Italian house, enemy fire was growing in intensity and accuracy. All John Haselden could do was to try and get the wounded away in the remaining trucks before the rest made a run for it. Four casualties were humped onto one vehicle together with the MO while Haselden prepared to ride shotgun in the other (the wireless truck). Buck and the SIGs seem to have been with him. Steiner appeared, still in his DAK colours, and Buck yelled at him to find British kit even though he himself was still fully masquerading as a German officer.

Barlow was to drive the wireless truck, but it was obvious the enemy were wise to the move and were setting up a block. As the vehicle burst through the ring, Haselden had already spotted this and dismounted to take the Italians on single handed. Buck, Russell, Berg and Steiner charged up after him, a suicide club indeed. The charge was magnificent, but Haselden was the first to be hit. Lieutenant MacDonald raced up to pull the colonel clear, but a grenade finished Haselden off. MacDonald was left dazed and scorched by the blast. Berg went down wounded, but Steiner managed to drag him back.[50] It was now *sauve qui peut* for those who could. There was no way through the steel cordon.

Immediately before the attempted breakout, John Poynton had raced back to Haselden's HQ seeking fresh orders. He'd probably anticipated he'd be told to destroy the captured guns and then get out as best he could. Poynton loaded up with explosives and returned to George

Harrison and his sappers. Nowhere was safe now; bullets hummed like bees and random shells were still falling. With each moment the vice was tightening. Methodically, Poynton's shrunken team blew the guns. Then they had to get back, perfect targets in daylight. Harrison and another of his RE men didn't make it, but the rest did. Sergeant Swinburn, true to the spirit of his Border Reiver ancestors, was holding the beleaguered HQ. Poynton had seen armour moving against them, just to lengthen the odds that bit further; planes were ranging overhead.[51]

Despite the severity of his injuries, Graham Taylor was among the 'walking wounded'. This stretched the definition, as some could barely move, but as they weren't technically stretcher cases, the injured officer volunteered to lead them down onto the beach where some means of escape might present itself. As they stumbled and clambered towards the temporary haven of the cove, Taylor could see the battle raging out to sea. He could see the crippled *Sikh* still firing and some of the MTB flotilla still lurking offshore, but there was only one in the bay itself, and that was hopelessly aground.

On the path they suddenly encountered Mike Roberts. His news was hardly calculated to raise the spirits. He confirmed Campbell was down, shot through the thigh. He explained the commandos had run into very stiff and determined opposition at Brighton camp (Landsborough insists the wounded Campbell was with Roberts at this point, though this seems to be open to doubt). Lieutenant Duffy was dead and very few were likely to make it back. Bill Barlow's dash with the wounded had also come to grief. He got back to the Fusiliers' position and begged Miller to re-site his guns to cover an attempt to get the wounded back from the wadi in which they were sheltering to the relative safety of the bay. The Fusilier obliged, his Vickers sweeping the higher ground opposite and keeping Axis heads down. Ammunition was perilously low.[52]

The furious rattle of the RNF machine guns kept the enemy sufficiently occupied to allow Barlow and his men to get the badly wounded up from the *wadi*. He was the senior officer of this small group. Their choices were pretty stark unless they'd a mind simply to surrender, which they hadn't. One way out was back into the desert and hope to be rescued by the LRDG, or they could attempt to make their way along the coast eastwards to Mersa Shegga, which was only 9 miles away, but the shoreline would be crawling with Germans. These choices were not ideal.

Pilot Officer Scott, who could be excused for wishing himself elsewhere and in the lesser tumult of the skies, had abandoned his lonely vigil and made a dash back to HQ. It was quite a sprint, as every Axis gun in North Africa seemed to be firing at him. A German E boat, nosing unexpectedly into the cove, also opened up with its formidable firepower, but only succeeded in shooting up some of the Afrika Korps. Scott, dodging from rock to rock, somehow jogged clear and fell in with Mike Roberts and Lieutenant Murphy, together with survivors from Campbell's commandos.[53]

The Italian house would never be a pretty seaside villa again. Small-arms and-mortar fire were raining down on the makeshift defences. It was daylight now and there was hardly any cover. The place was turning into a regular Alamo. More enemy were massing, getting steadily closer, and ammunition stocks were nearly exhausted. John Poynton and Sergeant Swinburn were in charge. The Axis came in at a rush, but sustained fire drove them back. Poynton wasn't beaten. He told Swinburn he'd lead a group of volunteers up onto some higher ground to the rear. The rest would cover and then leapfrog back in their wake.

He took his fellow gunners and those sappers still on their feet. Off they went. Bullets sprouted around them. This clearly wasn't going to end well, but suddenly the panting lieutenant tripped over one of their Italian prisoners who'd been cowering overlooked by both sides. Poynton's arrival, accompanied by so much automatic fire, provoked a collective panic and the captives rose as one man and bolted, happily in the same direction as the commandos wished to travel.[54]

Survivors later likened the gunnery officer to a dog driving a stampeding flock of sheep, driving the Italians to the top of the ridge he was seeking, despite a final burst of enemy fire that nearly did for everyone. Poynton and his team slid into cover. The Italians kept on running. The ruse had succeeded but with what point? Swinburn had signalled that he couldn't follow; a second group wouldn't be so lucky and the enemy certainly had their range.

Poynton could see the beached MTB beckoning like an oasis. They ran again, this time to the next ridge. Mortars stonked them and machine guns tracked them. Bombardier Bedward and Gunner Riley were killed outright, and more men were wounded. Then what Poynton took to be other remnants of the commandos turned out to be Afrika Korps. The game was up and they surrendered. Nobody could have done more.[55]

Swinburn kept on fighting. Minute by minute the odds grew heavier, but the commandos managed to create a kind of improvised blockhouse by linking some tin sheds. This redoubt had room for 18 men. The remaining eight held the sand-bagged verandah of the main building, now in some need of repair. Rounds were pinging off or punching through the tin sheets, ripping into sandbags and further pock-marking the already scarred walls of the main structure. The commandos' salient had shrunk to this tiny perimeter.

As the enemy pressed ever closer, the commandos chucked grenades, but the bombs couldn't clear the nearest ridge. Undeterred, Swinburn got another commando to hold open an empty sandbag while he pulled the pins from two grenades and placed them inside. Leaping to his feet, the big Geordie, an admirable target, whirled the sack sling style and sent it on its way. As this appeared to have the desired effect, he repeated the performance several times and cleared the Axis from their immediate vicinity. Amazingly, and despite their best endeavours, they failed to hit him.[56]

Most of the commandos were armed with automatic weapons, Tommy guns. Whilst these were very effective at close quarters, they lacked the range of Lee Enfield rifles and were far more prone to jamming. They also consumed ammunition at a prodigious rate. An enemy machine-gun team had found a particularly good vantage and opened up, the jagged, tearing sound of the fast-firing MG42 unmistakable. Rounds clawed at the flimsy sandbags and hammered the shuddering tin plate huts. Swinburn now went into action with a Bren, firing from the hip. Again he was exposed and tempting fate, but again he came through safe and the enemy were suitably discouraged.

Brilliant as his defence was, it was only a matter of time before it ended. Fire from the porch side of the building slackened and the place was overrun. Grenades were practically showering down around them. Private Mackay waited for the bomb that had just landed by his left foot to explode and kill or maim him. It went off, but amazingly he was unscathed. There was nothing to be said for going on, as most had only a few rounds left. Sergeant Swinburn took off his tattered shirt and waved it above his head. His luck, which he'd surely pushed to the limit, held. The shooting stopped. Force B would fight no more.

With Allied briefings now in Axis hands, Deindl, at 0700 hours, asked Regia Aeronautica to take to the skies and give him a fuller overview. In fact the Italians, unusually quick off the mark, were already sending up patrols. He needed to ascertain fully the status of British units on land and what was happening out to sea. Barely 15 minutes later his construction battalion was reporting that the attack had been seen off, and that 'the threat of invasion is lifted'.[57]

Nonetheless, the general was a cautious man and the high alert status was maintained for the moment. At 0830 hours the officers of both Axis powers met for a situation report. It was decided that DAK would maintain overall responsibility for everything north of the Via Balbia as far as Mersa Matruh and El Krim. Close control of the harbour, the port and its defences would stay with the Italians.

As the morning wore on, Deindl had increasing reasons to feel well pleased. Those marines still holding out under Major Hedley were rounded up by a composite formation comprising 5th Company, 85th Construction Battalion, 778th Landing Company, bolstered by two Italian units and led by the capable Rippich. The victorious gunners commanded by Hartmann and Nitzki were sent down closer to the bay itself, tightening the noose on what was left of the marines and shore parties. Guard Battalion Afrika was also engaged in mopping up.

All succeeded in taking prisoners. What was left of the landing craft, weapons and kit fell to the victors. For most of the Allied soldiers and marines, there would be no escape, although some were still ready for the attempt. Out to sea, however, the drama was far from over. The navy had suffered cruelly and their tribulations were far from over.

He lived, before the baleful sun
Was risen to burn the yellow sand
To which from out the seas he ran
And then, a moment later, died.
His voice, as stumbling through the surf
He shouldered friends in the khaki wave,
Was mix't with theirs, as strong and rough,
And then, no call or moan he gave,
He laughed, it mingled strangely with a sigh
His thoughts we knew, were far away
And lonely, as the sightless eyes
That saw no beauty in the bay.
Yes, lonely and quiet, as the single grave
Shallow dug beyond the clean washed sand
Safe from the curl of the grasping wave
He lies, and has passed the barren land.

E. Yates, *Beach Casualty*

CHAPTER NINE

RETRIBUTION

Operation *Agreement* had run, almost literally, into the sand. The marines had been destroyed as a fighting force, as had Haselden's team. He himself was dead. One destroyer had already been lost and the other was far from getting clear. Nothing had been achieved. No part of the port had been taken into Allied hands, nor had any significant damage been inflicted on the Axis infrastructure. This operation wasn't going to stop Rommel; it barely inconvenienced him. The brief flicker of hope at the outset, that pale shadow of gaining the initiative, had vanished like the desert haze.

Commander Blackburn had never managed to gather his MTB flock once the increased surge in speed had scattered them. Aside from the pair that made it, none got anywhere near the cove. Most did not see the signals from shore. MTB 309 had swiftly got clear of the cove with the crew of the abandoned 314. Blackburn later complained that neither of these two boats had let him know they'd arrived. It's hard to see if this would have mattered. The only real advantages the little boats possessed were speed and secrecy abetted by the blanket of darkness. The last two vanished with the rising light. It wasn't as if they intended to simply give up, but the tiny flotilla, dispersed before an alert and powerful defence, could never hope to achieve anything of worth. They came back in time and again, and every time the guns were waiting.

By 0545 hours Blackburn, with only four craft, had attempted 'balaklavering' into Mersa Umm Es Sciausc, a brave attempt that was met by a wall of fire. The fearsome Eboats were also active. If destroyers were not intended for big gun duels, then MTBs most emphatically were not. Blackburn remained game for another go, but the rising sun nipped this venture in the bud. He next considered trying to force an entry into the harbour, but this was now verging on the fantastical. Bobby Allan's section of the flotilla (MTBs 260, 261, 262 and 263) was completely out of contact with Blackburn, Jermain and the others. His boats came up to the coast a bit later and found a very warm reception. Despite the odds, several torpedoes were loosed at the boom. Certainly, the flotilla did not lack gusto, despite post-operational reports to the contrary.

The small-boat crews could now see the unequal duel being fought out westwards and attempted to get closer and render aid to the stricken *Sikh*. Commander White recalled that this was around 0730 hours and that Blackburn had asked what his boats could do. White replied regretfully 'she must be left'.[1] The Macchi fighters, like patient hawks, were already circling. The little boats would be seeing much more of these nimble predators.

Besides, Blackburn could by now still count only seven of his full complement of 16 vessels and knew nothing of the rest. He recalled, 'I reluctantly gave the order to MTBs and MLs in company to retire to Alexandria'. This would be more easily ordered than accomplished; the ordeal of the small craft was only just beginning. Blackburn has certainly been criticized for his lack of familiarity with small-boat operations, but he was highly experienced otherwise and he knew this coastline well from his days commanding *Ladybird*.[2] He was in fact the only naval officer involved in the operation who had such detailed local knowledge.

Regia Aeronautica was in the air and Il Duce's prized air force would not let him down, not on this day anyway. 13th Air Force Group commanded by Major Lorenzo Viale was in the skies. The unit was made up of three operational squadrons, mainly Macchi MC200 and a smaller number of MC202 fighters with some outmoded biplane fighter bombers.[3] On a dawn reconnaissance they picked up all of the British ships engaged, including the MTBs and MLs. Nobody at GHQ had or at least should have intended that the small boats would be operating in broad daylight. They were overloaded with men and kit, and worse, their reserves of fuel, necessary for such a long passage, were all deck-mounted. Jermain's early suggestions had been ignored on cost grounds, the ultimate in false economies.

Most of those soldiers crammed onto the decks, with the obvious exception of the sole RNF platoon that landed, never saw the beach. They did not, however, lack for excitement on the arduous return journey. Both the Fusiliers' and the Argylls' detachments would be very busy indeed during the murderous gauntlet of their withdrawal. The Jocks lost Second Lieutenant R. W. McLaren killed and several others wounded. Each time the hawks circled and struck, the Tommies opened up with rifles, Tommy guns and Brens.

Denis Jermain seems to have taken on the mantle of tactical leader as they fled. Unlike Blackburn, he had ample form for small-boat operations. It was a long way, 360 miles, to Alexandria. David Jefferson takes the view, rightly or otherwise, that Blackburn's sight was somehow defective and he failed to see enemy planes closing.[4] This may be unfair. Commander Blackburn's disadvantage was that he lacked the necessary tactical experience. Jermain possessed far more, the whole show was fast becoming a small-boat raider's nightmare.

The preferred formation when facing attack from the air was the 'loose diamond'. This gave individual commanders room to manoeuvre as circumstances dictated, but also allowed the flotilla to put up an effective combined barrage. It was the best that could be done. Generally the enemy came on in waves of not less than eight planes, in regular unrelenting onslaughts. Prevailing wisdom was that MTBs, fast, well-armed and handy, had little to fear from enemy aircraft and that drawing the enemy away from the larger ships was good work in itself. There was recognition of the fact the Fairmiles were underpowered and under-gunned.[5] It is highly unlikely that Jermain, Coles, Gray or any of the other crew would have agreed, however. The losses speak for themselves; even the fast MTBs were terribly vulnerable from the air.

The first casualty was MTB 312 (Lieutenant Jan Quarrie). She was isolated and her decks crammed with that fatal fuel. The Macchi fighters swooped like hawks and she was enveloped in fire. It is impossible to imagine the horror of being on so small and vulnerable a craft, completely crammed, providing target practice for a determined foe who knows he holds all the aces. The boat was raked from stem to stern; the fuel blew up creating an inferno. She blazed and the only hope for survivors was the flimsy landing craft she was carrying. Most did get clear, however, and were picked up by MTB 266 (Lieutenant Richard Smith).

Another boat, MTB 308 (Lieutenant Roy Yates) survived the first run of Italian fighters. She escaped their attentions and those of the Stukas that came after, but one of her engines was hit and put out of action, crippling her normally impressive agility. She and MTB 310 were then attacked by a brace of Ju 88s flying out of Crete. This was around 0800 hours and the German aircraft came back in for several more runs. Charles Coles was an eyewitness to what occurred next. He watched a lone Axis plane come in from a shallow dive and attack MTB 308. The MTB shot at the attacker from all her guns, but the aircraft, impossible to say exactly why, simply did not pull out of her dive, smashing into her intended victim in an unfortunate end for both combatants.[6] Nobody survived.

Coles relayed this story to Sub-Lieutenant Nigel Gray of MTB 310 when both were POWs in Italy. Gray's own boat, commanded by a Canadian officer, Lieutenant Stewart Lane, was next. First the Macchis struck and then came the Stukas, then another wave of Italians. About noon, the Ju 87s came back for another go and this time got it right. One bomb plunged clear through the bow section, scattering her planking like twigs. Astonishingly, nobody was killed outright, though the skipper was badly injured. The survivors, sailors and soldiers, got off in the assault boat as the fatally damaged MTB began to settle.[7]

Their ordeal was only starting. For eight terrible days they drifted in a hot, listless sea, as wounded and dehydrated men lost consciousness. Only three made it through alive. Lieutenant Lane was one of those who died and was buried, like the others, at sea. Burnt by the relentless sun, hallucinating from lack of water, the trio were finally rescued by enemy soldiers as they drifted inshore. The Axis had held back for a while fearing a trap, but at least Gray and the other two in the lifeboat survived.[8]

Coles, during a particularly determined and sustained attack, noticed an army medic who had previously and vehemently declared himself a non-combatant zealously and strenuously passing up belts of ammunition to the sweating gunners. 'I thought you were a non-combatant?' the sailor asked of the soldier. 'Let's forget about that, shall we?' came the shamefaced reply.[9]

If the MTBs were highly vulnerable, it was even worse for the slower Fairmiles. There were three of these, carrying the demolition teams.

Those earlier mechanical troubles experienced by MTB 268 had meant that, as she turned back from the outward passage, all her passengers and gear had to be stowed aboard ML 353 (Lieutenant Michelson). The tiny flotilla within a flotilla had its own CO, Commander Nicoll, with Lieutenant Commander Ball as the boat's skipper. The events of their return passage were chronicled in a subsequent report[10] made by Sub-Lieutenant G. R. Worledge RANVR (Royal Australian Naval Volunteer Reserve), the Australian skipper of ML 352. The launches were much slower, with 18–20 knots their best speed from the Hall Scott petrol engines.

During the tense hours of darkness on the night of the 13th about three miles out, both 352 and 353 were told to heave to whilst Nicoll in the other launch, 349, crept in closer for a recce. Searchlights and active gunners were much in evidence, but he managed to avoid detection. The other two boats lying to lost contact with Nicoll's craft and Worledge decided they should go it alone. Relying on their ASDIC* kit for direction and range, they looked for the cove at Mersa Umm Es Sciausc. They couldn't find the passage and dawn showed they were only three cables (203 yards) away from the harbour boom, with enemy warships clearly visible. This plainly wasn't good.

As another opportunity for Axis gunners to practise their marksmanship offered itself, the launches headed out to sea at maximum revs. They put down smoke as the enemy destroyer added her firepower to the barrage. Worledge got clear and sighted Nicoll's missing boat further offshore. ML 353 was less lucky; she was taking palpable hits and survivors were taken off by 349. She still didn't sink, even though she burnt down to the waterline, and demolition charges had to be fixed to finally dispatch her. The surviving craft made a run for it, engines

---

* ASDIC was an early form of sonar equipment used to detect submarines.

straining, but the enemy hawks were on their tails. Worledge's launch took severe punishment. A reserve tank with 400 odd gallons in it was shot up and spilled. The port engine gearbox casing was shot away.[11]

Efforts to pump the rest of the petrol from the ruptured tank foundered as the auxiliary pump motor had become another casualty. It got worse (if this was possible), as the main engine bilge pump was another casualty and sprayed fuel into the engine room bilge.[12] By now it was broad daylight, after 0800 hours. The Axis had neither given up nor gone away. The next attack ignited the swilling gasoline, which blew a great rent in the small boat's port side.

There was little hope of extinguishing the fire, which now raged freely. Despite this hopeless position, the gunners firing the boat's two-pounder kept on banging shells at the enemy fighters. Soon the ammunition was going up and Worledge gave the order to abandon ship. Survivors clung to the small ship's dinghy, which towed a series of rafts. They regularly had to drop the tiny sail in an effort to avoid detection. That didn't work and at approximately 1130 hours they were captured by Il Duce's destroyer *Castore*. The Italian navy was having a good day.

What was left of the flotilla made it back, limping into Alexandria's Mahroussa jetty in the late afternoon. There were no drums and cheers for them, only a queue of ambulances for the many wounded, carried supine from their scarred and ravaged boats. All vessels bore the hallmarks of fighting and of defeat. Losing is like contracting a contagious disease; nobody really wants to know and there are neither plaudits nor sympathy. Jermain and the other skippers had fought a damn good fight. They had struggled with a far longer passage than their role normally required, loaded with men, gear and fuel. They had no fighter cover and had been forced to operate in daylight off a well-defended enemy shore with powerful and determined air forces. Their whole mission had been flawed from the very start.

That wasn't what anyone higher up the command chain was interested in hearing. Things had gone badly wrong and what were needed were scapegoats. The returning officers would do nicely. It was suggested that the requisite elements of dash and fire, of derring-do, of the Nelson touch, were lacking. Indeed, Jermain and his comrades might be considered distinctly timid, even cowardly.[13] This was downright unfair and completely wrong. Commander Blackburn clearly lacked training in and experience of small boat operations, but then there hadn't been the time or the detailed planning/training needed to remedy this very obvious defect.

He may not have been willing to listen to his subordinates, but had shown no lack of either courage or dash. The plain fact was that, once split up, their chances of getting all the boats into the cove were minimal and, once they'd been rumbled and the sun began to rise, they were totally and hopelessly exposed. It had been a very bad plan, but the survival instincts of those involved and who never left harbour were going into overdrive. Admiral Harwood, stepping smartly backwards, condescendingly noted that, in light of all that had happened, they had encountered a very difficult task, but there was no doubt that chances had been missed.

The small-boat officers themselves highlighted the lack of planning and inadequate training, correct on both counts. Jermain and Allan also felt the higher echelons lacked real understanding of the capacities and also limitations of smaller craft. Normally MTBs cruised in groups of four; 16 was too many. They were not designed to be employed over such long distances nor as improvised troop carriers. An MTB is not a destroyer. The boats had not trained or operated together as a single unit. Tacking on the slower Fairmiles added more unhelpful elements to a dangerous mix. These were the problems; lack of resolve wasn't one of them.

Jock Haselden was dead. Most of those who'd survived the fight had now surrendered, but not all. Tommy Langton had got back late to the HQ and found the bullet-riddled ruins uninhabited. That battle was over. His wasn't. Again he retraced his exhausted steps to the temporary sanctuary of the cove. This too was deserted but for the shell of the abandoned MTB, still hopelessly aground. This must have been a surreal moment for him, alone, the wrack of war all around, lightning flashes of gunfire resounding from the sea battle westwards. He went aboard; clearly the boat couldn't be got going, but he picked up such rations as could be had.

He wasn't alone for long, as soon he was joined by a handful of other survivors, lieutenants Sillito and Russell and Buck (possibly), Berg and Wilenski (Goldstein) and probably Weizmann (Opprower) (authorities vary).[14]

Langton resumed his ambitious and doomed efforts to get the boat's engines started while Russell manned the gun. He later recalled that he

> … operated the twin Lewis gun, which was mounted on the forward deck, at what I took to be the enemy. We were being shot at spasmodically … Langton and Watler who was a mechanic went below to look at the MTB's huge engines but neither could get them going at all, so after gathering more food and water, they shifted over to one of the equally abandoned assault craft lying alongside her, being joined by the others.[15]

They were forced to rely more on oars than engines as they attempted to row the ungainly craft out of the cove and attempt to escape by sea. There was no escape, however. It was light by now and as they nosed out into open water, leaving the cover of the sheltering bluffs, they came under heavy fire. Tommy Langton saw some of the ongoing action:

[I saw] some of our own men dodging along the west side of the bay and there were large explosions coming from behind them. It was impossible to tell who they were but I think they may have been the REs dealing with the guns on the point.[16]

They rowed back to the beach.

Back on solid if far from friendly ground, they moved up off the sand, through yet another belt of mines and into a sheltering wadi. They were to see much of such sheltering wadis in the weeks to come. Soon, this handful was joined by Sergeant Evans, and they all began the very long trek east. They constantly had to duck from prowling planes or searching ground patrols, now just the foxes no longer the hounds. At one high point Tommy Langton looked back and saw the sea battle still raging, with gallant *Zulu* seeking to draw clear her stricken mate, shells bursting all around. The ridge wasn't safe, as enemy guns from 'Brighton' sought them out. They scrambled on into another sheltering defile where they came across another larger group of 15 to 20 survivors.

Most of these were RNF who, after firing off their last rounds, had spiked the guns and made for the cove led by lieutenants McDonald and Barlow. Altogether, they were what remained of Operation *Agreement*, and their only objective was escape and evasion. Few as they were, they were too many for a single group, so they split up. Sillito and McDonald led their team east via the coast, hoping against hope they might be picked up by the MTBs. 'I don't think they had the slightest chance of succeeding', Russell dryly observed.[17]

He was right of course. The Guardsman-turned-SIG now led his own squad, together with Langton, Barlow and eight others. They struck off south-east to find a landward route. Nobody would have given much for their chances either. And this was a big pack with the scent fully in their nostrils. Lying up in another defile, their luck held that first day. As darkness fell, they opted to split into still smaller groups, three in all, each with an officer and a couple of men. They divided their meagre share of water and rations. They were on the run.[18]

***

The Italians were not slow in claiming the victory. In fairness, this was enough of a rarity for us to understand their enthusiasm. This was despite the fact the Germans had largely fought an independent and highly successful defensive action. The New Legions boasted:

> During the night three heavy lorries crammed with British prisoners and guarded by German troops arrived at the town [Tobruk], having successfully passed through all the roadblocks. But the British were not prisoners and the Germans were not Germans – and large quantities of arms were concealed in the trucks. In a small bay down by the port ... they massacred a group of Italian artillerymen in their sleep, having first silently knifed the sentries ... A typically barbaric bit of Tommy thuggery of course. But we had completely broken up the raid by morning. Almost all the British who landed were killed; there were very few prisoners. The massacre at El Adem had been dearly paid for.[19]

It would be harder to say who would have scoffed more loudly at this bombast, the British or the Germans.

Nonetheless, the Italian fighters had done well. They were quick off the mark and relentless in pursuing their attacks. That was their role of course, but they didn't lag behind their generally more feared Luftwaffe allies. These successes earned rapturous praise from Rome – 'magnificent daring in defeating the invasion force', as the Italian official history put it. The sector commander, General Marchesi, who was in charge of the 5th

Squadron area to which 13th Fighter Group was attached, enthused over such 'magnificent results'.[20]

If the small boats had suffered terribly, the big ships had it even worse. *Zulu* had barrelled east after abandoning her doomed attempts to save her sister destroyer. Her own survival was now very much at stake. Damaged but still capable of 30 knots, she was running for her life with an awful lot of sea miles between her and safety. From the bright blue skies at about 0850 hours a single Ju 88 came charging in. The bomb missed by a good 50 yards but there would be many more to come. Throughout the late morning and early afternoon, three further attacks, each delivered by half a dozen planes and more, burst around her. She emerged unscathed and what was identified as a potential enemy warship turned out to be non-combatant; so far so good.[21]

Help was not that far away, as HMS *Coventry** and her destroyer escorts were steaming to *Zulu*'s aid. This time there was air cover. A score of Bristol Beaufighters† from No. 201 Naval Cooperation Group had been scrambled that morning. They flew at 8,000 feet, rotating cover initially from a couple of planes, then six, then four, reducing to one only in the hours of darkness.[22] The first brace were over the flotilla by 0500 hours. This was clearly good. Communications, however, so utterly vital, were not.

Two hours elapsed before radio contact could be established. The Beaufighters were sending on their HF (high frequency) of 4,350 kilocycles and this initial message was the only one the ships received. *Coventry*'s fighter direction officer (Lieutenant Gardner)

---

* HMS *Coventry* was a C Class light cruiser that had gone into service in 1918 but had subsequently been converted into a light anti-aircraft role. She weighed in at just over 4,000 tons with a complement of 327. In terms of speed, she was very nearly as quick as a destroyer.

† The Bristol Beaufighter – the 'Beau' – was a highly versatile twin-engined plane. It was essentially designed as a heavy fighter, though rather heavy and slow for this role.

and radar specialist (Sub-Lieutenant Shales) were in touch with the RAF throughout but not with the individual planes, so quite who was overhead when or indeed if at all remained unclear. Directing planes onto potential targets was an imperfect art at best. A number of the 'Beaus' failed to show their IFF (identification, friend or foe) beacon until they came in very close. Details of the strengths and call signs of the fighter patrols were equally elusive.[23] For their part, however, the fighters thought everything was working well! This was clearly all very worrying.

At the outset, the atmosphere aboard *Coventry* and her escorts had been relatively relaxed. Captain Dendy had been mainly worried by the possibility of hit and run attacks from predatory Eboats.[24] Early reports had suggested the operation itself was proceeding as planned. When reality struck home after 0630 hours and the depressing truth began to emerge, the mood switched. Admiral Harwood ordered his ships to move fast and converge with *Zulu*. Another problem now reared its head. The Hunt Class destroyers had a limited range and they risked running out of fuel.

Captain Dendy quite prudently slowed down to 20 knots as each ship reported on her fuel stocks. They would have just enough fuel to get to the RV and back safely to Alexandria, but there was no margin for error or any contingency for the unexpected. War tends to throw up the unexpected at fairly regular intervals. Worse, enemy aircraft had been detected shadowing the ships from 0700 hours. They hadn't attacked, they were just observing, at least for the moment. Within 30 minutes, fresh signals came in from *Zulu* advising that due to the damage she'd already sustained she wouldn't be able to maintain full speed. This produced a domino effect. If she couldn't get far enough westwards for the RV, the rescuers would have to go further east, so using up their scant reserves of fuel. *Coventry* could go it alone, but that would leave her completely unprotected, not just from air attack but at the convenience of any U-boats around. Dendy decided to turn back east to re-fuel.

Before this draconian but understandable move could be put in train and perhaps happily before the signal to Admiral Harwood went off, *Zulu* signalled again to confirm she could still keep going at 30 knots. This was faster than both the Hunt Class ships and *Coventry* – the original plan was therefore still viable. Two of the destroyers, *Aldenham* and *Belvoir*, were so low on fuel they had to turn back, leaving a round half dozen with the light cruiser.[25] Harwood never got the intended signal, which was probably just as well.

The Luftwaffe hadn't forgotten them and by 0800 hours, Allied radar detected large swarms of enemy planes taking to the air. Providentially, the first wave missed the convoy completely and it would require an estimated hour and a half for them to return, re-fuel and get back in the air. Time mattered; it was the real enemy. Every minute that passed as *Zulu* strained eastwards was a minor victory. She still had a very long way to go and the Axis wouldn't be likely to miss a second time. This initial failure did however give the RAF more elbow room and at 0915 hours another half dozen Beaus were sent up.[26]

Captain Dendy, now that the Axis clearly knew where he was and must be pretty sure what he was about, could see no point in maintaining radio silence, so decided to invite the RAF fighters to seek out the enemy on a pre-emptive basis. This could draw the sting from the Axis bombers and deny them the initiative. The trouble was, he couldn't establish any form of radio contact with Allied aircraft. Signalling by Aldis lamps wasn't enough to get the fliers to check their radios. Maddeningly, nothing happened and the opportunity was lost. This lack of communication was to reap a very bitter harvest. The ships were instructed at this point to steer further away from the coast, a 90 degree turn. Dendy signalled he'd turn west once more at 1130 hours and hoped to meet up with *Zulu* two hours after that. By 1020 hours two of the Beaus had sighted *Zulu* and, in this instance from 8,000 feet, radio contact was fine.

Various alarums followed. Potential enemy aircraft were detected and the two watchers, 'Charlie One' and 'Charlie Two' were sent off to investigate. Cloud cover frustrated attempts to intercept and the fighters could only report no sightings. Charlie One was very close to the suspected mass of enemy before he finally detected them. He radioed back 'there's a lot of planes ahead of me'.[27] The men aboard *Coventry* had only a moment before they came under determined attack. Fifteen Stukas came screaming down in their devilish dive, line astern at 90 degrees, the fearful dirge from their sirens wailing.

The ship's guns responded and the destroyers joined in, sending up a box barrage. Bombs whistled down and a stick caught *Coventry* – the worst of bad luck, as the hits destroyed her radar. The flotilla had been surprised, and the sudden fury of the bombing was exacerbated by the loss of the two ships sent back to refuel. Both *Coventry* and *Croome* were targeted, though the more nimble destroyer, by dint of some nifty shifting, got out of the way. The bigger ship was less fortunate. The Luftwaffe was ahead of the game and the RAF screen had failed.

Inevitably, there was much post-mortem debate as to how this could have arisen. Dendy felt the enemy might have cleverly used IFF, which confused the radar operators. This was exacerbated by the fact the kit itself had a 'black spot' astern – inevitably this was the dive-bombers' preferred line of attack. By this phase of the war the Ju 87, the infamous Stuka of *Blitzkrieg* legend, was considered obsolete, slow and vulnerable to fighters, and not even that effective as a bomber. Technically, this was no doubt true, but when they're screaming down from above you and the bombs are bursting, a more subjective test will apply. Conventional wisdom also dictated that dive bombing was pointless unless the cloud cover was much higher. Clearly the Luftwaffe disagreed. As the attack went in, the Beaus did try to intervene but the raiders were getting clear away into the clouds. None was knocked down but at least one Beau kept up the chase for 40 miles. Although a couple of Stukas may have been hit, there was no confirmed kill.[28]

These Stukas, from 3rd Group of 3rd Ju 87 Wing, flying from Daba and Fuka aerodromes, were led on the raid by Lieutenant Gobel. His attack was pure textbook. Even the latest variant of the Ju 87 might now be old fashioned, but their pilots knew them very well and their screaming sirens had struck terror in Poland, France, the Low Countries, Yugoslavia, Greece, Crete, Russia and the Western Desert. A full quartet of bombs straddled *Coventry* and her decks were raked by 20mm cannon and MG fire. One projectile blasted a huge chunk out of her bows ahead of No. 1 gun, tearing and blazing down to the waterline.[29]

The next two both seemed to strike the deck area beneath the bridge, taking out the communications, radar, chart house and most of the bridge, penetrating into the bowels of the ship. Smoke and fire followed. Warships are crowded spaces, crammed with crew and kit and supplies. Onboard explosions create havoc. Men are burnt and dismembered. The fourth hit was perhaps the worst, and was ultimately mortal. The bomb struck behind the after funnel, sliced down into A boiler room before exploding. The radar room was among the areas devastated. The old ship staggered, shuddering beneath the weight of these blows. None of her surviving crew would have been willing to attest to the obsolescence of the Ju 87. *Coventry* wallowed and came to a halt.[30] Though casualties were high, an insistence that ratings keep their anti-flash kit on all times when at action stations had saved many from even more terrible burns.[31]

Peter Smith relates an account from the 18-year-old paymaster Geoffrey David who, just before the raid, had heard over the ship's speakers that *Sikh* on which his brother was serving had gone down. He'd barely had time to take in this awful news when the bombs hit. The explosions were very loud indeed and then came a moment of silence, as David remembered: 'I caught a glimpse through the wardroom skylight of debris flying through the air ... in the silence I heard the comforting rumble of the ship's turbines suddenly die away to nothing'.[32]

The lad was shaken, embarrassed at his own perceived weakness. His was a savage baptism. 'After picking my way over a scatter of debris, and seeing to my horror a headless corpse draped over the side of the sea boat, I got almost as far as the break in the forecastle, but then found my way barred by a fire just abaft the bridge.' He tried to get around the starboard side, but it was no better. 'I noticed a wounded rating lying propped against a stanchion, and completely black all over – presumably from flash burns. He was alive and moaning faintly.' There didn't seem to be much he could do for the injured man. A blank crater had by now opened up in the ship's innards. The fighter direction officer suggested he should just keep smiling. Next came the order from the skipper to abandon ship.[33]

Claude Nice was one of the gun crew working the forward turret. He recalled how swiftly the raiders seemed to pounce, with a single Stuka seeming to appear directly above their gun. Then the bombs fell.

Most of the forecastle had ... disappeared, and a fierce fire was raging beyond the breakwater. Amazingly, the ship remained on an even keel as she slowed down. The paint shop had been in the blown out section and when we on the gun surveyed each other we realized we were all covered in colours of all shades.[34]

This was all the amusement to be had. Many had died and more were injured. Getting all the wounded off the doomed ship and into boats was strenuous. Mercifully, the attackers had not returned.

After the event, there was much soul-searching as to why the radar hadn't picked up the Luftwaffe. A number of explanations were put forward, but most probably a combination of factors was to blame. It seems the radar did pick up enemy planes, but not the numbers, and it then confused these with the previous observation aircraft. The Beaufighter hadn't been aware of the enemy presence until it was too late, due to confusion over proper height finding.

Dendy's immediate assessment, as the Stukas broke off, showed significant damage. There was fire raging forward and as the 4-inch magazine had been flooded the pom-pom ammunition store couldn't be reached. The bow section was pretty much gone, the bridge or what little was left of it was burning, communications equipment was smashed completely, as was one boiler room. The ship could still make way, but the fires were spreading.

The captain had a difficult choice to make; the loneliness of command must have seemed acute. It was possible, just, for the destroyers to take the crippled cruiser in tow. But they were still well within bombing range and the Stukas were bound to return. It was daylight and much of the day remained, and Alexandria was 160 miles east. *Zulu* was still in danger. *Coventry* had many badly wounded aboard. He made the only decision possible. The old girl's time had come. *Coventry* had to be abandoned and sunk.

Beaufort and *Dulverton* came alongside to help evacuate the badly burnt and maimed casualties. The usual last rites, ciphers, papers, log books et al. were consigned to the deep. By the time last survivors were got off, the flames were rapidly engulfing the shattered hull and exploding ammunition blazed a final explosive eulogy. Ironically, scuttling charges placed but left unprimed couldn't be detonated as the final bomb blast had disabled them.[35]

Once everyone was off, the stubborn old ship refused to go down. Dendy, aboard *Dulverton*, ordered Lieutenant Commander Petch, his senior subordinate, to finish the job with torpedoes, but the Hunt Class ships didn't carry torpedo tubes, aside that is from the pair which had already been sent back earlier for re-fuelling! *Beaufort* and *Dulverton* opened up with their guns and fired depth charges. By bitter irony, none of these seemed to have any effect and the funeral pyre that had been *Coventry* continued to blaze. *Croome* came up and added her salvo, firing 4-inch semi-armour-piercing rounds. Still *Coventry* wouldn't sink. *Croome* alone pumped 124 shells into the blazing hulk with nil result. She then tried 18 depth charges, intended to explode beneath the keel and blow great holes in the hull. This didn't work either. *Hursley* was next up and shot off a further 22 depth charges, another prodigious barrage for no result.

Zulu was getting close, only 15 miles out. Now she did carry torpedoes – what a cruel irony that the rescued had to finish off the rescuer. It was nearly 1330 hours. Harwood, back in Alexandria, could only feel his fears deepening. *Coventry* was lost, the destroyer escort was split up and the enemy must surely return at any moment. The admiral signalled that Force D must close up and fall in with *Zulu*. By yet another dark twist, the signal was not fully received and the force kept going as it was. This meant *Dulverton, Beaufort, Exmoor* and *Hursley* were returning to Alexandria while *Croome* and *Hursley* remained with the blazing hulk of *Coventry* as *Zulu* closed up on them.[36]

There were some sound reasons for this: *Exmoor* was very low on fuel and *Beaufort* crammed with wounded, some in a very bad way. It was also hoped the Stukas might prefer to pursue the larger group of quarry. *Coventry*, despite the odds, continued to float. By now the first two destroyers to turn back had reached Alex and were re-fuelling. As the other four steamed back (they'd arrive at 1935 hours), five of the badly wounded died and were buried at sea. Even when the force had been together, communication with the Beaufighters had been near impossible; with the flotilla effectively scattered, this became even more difficult. What followed could have come from a *Carry On* movie, except nobody was laughing. With *Coventry*'s communications gone, the ship's radio officer who took over had such a broad cockney accent the pilots couldn't understand him! To all intents and purposes, the fighters were now flying blind.

At 1430 hours *Zulu* joined *Croome* and *Hursley*. Her first job was to put torpedoes into *Coventry*. The newcomer had to be reassured there were no survivors left aboard. By now the Luftwaffe had found them again and the first wave came in just as *Zulu* was closing up with the other two ships. These planes were Ju 88s from Crete and there were a lot of them. On their initial pass, however, they scored no hits and, at 1449 hours, *Zulu* fired two torpedoes into what remained of *Coventry*. To send the charges straight and true Commander White slowed to 12 knots, immediately increasing revs as the torpedoes achieved what so much gunfire and depth charging had failed to do. *Coventry* sank.

Half a dozen Stukas plunged down. They missed and the three ships, free of the burden of the stricken, stubborn cruiser, fled east, 1½ miles apart, with *Hursley* leading the charge, followed by *Zulu* and *Croome* in line astern. *Zulu* could still manage 30 knots but had to be content with slightly less as the Hunt Class ships could only get up to 25 knots. It was a race against time to cover the distance.

One eyewitness to *Coventry*'s final death agonies was Luftwaffe Major Gerhard Stamp.* He was flying with 1st Group of 1st Training and

---

* Gerhard Stamp (1920–88), holder of the Knight's Cross and Iron Cross, was credited with personally sinking 35,000 tons of Allied merchant shipping and the destroyer HMS *Defender*. He continued in the West German service after the war almost to the date of his death: https://en.wikipedia.org/wiki/Gerhard_Stamp, retrieved 15 July 2015.

Development Wing, the notorious Helbig Flyers. They were specialists in attacking ships, equipped with Ju 88s and based at Heraklion. Their 'kill rate' was impressive. His crack crew had been sent to an airstrip south of Mersa Matruh from where, after the Stukas had bounced *Coventry*, they were sent aloft to pursue the surviving destroyers. The Stukas, young lions, weren't good enough to catch the fast-moving warships, but the old hares might do better. In fact the Ju 88s were stood down and flew back to Crete but, as they passed over, they saw the crippled cruiser ablaze in the bright blue sea. Stamp also saw the torpedoes hit and he incorrectly assumed these had been fired by one of the Axis's own U-boats.[37]

Doggedly, the RAF continued to send up pairs of Beaus, so there was a continuous standing patrol of four. The bad communications and the dispersal of the ships hampered effective protection; the Royal Navy rather caustically observed that beaufighters were poor day fighters against modern bombers. *Croome*'s skipper commented that by late afternoon on the 14th decent communications had been established with the fighters, but the real problem was how best to deploy them and get them into the best position to intercept. He praised the courage of the individual flyers, who had certainly not failed to take the fight to the enemy when the chance arose.

At least one Beau, just after 1500 hours, was shot at and shot up by the Royal Navy's guns. He had sent out the ID colours for the day, but this didn't seem to dampen the gunners' enthusiasm. He had to get smartly out of range. He didn't give up but kept shadowing from a safe distance and was even able to take on some prowling Stukas, taking palpable hits from their returned fire.[38] An hour later, he got close in again and this time the Luftwaffe was out in force. He attacked a Ju 88 and peppered the Axis aircraft with cannon and MG fire, setting, as he thought, both engines on fire and forcing two other aircraft to bracket the damaged plane like aerial shepherds. By then he'd run out of ammunition. He counted ten Ju 87s and 18 Ju 88s on the raid.

Hursley's skipper, Lieutenant W. J. P. Church, had a ringside seat. This onslaught was the worst they'd experienced. Despite the blast and fury, almost miraculously, no damage or casualties were sustained. This time the radar was really proving its worth, showing the hostile swarms 7 miles out. A prodigious quantity of 4-inch shell and Oerlikon rounds were put up in the box barrage. Brave *Zulu*, however, which had done so much and come so far, but not quite far enough, was less fortunate. Lieutenant Church reported she took a direct hit to the engine room just after 1600 hours and soon stopped, dead in the water.

Three separate formations of enemy dive bombers had come in from all sides. Clearly the bigger destroyer was their prime target. Commander White delivered a virtuoso performance, his sleek warship swerving and ducking, dodging the hurricane of bombs raining around. All but the last, which he recalled 'hit the ship's side, entered the engine room and burst. The engine room, No. 3 boiler room and gear room flooded and the ship settled down about two feet.'[39]

She wasn't done yet, however. The two Hunt Class ships closed up. *Hursley* attempted to fix a viable tow whilst *Croome* took off many of the survivors, leaving just a skeleton crew aboard. *Zulu*'s towing wire had all been expended earlier trying to save *Sikh* and *Hursley*'s gear wasn't to hand, so a heavy rope was thrown across. This lasted less than quarter of an hour, but by then a proper towing wire had been sorted and the slow business got under way. The Axis planes hadn't finished, however, and there weren't enough personnel left aboard the crippled ship to man the big guns, only the Oerlikons and pom-poms.

Just after 1700 hours the enemy planes circled back in again. This time, the ships' combined wall of fire was sufficiently daunting to see them off. This barrage, it should be said, was equally dangerous to the Beaus.

To a naval gunner, any twin-engined aircraft looked pretty much like another, and nobody was keen on taking chances. The rest of the Hunt Class ships were already en route back to Alexandria; Admiral Harwood signalled they should turn round to assist if their fuel stocks permitted. Generally, they didn't. Nonetheless, *Hursley* at least did turn back. The admiral blasted out an APB (all points bulletin) to all navy ships to lend a hand. As Peter Smith rightly observes, the code word for this, 'Anger', was undoubtedly entirely appropriate to Harwood's mood. The army's botched plan was claiming a fearful toll of his precious ships and sailors.

The destroyer *Aldenham* with *Belvoir* and a tug, *Brigand*, steamed out of Alex to help and the RAF continued providing air support till night. By 1749 hours, *Zulu* still hadn't moved, however. She had 'two degrees of port rudder on her and she could not be got out of it and the towing speed, only four knots, was further hindered by her constant yawing'.[40] The relatively diminutive Hunt Class ships didn't give up, edging around the wallowing destroyer. The Luftwaffe didn't give up either. At 1915 hours and again 25 minutes or so later, four Ju 88s came back. This time, however, they didn't have it all their own way. Gunners, sailors and marines banged off whatever weapons they had and finally had the long overdue satisfaction of seeing one of the Axis planes brought down by *Croome*. One of her 4-inch shells caught a fleeing Junkers and blew the bomber apart in mid-air. The Beaus also did their bit, chasing off the survivors.

Now it was back to the painstakingly difficult business of getting *Zulu* under tow and under way; the damaged destroyer needed to straighten her rudder and attempt to steer east towards their distant salvation. Lieutenant Church described the difficulties: *Zulu* appeared to be carrying a little port wheel so that she towed crab fashion on the port quarter with the result that she pulled me around to starboard until I was ready on 170 degrees, a most undesirable course.[41] Getting her round was a very slow and complex manoeuvre. It took till 2200 hours. They crept forward at 6 knots, then moving up another three knots. *Croome*'s radar was unserviceable due to damage from near misses so she'd be blind in the dark, and she was down to 70 tons of fuel.

More hearteningly, the refreshed and revitalized Hunt Class ships *Dulverton, Beaufort* and *Exmoor* were racing back from Alexandria. However, *Zulu* was already losing her last battle. She had survived many and had fought a magnificent fight, but the pumps simply couldn't cope with the water spreading inexorably through her ruptured vitals. Lieutenant Church was still trying to save her; his much smaller vessel was straining every bolt and sinew to drag her unresponsive charge to sanctuary: 'gradually she came round to port thereby pulling me round to starboard again. In trying to follow she was using 15 degrees starboard wheel ... I tried towing her to starboard in the hope she would eventually come right round'.[42]

Commander White had come to the painfully correct conclusion that his ship could not survive and was endangering the other. He signalled both Hunt Class ships to take off survivors, but then it was as if the old lady decided she'd had quite enough and simply gave up. She rolled over, capsizing, with the tow still dragging. This was successfully cut before she could pull her rescuer down into the same watery grave. This was not altogether easy, 'for in trying to knock out the forelock of the slip it got bent and could not be moved. After some anxious moments, the tow was slipped, just as she was sinking'.[43]

Despite the suddenness of her final demise, all left aboard *Zulu* got off into the water and were safely picked up, including some who were badly wounded. One of these remembered:

'Croome', leaping into speed, swiftly came in. They saw heads bobbing in the water. But it took time to get into position to pick them all up. They saw Commander White swimming strongly ... Lieutenant Burnley, in spite of his badly damaged arm, was supporting a drowning man. They could see him joking and encouraging him as the life came back into the seaman.

This was the final act in the long chase. The rest of the ships came safe home and the end of *Zulu* really marks the dying stages of Operation *Agreement*.

The fight was over, but the drama was not. David Russell, Tommy Langton and their comrades had not yet given up. Though the operation is rightly judged as a complete failure, the courage and determination of the survivors remains an inspiration. These escapees needed to demonstrate even more grit, and they certainly did so.

David Russell and his two companions travelled by night, lying up during the still hot late summer days. The enemy had not forgotten them, but even so, by 19 September they'd got as far as Bardia. Between them they had only 1½ bottles of precious water, and rations, very meagre at best, for only two days. By the old airfield at Gambut, they chanced on a treasure trove of a quarter full tin of jam and some additional water. Not much, but such manna in the desert can be the difference between life and death, or at least between freedom and captivity.[44]

They'd been kept going by the hope that the Royal Navy would send additional boats to Mersa Shegga, which lies 9 miles or so north of Bardia, on the night of 18 September. Perhaps ominously, the naval operation orders ended with the statement that 'this beach is recognizable by the wreck of a schooner lying at its northern end'.[45] They got close, close enough to attract the hostile attentions of Italian coastal troops. In the rush, Private Watler was left behind. A brave, tough and resourceful character, he was suffering badly from a chest infection and his hearing had been damaged.[46]

Having, as it seemed, been written off by the navy, Russell decided it would be easiest just to highjack a truck from one of the Italian convoys motoring along the main highway between Bardia and Tobruk. They had no more luck with this, though they did bump into a friendly Arab who gave them bread and took them to water. Their guide warned them there was no more to be found this side of the El Alamein line. Still undeterred, Russell opted to march inland towards the Djebel el Akhdar and seek out a British agent he knew to be operating in the region. By this time Weizmann was in a bad way and, after 17 days on the run, could go no further. Russell with great reluctance agreed to leave him.

Weizmann was found by Arabs, who handed him in to the Italians, who in turn gave him over to the Germans. War without hate didn't extend as far as the Gestapo, and the injured man was beaten and abused for five long, nightmarish days. He was advised of his own imminent execution and stood up in front of the firing squad with his open grave awaiting him. It was an Afrika Korps officer who in fact saved him and got him sent to a POW camp.[47]

Russell had more luck with friendly Senussi and kept heading west, passing over the old battlefield of Gazala where Italian troops, immersed in their drill, simply seemed not to see the ragged enemy crossing their path! It was west of Mekili where he encountered yet more Arabs, this time active as agents for the Allies. On 18 November, after two months of evasion, he was able to dispatch one of his new friends in pursuit of a flying column of what he took to be British armoured cars he'd managed to glimpse. They were in fact South Africans, but that did just as well.[48] He was home free. By one of war's nasty little ironies, Russell would, as a captive, most likely have survived the war and come safe home at the end. His great courage and steadfastness ensured that he would not.

Tommy Langton had three men in his group. He and Barlow had parted, but met up again just after a wild scramble through a wadi on the night of the 14th September. Barlow went missing during the chase, but the rest got through the outer cordon. Langton now had Sergeant Evans (Welsh Guards), Corporal Wilson, both Leslie brothers and Private McDonald (all RNF), together with Hillman from the SIG. Hillman was suffering from a badly cut foot and was hobbling with only one boot. As his fate on capture would be certain death, he was renamed Kennedy to hide his being Jewish.[49]

Like Russell's team, they could only move under cover of darkness, their tiny supplies dwindling and then gone. Hillman, even if injured, was a tremendous asset on account of his linguistic skills. He was able to communicate with a party of Arabs who took them in on the 19th, providing much-needed sustenance. Their hosts confirmed they'd known all about the planned raid on Tobruk, though the LRDG's epic journey all the way up from Kufra astounded even them. The escapees were passed as human cargo across a chain of tiny settlements. They covered some 70 miles from Tobruk before they encountered an Italian outpost at the coastal mouth of Wadi el Mreisa, 10 miles north of Bardia. Tantalizingly, their guides informed them that British boats had earlier crept in here to search for survivors.

They skirted the next post and reached yet another major defile, the Wadi Kattara. Here they found two fellow evaders, Private Watler, Russell's missing trooper, and an Indian army soldier from 3/18th Garwhal Rifles, something of a serial escaper from the fall of Tobruk who'd been lying up there for three months. They were stuck in this inauspicious sanctuary for four long weeks. They did attempt to get signals ready to attract passing Allied aircraft, but instead they were bombed.[50]

Their hosts operated a thriving sideline in selling eggs to the local Axis units, a handy source of information. Enemy morale was low.

It rained, creating the dank, grey veil of autumn. Evans and one of the Leslie brothers contracted dysentery, the soldier's curse from time immemorial. Both became so weak they had to be left out for the enemy to find. The other Leslie would not be parted from his sick sibling. That left five.

Langton went on with Wilson, Watler and Hillman. They had a map, cans of bully beef, goat's meat and 10 bottles of water. They kept heading east, passing unnoticed through the frontier wire and crossing the surreal junkyard of industrial warfare, rusting in a primeval landscape. On Friday 13 November, which at least for them proved anything but unlucky, they encountered an Allied unit. They had reached Himeimat, some 30 miles south of Alamein.[51] And that, with Russell's deliverance a few days later, was really the end of Operation *Agreement*.

Admiral Harwood said 'I much regret the heavy losses, but I feel it is better to have tried and failed than not to have tried at all'.[52] He did, naturally, have to put on a brave face, in public at least. Behind the scenes the blame game was going on at full swing and would continue for some time. Montgomery stood clear, but wasn't shy with his criticisms. In terms of the unrealistic scale and complexity of *Agreement,* he might have reflected more fully on these whilst planning or conceptualizing *Market Garden*, where not dissimilar planning failures resulted in an even worse disaster.

This failure had been expensive. Some 280 naval personnel, 300 marines and 160 soldiers and commandos had become casualties, though many of these were captured rather than killed or wounded. HMS *Coventry*, the venerable light cruiser, together with the destroyers *Sikh* and *Zulu*, four MTBs and two Fairmiles, all went down, a diminution of strike capability the Mediterranean Squadron could well have done without.[53]

Axis personnel losses were minimal, perhaps a dozen Germans and an unaccounted (but probably quite high) number of Italians killed in the early stages of Force B's attack. The Official History pithily sums up the causes of failure: 'the great hazards of the plan, the distance to the objective – beyond the reach of all but a few of the British fighters – lack of experience of landing operations and of suitable craft, and underestimates of the enemy'.[54] This is essentially correct, if nicely understated. The plain facts are that it was a bad plan, hastily extemporized, without a single guiding mind behind it. Haselden's original concept had been hijacked and expanded beyond all recognition.

In those moments in between of what is
And what was meant to be.
There in silence you will find me.
A faceless face, an unknown name.
The unknown soldier, my simple grave.
There friends and family came not visiting.
There my widow could not weep for me.

In life I was not alone.
In life, I was not unknown.
I had a wife, a son, a home.

Samantha Kelly, *The Unknown Soldier*

CHAPTER TEN

'A MOST INGLORIOUS EPISODE'

It was to be no better at Benghazi. MEF (Middle East Forces) instruction no. 140 had detailed plans for what would become Operation *Bigamy*.[1] Stirling was to strike hard at the Axis-held port and seek to block the main entrance and destroy shipping, oil storage and pumping facilities.[2] This was a pretty ambitious set of objectives. Stirling would lead Force X, comprising L Detachment SAS, LRDG patrols S1 and S2 (as it turned out), naval and SBS detachments, plus an RAF liaison officer and two Stuart light tanks (though quite what use these might be is hard to fathom); in all 14 officers, 200 men and 95 vehicles.[3]

They would strike Benghazi on the night of 13 September with SBS attacking whatever floated in the harbour and the navy sinking a blockship across the entrance. Having suitably chastised and diminished the Axis here, they'd then move en bloc to Jalo which, as it was hoped, would have been captured by Force Z coming up from Kufra. If the place hadn't fallen, Stirling's raiders would make sure it did and then settle down for a burst of profitable foraying against Rommel's supply lines.

Just to further complicate an already complex plan, Stirling would initially be acting under the orders of GHQ except for the approach march and attack on Benghazi, when he'd be under the joint jurisdiction of the commanders-in-chief from HQ, Commander-in-Chief Mediterranean at Alexandria. Once Jalo had been secured and the Forward Operating Base established there, the garrison would come directly under 8th Army.[4] This was adding additional layers of complexity, not to say obfuscation, onto what was already a very convoluted plan.

Paddy Mayne led the initial party up from Kufra on 4 September with five officers and 118 men, guided by S1 Patrol, all transported in three-tonners and light trucks or Bantams.* Captain Cumper, originally a sapper, left the oasis a day later with a further handful of officers but only 73 men in five three-tonners and a score of Bantams. Stirling himself went off on 6 September in command of the rump of Force X, 20 officers and 35 men, driving 11 three-tonners and another 20 jeeps. By 11 September the whole team minus S2 Patrol had reached the RV and the final LRDG element joined them there on the 12th.[5] There were only two casualties during the march: a cluster of three thermos bombs destroyed the navy officer, Lieutenant Ardley's car, killing him and badly wounding his driver, Corporal Webster.

Mayne had got to the RV on 9 September and immediately sent out a recce patrol under the intelligence officer, Captain Melot, with 2nd Lieutenant Maclean and a single trooper from the LAF (Libyan Arab Force). Their initial brief was to make contact with an ISLD (Inter-Service Liaison Department) representative known to be active in the

---

* The original model of Jeep manufactured by American Bantam Company.

locale, but who in the event could not be traced. On 10 September, this Arab volunteer braved the lion's den alone at Benghazi, in civvies, and made it out undetected a couple of days later.

His news wasn't good. The Axis appeared to be fully alert and had beefed up surrounding garrisons accordingly. Some five thousand Italians were at least said to be stationed at El Abiar, 30 miles east of the port, and a DAK battalion based to the north-east had been reinforced by more Italian troops. Worse, much of the shipping had now sailed, leaving the larder fairly bare. Bizarrely, when this disquieting news was communicated to GHQ MEF, no alarm bells appeared to start clanging.[6]

Prior to the main attack going in, Stirling's men would need to take out the old fort atop the escarpment before the town. This was functioning as an enemy radio station and clearly couldn't be left intact. Melot, with two other officers and 10 men, attacked the place and put the enemy communications out of action, killing five of them and capturing a sixth. Melot was shot, along with Captain Bailey, whilst another man went missing. With such a knowledgeable officer out of action, the raiders had to rely on their Libyan volunteer who'd done so well during his recce. He proved less successful as a guide and led the attackers in an aimless tour of the escarpment.[7]

They weren't in position for the final approach to the target until 0430 hours on 14 September, four hours behind schedule. Stirling then took the bold decision simply to barge down the nearest available track, which came in from the east. Very soon they came to a substantial barrier, apparently unmanned. This was a form of cantilever gate, supported by an earth-filled gabion. Captain Cumper prised the portal open and the first half dozen jeeps passed through. In an instant, the night air erupted in flame and fire poured down on them seemingly from all sides, with small-arms and mortars pattering out their fearful dirge. Clearly, they were not unexpected. The Allied troops fired back with gusto but two of the jeeps barrelling into the ambush were wrecked.[8]

Even the most optimistic officer could hardly hope to get any further. It was no longer about getting in undetected and more about getting out with minimal loss. David Stirling was a bold and determined commando but never reckless or careless with the lives of his men. It was time to go and quickly. They pulled out to the east, remarkably getting free of the fire-fight with no more damage. The harsh light of dawn brought the enemy fighters, first three and then seven, swooping to strafe their exposed vehicles. In accordance with usual practice, the trucks raced off in differing directions, splitting the target and seeking any available cover. Five three-tonners and seven jeeps were shot up and written off in the chase.

Their original planned RV was 25 miles east. There was no respite. Time and again the Axis eagles came in for the kill. One came too close too often and a Free French squad brought it down with their twin Vickers guns. It was still pretty one sided and the running fight went on for five gruelling and relentless hours during 15 September. Three men died and four more were wounded. When darkness finally brought respite, the survivors split into three teams. Paddy Mayne led one, Captain Scratchley a second and Stirling the last, which acted as rearguard. Straggling over the hostile sands they got to Jalo a couple of days later, having lost another half dozen vehicles during the trek. The LRDG patrols, past masters in this deadly game, had made their own escape.[9]

Jalo Oasis had been attacked on 16 September by a battalion of the SDF, supported by a light AA battery and some meatier 3.7-inch pieces from the Sudan Artillery Regiment, the guns commanded by Lieutenant Colonel A. B. Brown detached from the King's Own Yorkshire Light Infantry. This was to be Operation *Nicety*, but it didn't go nicely at all. The enemy was alert and ready. The attack may have caused some losses,[10] though this rather smacks of face-saving but strategically achieved nothing. A second attempt was aborted. What remained of Stirling's force did manage to link up with the SDF rearguard and make good their escape. Stirling himself with his round-up party also made it out, but one officer and 16 troopers were missing. Captain Bailey and three soldiers were too badly injured to endure more jolting over the harsh terrain, so one medic, under a flag of truce, arranged for the enemy from Benghazi to collect and care for these wounded. Happily, the Axis commanders were punctilious and obliged.[11]

In a final flourish of what must have been very bitter irony, the missing ISLD officer subsequently appeared and advised that the Axis had plainly been forewarned and made ready. So seriously did they take the threat of Stirling's raiders that the whole civilian population had been moved out and more MG teams moved in.[12] This must have added considerably to Stirling's sense of failure. The mission had been hopelessly compromised from the start and suggests that in the case of the Benghazi raid, all that loose talk in the Delta must in fact have been picked up.

It was failure all round, except at Barce. Here LRDG conjured a very different story.

Operation *Caravan* was, from the outset, purely an LRDG affair. The dynamic Jake Easonsmith (later killed tragically in the ill-starred Dodecanese campaign) led a force of two patrols, T1 (Nick Wilder) and G1 (Alastair Timpson). Some support personnel including, providentially, Dick Lawson the MO, were along from B Squadron's HQ detachment. 'Popski' and two Senussi drawn from the LAF provided the intelligence cell.

There were a total of 47 raiders in 12 trucks and five jeeps. They had some heavyweight company from a brace of Mack 10-tonners as far as Ain Dalla. The group drove out of Faiyum Oasis on 1 September; their target was 1,150 miles away in Jebel Akhdar. Dick Lawson, as MO, was in demand from the start. As they traversed the Egyptian Sand Sea, Timpson was injured as his vehicle careered over a razorback dune, the old perennial hazard. Another trooper was paralysed. Both were evacuated by air from Big Cairn.[13]

Easonsmith made up for lost time, dashing over the firmer *serir* (gravel desert). It wasn't until 10 September that they debouched from the western rim of the next belt of sand sea. The dunes end abruptly, as if tidied up by a giant's broom.[14] The raiders crossed the ancient camel road from Jalo to Siwa, the timeless desert highway that had witnessed its fair share of invaders come and go over the centuries. After another 200 miles of changing terrain, moving from the stripped and scorched earth to the border of vegetation, spare and clinging to begin with then thickening into a form of rough savannah. The two Arab irregulars were dropped off a few miles short of Barce to contact locals and bring back up to date intelligence.

On 13 September, 15 miles south of their objective, the patrols halted. Here, Easonsmith gave a detailed briefing and the men prepared for action, guns cleaned, ammunition and vehicles checked. Under cover of the velvet, late summer darkness, balmy and alive with insect noise, they drove boldly towards their target. At one police post, a single native copper came out to challenge them and found himself an LRDG 'volunteer'. Hamed, as he was called, would spend several months of cheerful servitude before being got safe home.[15] As Hamed was being pressed into service, there was movement from inside the roadside blockhouse. Only one Italian officer came out to investigate and was promptly shot. The rest of the gendarmerie left via the rear door. In the excitement, two trucks banged into each other and both had to be dumped.

When the patrols, still combined, got as close as the village of Sidi Selim, Dick Lawson was left there with T Patrol's radio truck as rearguard and rally point. As the rest of the vehicles struck the main highway to Benghazi and breasted an escarpment five miles out of Barce, they encountered a pair of Italian light tanks. Easonsmith drove towards them unhesitatingly, as no one was expecting raiders this far west. The tank crews received a most unexpected surprise when the LRDG opened up on them at point blank range. They caused no further trouble.[16]

Just outside town, at the principal crossroads, Easonsmith divided his forces. Nick Wilder, with T1, would attend to the airfield while Sergeant Dennis, leading the Guards after Timpson's evacuation, would attack the downtown zone and barracks. Wilder drove around the outskirts till he reached the aerodrome. Shooting up those light tanks earlier did not seem to have alerted anyone and the raiders drove through the gates unopposed. Belatedly, the garrison woke up and several came running out. This became their final deployment.[17]

As the Italians sprawled in the dust, tracer set a nearby petrol tanker ablaze, the most perfect illumination. Grenades were chucked into the airfield's canteen and the attackers, down to four 30-cwt Chevrolets and a lone jeep, raked enemy aircraft with a storm of bullets. Those that survived the hail of incendiary rounds were each awarded an IED (improvised explosive device). Thirty-seven planes were attacked and at least a score of these were complete write-offs. By now, the surviving Italians had woken up and were blazing away at everything and nothing. Despite this enthusiasm, the patrol came through without a single scratch.[18]

Behind them, the airfield was wrecked and ablaze. Wilder's trucks charged headlong down the long straight street to the station at the far end of town. Two more light tanks barred the far end; their shot whistled up the road, happily firing too high. Wilder rammed the first tank with sufficient force to push this into the other. The Chevy was a write off, but after a bunch of grenades had been deftly rolled beneath both armoured vehicles, so were they.

Wilder and his crew, unharmed, jumped onto the jeep. The over-laden Willys roared towards the station, Wilder on the Vickers firing bursts of tracer. Blinded by white light from the rounds, the jeep's driver struck the kerb and the vehicle did a somersault, spilling its stunned passengers. Wilder was pinned and knocked unconscious. The following truck righted the jeep, which was still operational, collected Wilder and drove on. Trooper Craw and his truck became separated at some point in the melee and got lost.[19]

Sergeant Dennis and the Guards were keeping up trade at the other end of town. As their trucks rolled past the hospital Kennedy Shaw recalled that two sentries challenged from the darkness: 'Dennis rolled a four-second grenade between them and turned them from sentries into patients'.[20] Next it was the barracks' turn; two more sentries were disposed of, then the trucks drove around the site, bombing buildings, generally shooting up trenches and anything that moved. Dennis only finished the attack when he'd run clean out of bullets after playing dodgems with another pair of light tanks in the hospital grounds. Trooper 'Jock' Findlay's truck was mislaid sometime during this mad caper.

As it later turned out, Findlay had missed the road out of town and soon picked up a vengeful posse of Italians, who chased his lone vehicle across the plain as dawn was breaking. Ahead of them, the escarpment rose dizzyingly, far too steep for any two-wheel drive vehicle, so they abandoned the truck and set it on fire. After a day of dodging their pursuers, Findlay found himself alone. He walked eastwards for three days before being picked up by friendly Bedouin. He wasn't recovered until October, as Kennedy Shaw remembered: 'There he stood, surrounded by goats and sheep, a tall, bearded figure in Arab gear with a big, beaming smile on his face. 'What took you so long?' he said'.[21]

Jake Easonsmith was on his own where the patrols had split, as ever determined not to let others have all the fun. It probably isn't a commander's job to get too close to the action, but the temptation was overwhelming. He first attacked some small bungalow-type units, which might have been officers' quarters. Next he took on a further pair of light tanks before terrorizing a central piazza, scattering grenades amongst startled Italians. Next one up was an MT park containing a dozen vehicles; none of these would be going anywhere soon. By 0400 hours both raiding parties were back at Sidi Selim; 10 of the original 12 vehicles had come through, three jeeps and seven trucks in total. All they had to do now was to sweep up the two vehicles left earlier at Sidi Raui and be on their way.

For once the Italian complement there proved capable of aggressive action, setting up a neat ambush in a narrow defile south of Sidi Selim. All hell suddenly broke loose. Three men were wounded and Dick Lawson's car temporarily immobilized with a shot-out tyre. Calmly Sergeant Dennis backed up to shield the stricken vehicle with his own while the wheel was changed. This accomplished, everyone got clear and the two broken trucks were recovered under tow. Clearly, it wasn't possible to drag both of these all the way back, so they had to be got going. This meant another halt and the posse caught up. Jake Easonsmith kept the Italians, local Arab levies, busily occupied in a bold flanking attack with only his own jeep until the column got moving again.

It was all going rather well, too well in fact. Luck finally deserted them when G Patrol's wireless truck broke down in, inevitably, a totally exposed location. Frantic efforts to get the vehicle under any kind of cover took just that bit too long and the fighters found them. Carrying out an attack after a concealed approach march was one thing, getting away with it quite another. Stung by losses and humiliation, the enemy's vengeance came roaring out of a shining sky. From late morning till sundown, the patrols were attacked relentlessly. By the time darkness brought relief, only a single truck and two jeeps remained serviceable. These would have to ferry 33 men back to Kufra. Worse, there were now several wounded. Nick Wilder had been hit in both legs and Trooper Parker in the stomach. Dick Lawson performed prodigies, working unconcerned and incessantly during the strafing.

Given the fury and duration of the bombardment, it could have been much worse. It did get somewhat worse just as darkness was falling. Jake Easonsmith had wisely unloaded all of the precious water and rations, dispersing them around. It seemed safe to load all of these onto one of the two surviving Chevys, but just as this essential cargo was being stacked, the fighters came back for a final pass and hit the lot.[22] This was both galling and serious, but Easonsmith had foreseen this dire possibility and had earlier created an emergency dump located some 60 miles south-east of Barce at Bir Gerrari.

As dusk fell on 14 September, the party set off. Dick Lawson had one jeep and one 30-cwt truck with his group. He took the six wounded men, plus driver, fitter and navigator. They had 700 miles to cover. Two marching detachments moved off at the same time, only a single jeep between them carrying supplies or such supplies they still possessed. The ground was hard and unyielding. Lawson's jeep gave out, the tank holed by a random round during the attack. Next, the second jeep stalled; its sump was fractured, though this was repairable. One man became lost in the darkness, probably having succumbed to exhaustion. He could not be found. They kept walking, dodging aerial sweeps. At last they had some good luck as they came across a Bedouin encampment, were able to buy food and milk. More good fortune occurred on 16 September – they discovered blessed water.

Next day, as dawn broke, they heard vehicle engines with a reassuringly friendly beat. Easonsmith fired off several flares, but to no avail. Barely an hour after, as they trailed on disconsolately, they stumbled upon John Olivey and his patrol – salvation! When they reached the stash at Bir Gerrari, Lawson had already passed through and deposited a note. This still left the second walking group unaccounted for. With Captain John Olivey's Rhodesian troops, Easonsmith combed the area for the missing men; they'd been sighted by local Arabs. By the evening of 19 September the eight missing troopers were finally located, though two injured men, who'd been left behind, could not be traced.[23] When the combined groups reached Landing Ground 125, they discovered Captain Ken Lazarus of the lRDG with two of Dennis' guardsmen who had been left behind in the fracas; the wounded men had been taken off by the RAF.

Two days afterwards they had traversed the sand sea, and went on to Howard's Cairn where Arnold with the supply section was waiting. By 25 September, all were back at Kufra. The LRDG attack of Barce was the only one of these September raids to succeed. The Axis had lost perhaps 30 planes and as many dead. That the raiders could strike so far behind the lines was a significant dent in Axis morale, however, and a comparable boost to the Allies. LRDG had suffered none killed, half a dozen wounded, ten POWs and lost 14 vehicles. All of the men missing in the desert were recovered. One MC, two DSOs and three MMs were awarded[24]; all in all, a very impressive undertaking.

Barce was the only successful element of all the great September raids. The rest all failed and at considerable cost. The National Archives lists the lessons to be learned from the failure, primarily of Operation *Bigamy*, though much of what was said could apply equally to Tobruk.

Lack of security was realized, belatedly, to be a problem; this one is so obvious it hardly seems necessary to underline – 'too many people knew of the Benghazi operation, and a very much higher sense of security was necessary'.[25] The lack of precautions led to the other failures. Once an enemy is aware, then surprise, the key to Special Forces' success, is lost. It was also considered wise not to rely on Arab guides. This is possibly unfair, as navigation over such sterile terrain in the dark is a significant challenge for anyone.

The post mortem also points out the perils caused by enemy aircraft – again, this is scarcely ground-breaking. That the Axis planes should be 'neutralized' is clearly desirable, if rather more difficult in the accomplishment.[26] The lack of co-ordinated intelligence gathering, mechanical failures and general overloading of vehicles are all pointed out. In the last analysis, poor security derailed the attack on Benghazi even more surely than it did the bigger affray at Tobruk, where we cannot say for sure the enemy was actually forewarned.

A list of what went wrong with Operation *Agreement* could fairly easily be summarized as 'everything', and this would not be too blasé or cynical. Attempting to list the failures has to start with the overall concept and planning. Haselden's original idea was sound; although it was risky and bold, it did not quite approach rashness and was essentially do–able. Once the whole plan grew so astonishingly, however, involving air and sea elements, it got totally out of hand and into the near fantastical area of wishful thinking. It grew too big with too many interdependent elements and too many split-second timings. At the time, the failure to light the landing beaches was stressed[27] and this is undoubtedly correct. But it was a failure of intelligence and communication that the SBS Folbot team and the officer commanding the submarine *Taku* did not appreciate just how vital their assigned role was or the dire consequences of failure.

The lighters, badly, cheaply and wrongly put together, were another prime cause. Their limitations were not picked up because of the inadequacy of training and rehearsal. Properly undertaken, this would have revealed the inherent problems. Sending in the bombers before rather than after, as the original *Waylay* plan had called for, was another principal error. The enemy's defences were not compromised, very little real damage was inflicted and the Axis's ability to deploy to meet the attack was barely inconvenienced. Lack of adequate aerial reconnaissance prior to the raid and the bland assumption that only Italian troops of questionable quality would be present were avoidable mistakes. Lack of adequate communications was another.

Whilst we armchair strategists, writing with the inestimable benefits of hindsight and under no operational pressure whatsoever, find it easy to be critical, in war mistakes will be made. What the many successes of the LRDG had demonstrated was the need for limited objectives and getting in and out fast – the fewer cogs the better. Barce, the sole success in that September, underlines the point. Later, in 1943, the LRDG were to become victims of similar muddled objectives and slack planning when they were pitch-forked into the mess of the Dodecanese campaign. Military success cannot rely entirely on wishful thinking and political expediency. This led to disaster in Norway, Greece and Crete, nearly losing the Allies the Desert War in the process.

Operation *Agreement* and its outcome was very quickly overtaken by events. Montgomery had been careful to distance himself from the raid, though he was by no means slow in adding his powerful voice to the wailing chorus of mourners when it failed. The next month, October 1942, he launched his great offensive that became the Second Battle of El Alamein. This was the deciding swing of the pendulum. In a hard fought struggle of attrition, Rommel's forces were ground down and finally hurled back.

For Rommel, the scale of this defeat was enormous. Assessments differ, but the Axis had lost something in the order of 30,000 prisoners, two thirds of them Italian, and perhaps as many as 20,000 dead and wounded. Most of his Italian formations had been decimated and such transport as could be found was reserved for German survivors. Out of nearly 250 tanks DAK could barely field three dozen, and though the Italians had more runners these were inferior and no match for Shermans. Well might the marching soldiers have lamented, many of whom would never see Rome or Naples, Milan or Bologna again. In a very short time the overall situation had changed beyond recognition, almost impossible to have visualized in September.

The Desert War wasn't over. Far from it: much hard fighting remained in the long dogged battle to clear the Libyan littoral and the intense struggle for Tunisia following the *Torch* landings in Vichy North Africa. Tobruk, battered but still functioning, changed hands for a final time. At Tunis, on 12 May 1943, General Armin and General Messe each formally surrendered their commands. At 1415 hours on the 13th Churchill finally received the telegram from Alexander he had waited so long to read: 'Sir, it is my duty to report that the Tunisian campaign is over. All enemy resistance has ceased. We are masters of the North African shores'. The War in the Desert was indeed over, but the bones of some 220,000 British and Imperial soldiers would remain.

When operations fail, there's always the compelling temptation to try to wrest some positive conclusions. In the case of the September raids, this is very difficult. There's no evidence that the Germans in particular were significantly perturbed. Their losses were trifling. Their plans worked and flow through the port hardly faltered. Many brave men were lost, together with a vast quantity of materiel including fine ships, which were virtually irreplaceable. It does have to be said that while the operation failed totally, this was no fault of those who took part. The courage, determination and resilience of the British and Allied fighting men were never more fully demonstrated. The plan failed, but the men did not.

Almost exactly a year after the raid, the Training and Staff Duties Division, Naval Staff produced an analysis of the mistakes made called *Fighting Experience – Operation 'Agreement'*. This contains some exculpatory opening remarks commenting correctly on the gravity of the situation for Middle East Command a year earlier when the strategic balance was hanging very much by a thread. What is admitted is that the length of the operation was too extended and lack of air cover a serious flaw.[28] A desperate situation often demands desperate remedies – the destroyers, as the report points out, were well camouflaged in Italian colours, though this hardly compensates for the subsequent lack of fighter support. It is admitted that the effect of the bombing was only to put the enemy on alert, but by September 1943, the myth of bombing effectiveness had not yet been fully dispelled.[29]

The damaging lack of communications and the delay in getting the success signals from Haselden's men through is noted, as are the signalling failures that did so much to account for the failure of the bulk of the MTBs to make a landing. The absolute necessity for clear and effective signalling is recognized as paramount. The severe effect of the heavy swell is also noted.[30] The need for effective use of compasses, for adequate training in high-speed flotilla sailing and manoeuvres, and the proper deployment of landing craft are all recognized. The report also contains the unnecessary warning that 'surprise attack by aircraft is likely to be fatal',[31] and the absolute need for secrecy and for proper aircraft recognition are also highlighted.

These platitudes aside, the report fails to acknowledge any of the fundamental failings that damned the raid to failure. This would have been the time to admit that such grandiose plans are virtually unworkable, that attempts at saturation bombing of tactical targets cannot be guaranteed and the overall effect works against the attackers. However, the abysmal security is brushed aside and equipment failures, particularly the disgracefully shoddy lighters and the lack of training beforehand, are not alluded to. The report is something of a placebo. It largely exonerates the failure, which is ascribed to the needs of the hour, and none of the fundamental errors is highlighted in a sufficiently robust style.

Of that remarkable group of men who made up the SIG, Russell was murdered in Yugoslavia, probably by ostensible allies, Tito's partisans, nearly a year later in August 1943. He was one of those who wondered about how he'd cope with peace – he needn't have bothered. Buck was captured after the raid and spent the remainder of the war 'banged up' as a POW.[32] David Jefferson recounts the experiences of another Operation *Agreement* survivor, Charles Coles, who met up with Buck in an Italian camp at Padula near Salerno. Buck did manage one escape attempt, but didn't get far. Coles later acted as usher at Buck's wedding to Celia Wardle. After a tragically short time as a married woman, the bride was widowed when Buck died in a plane crash on 22 November 1945, almost immediately after his marriage.[33]

'Chunky' Hillman, identified as J. Kennedy and one of the SIG present on the raid, won both an MM and MC. Austrian by birth, he detested the Nazis, surviving the war to command a field security unit in occupied Germany. He had a long career in the army and may have emigrated to Canada following his honourable retirement.[34] Maurice Tiefenbrunner ('Tiffin') also survived a very eventful war and fought for Israel in the 1948 conflict. He survived this struggle as well and finally, after many years living in West London, moved full time to the country and the cause he had served for so long. He died in 1997. Toward the very end of the war against Hitler Buck had apparently attempted to entice him into the SAS for service against the Japanese, but that was one fight he declined.[35]

David Lloyd Owen finished the war commanding LRDG and pursued a very successful military career. The unit itself continued to function after the Axis collapse in North Africa, fighting in the Dodecanese, Italy, Yugoslavia, Greece and Albania. It was disbanded in 1945, yet remains a legend. Stirling and the SAS also kept fighting until he was captured, another who spent the remainder of the war as a POW. The mercurial Mayne, a man of immense courage and stamina, never quite reached the same status and could never fully adjust to civvy street. He died in a car crash late in 1955. Denis Jermain had a very busy war and continued to serve with great distinction. He earned a DSC (Distinguished Service Cross) and Bar, being mentioned in despatches no fewer than five times, an astonishing testimony. He remained in the navy till 1973 and remained a keen yachtsman for the rest of his life. He died in 2007 at the age of 89.[36]

Operation *Agreement*, one of the great heroic failures of the war, passed very swiftly into relative obscurity, but for all the dreadful cost, the story of the men who took part deserves to be remembered, and failure perhaps almost as much as success builds another layer on the continuing toughness, resilience and humour of Britain's armed forces. That perhaps and the recognition that our Special Forces remain the best in the world is their true legacy.

Above all we should remember the SIGs. They were few but their service and sacrifice exemplifies what the Allies were fighting for: to remove a monstrous tyranny responsible for the industrialized murder of millions, most of them Jews. For the SIG this was deeply personal 'war with hatred'. It was also about fighting back.

APPENDIX

ORDERS OF BATTLE

ALLIED FORCES

Force A – Lieutenant-Colonel E. H. M. Unwin RM

11th Battalion Royal Marines (360 men and 22 officers)
Detachment of AA and CD gunners
Sub-section 295 Field Company RE
Detachment Royal Signals and RAMC
Force carried aboard two Tribal Class destroyers HMS *Sikh* and *Zulu*
    commanded by Captain St J. A. Micklethwait RN

Force B – Lieutenant Colonel J. E. Haselden Middle East Commandos

Squadron 1st SS Regiment – Major C. Campbell
Y1 Patrol LRDG – Captain D. Lloyd Owen
Detachment AA and CD gunners – Lieutenant Barlow RA

Sub-section 295 Field Company RE – Lieutenant Pointon RE

Special Detachment SIG – Captain H. Buck and Lieutenant T. C. D. A. Russell

Detachment Royal Signals – Captain Trollope

RAMC Medical Officer – Captain Gibson

Force C – Captain A. N. Macfie Argyll and Sutherland Highlanders

D Company 1st Battalion A&SH (97 men and 5 officers)

One platoon Royal Northumberland Fusiliers (32 men) – Lieutenant E. Raymond

Two sub-sections 295 Field Company RE

AA Detachment RA – Lieutenant Beddington RA

Detachment RAMC

Force carried aboard 16 MTBs and 3 MLs commanded by Commander J. F. Blackburn RN

Forces D and E

These comprised naval supporting elements including C Class light cruiser HMS *Coventry* (Captain R. J. R. Dendy RN) and four Hunt Class destroyers: *Hursley, Beaufort, Exmoor* and *Aldenham* from No. 5 Flotilla, with Submarine HMS *Taku* (Lieutenant-Commander J. G. Hopkins).

Royal Air Force

No. 201 (Naval Co-operation) Group and No. 205 (Heavy Bomber) Group, comprising 101 aircraft (35 heavy and 66 medium bombers including five B-17 Fortresses from the USAAF).

AXIS FORCES

German — General-Major O. Deindl

Staff Company Koruck Battalion

Detachment Field Police and 613th (Motorized) Military Police Company

Two companies of Wachbataillon Afrika

Reinforced Motorized 909 Pioneer Company (680 other ranks [ORs] and 35 officers)

Supply and rear echelon units (Major Hardt) *c.* 1,400 ORs and 40 officers

Luftwaffe personnel (Major Schewe), 292 ORs and 20 officers

AA units under Luftwaffe command, some 48 8.8cm Flak guns, 85 20mm Flak guns

Detachment of Kriegsmarine (Korvettenkapitan Meixner), 25 sailors and two officers

Italian *

Detachment of marines comprising 160 men of the San Marco Battalion (Lieutenant Colotto)

Detachments of coastal gunners

Detachment of field police 18th CG.RR Carabinieri Battalion

Detachment of Italian African Police, 25 strong

Various rear echelon and logistical personnel

Axis naval forces in Tobruk harbour comprised three Italian destroyers and some patrol craft with a German minesweeper flotilla

---

* with General Giannantoni (sick), actual command was devolved onto Colonel Battalglia, with senior naval officer Captain D'Aloja, but visiting Rear-Admiral Lombardi was the overall senior officer.

NOTES

INTRODUCTION

1. F. Harrison, *Tobruk: The Great Siege Reassessed* (London, Brockhampton Press, 1999), p. 29.
2. Ibid., p. 31.
3. http://en.wikipedia.org/wiki/Intercommunal_conflict_in_Mandatory_Palestine retrieved 14 April 2015.
4. M. Gilbert, *The Holocaust* (London, Fontana, 1987), p. 34.
5. Ibid., p. 41.
6. Ibid., p. 47.

CHAPTER ONE

1. TNA: WO HW1/643, forwarded to the prime minister as File CX/MSS/1671. TX.
2. No. 551781/42G.K. Chefs W.F.St/Qu F.H. Qu 19/10/42.
3. C. Herzog, *Arab – Israeli Wars* (London, Greenhill, 2005), p. 12.
4. Ibid., p. 13. Avraham Stern was subsequently killed in a confrontation with British police in 1942.
5. Ibid.
6. Raised on 17 October, 1939: see M. Chappell, *Army Commandos 1940–45* (Oxford, Osprey, 1996), p. 48.
7. Chappell, p. 17.
8. TNA: WO 201/732, cited in M. Sugarman, *Lions of Judah*, Association of Jewish Ex-Servicemen and Women, Jewish Military Museum (February 2002). Lieutenant General Terence Sydney Airey (1900–83) latterly served as chief of staff to General Alexander and was a participant in the Karl Wolff affair that sparked a row between, the USA/UK and Soviet Russia.
9. M. Sugarman, *Fighting Back: British Jewry's Military Contribution to the Second World War* (Middlesex, Valentine Mitchell, 2010), p. 154.
10. Ibid.
11. J. Bierman and C. Smith, *Alamein – War without Hate* (London, Penguin, 2002), p. 140; Leah would become the wife of Yitzbak Rabin and her sister married Major-General Avraham Yoffe.
12. Ibid.

13. Bierman and Smith, p. 140.
14. TNA: WO 218/159, 17 March 1942.
15. TNA: WO 201/732 1 April 1942, cited in Bierman and Smith, p. 141.
16. TNA: WO 201/727, cited in Bierman and Smith, p. 141.
17. Bierman & Smith, p. 142.
18. A joint British-Zionist counter-insurgency unit set up in 1938. Moshe Dayan was an early recruit.
19. Sugarman, p. 155; Shai was another German émigré, moving to Palestine in 1938 at the age of 16, volunteering two years later.
20. Reverend I. Levy, *Now I Can Tell – Middle Eastern Memoir* (privately published, 1978), p. 49.
21. Cited in Bierman and Smith, p. 143.
22. See G. Landsborough, *Tobruk Commando* (London, Greenhill, 1956), p. 31.
23. V. Cowles, *The Phantom Major* (London, Collins, 1958), p. 135.
24. Sugarman, p. 159.
25. Ibid.
26. A. Swinson, *The Raiders* (Purnell, London, 1968), p. 115.
27. Cowles, pp. 140–41.
28. Ibid., p. 141.
29. D. Lloyd-Owen, *Providence Their Guide* (London, Harrap, 1980), p. 99.
30. Sugarman, p. 160.
31. Ibid, PRO WO 201/727.
32. Sugarman, p. 160 .
33. TNA: WO 201/727.
34. T. Geraghty, *March or Die: France and the Foreign Legion* (London, HarperCollins, 2001), p. 213.
35. TNA: WO 201/727.
36. This was disclosed in the course of an interview with Carmi in 1999 conducted by John Bierman and passed on to Martin Sugarman by letter dated 6 August 1999.

CHAPTER TWO

1. Keith Douglas, quoted in R. Bowen, *Many Histories Deep – The 'Personal Landscape' Poets in Egypt 1940–1945* (London, Associated University Press, 1995), p. 89.
2. Bernard Spencer, 'Aegean Islands', quoted in Bowen, p. 121.
3. J. Lucas, *War in the Desert* (London, 1982), p. 74.
4. R. J. Crawford, *I was an Eighth Army Soldier* (London, Arms and Armour Press, 1944), p. 20.
5. Ibid., p. 19.
6. Terence Tiller, 'Flare', quoted in Bowen, p. 111.
7. Crawford, p. 27.
8. P. Warner, *Alamein, Recollections of the Heroes* (London, Pen and Sword, 1979), p. 30.
9. *https://www.google.co.uk/?gws_ rd=ssl#q=define+commando* retrieved 8 April 2015.
10. W. B. Kennedy Shaw, *The Long Range Desert Group* (London, Greenhill Press, 1945), p. 21.
11. B. Pitt, *The Crucible of War – Western Desert 1941* (London, Jonathan Cape, 1980), p. 223.
12. M. Morgan, *Sting of the Scorpion* (Gloucs., Sutton, 2000), p. 3.
13. Pitt, p. 224.
14. Morgan, p. 6.
15. Pitt, p. 226.
16. A. Gilbert (ed.), *The Imperial War Museum Book of the Desert War 1940–1943* [IWM] (London, Sidgwick & Jackson, 1992), p. 37.
17. Ibid.
18. The Lovat Scouts were the British Army's first sharpshooter or sniper unit, active in both world wars and finally stood down in Athens in 1947.
19. Bierman and Smith, p. 92.
20. Bierman and Smith, p. 97.
21. IWM, p. 196.

CHAPTER THREE

1. J. Strawson, *The Battle for North Africa* (London, Scribners, 1969), p. 16.
2. Strawson, pp. 26–27.
3. Bierman and Smith, p. 49.
4. N. Barr, *Pendulum of War – The Three Battles of El Alamein* (London, Jonathan Cape, 2005), p. 65.
5. Ibid., pp. 66–67. Each Panzer division comprised a reconnaissance unit, a twin-battalion Panzer regiment and a rifle regiment of three battalions plus supporting artillery.
6. Ibid., p. 67; the Motorized Light Division had four infantry battalions, each with an all-arms component.
7. Leslie Morshead, 1889–1959.
8. Pitt, p. 250.
9. R. Parkinson, *The War in the Desert* (London, 1976), p. 44.
10. Strawson, p. 33.
11. Ibid., p. 57.
12. Official History., Vol. 2, p. 159.
13. Parkinson, p. 55.
14. Ibid., p. 56.
15. Pitt, p. 355.
16. Parkinson, p. 79.
17. Official History, vol. 3, p. 57.
18. An expression dating from C. R. M. F. Cruttwell's outstanding book, *A History of the Great War, 1914–18*.
19. Official History, vol. 3, p. 145.
20. Ibid., p. 154.
21. Ibid., p. 214.
22. Ibid., p. 214.
23. Ibid., p. 233.
24. Parkinson, p. 110.
25. Ibid., p. 110.
26. Official History, vol. 3, p. 246.
27. Barr, p. 16.

CHAPTER FOUR

1. Barr, p. 185.
2. Ibid., p. 187.
3. Ibid., pp. 191–92.
4. Ibid., p. 193.
5. Official History, vol. 3, p. 367.
6. Barr, p. 199.
7. Ibid., p. 200.
8. Official History, vol. 3, p. 370.
9. Ibid., p. 370.
10. Ibid., p. 370.
11. Ibid., p. 371.
12. Montgomery of Alamein, *Memoirs* (London, Collins, 1958), p. 92.
13. Official History, vol. 3, p. 384.
14. Official History, vol. 3, p. 383.
15. Ibid., p. 386.
16. Ibid., p. 388.
17. Ibid., p. 364.
18. Barr, p. 185.
19. Barr, p. 187.
20. Ibid., pp. 187–88.
21. Ibid., p. 190.
22. Ibid., pp. 191–92.
23. Ibid., p. 193.
24. Ibid., p.196.
25. Official History, vol. 3, p. 367.
26. Barr, p. 199.
27. Montgomery, p. 90.
28. Barr, p. 200.
29. Ibid., p. 201.
30. Ibid., p. 203.
31. Ibid., p. 204.
32. Official History, vol. 3, p. 369.
33. Ibid., p. 370.
34. Ibid., p. 370.
35. Montgomery, p. 90.
36. Ibid., p. 93.
37. Official History, vol. 3, p. 370.
38. Ibid., p. 370.
39. Ibid., p. 371.
40. Ibid., p. 397.
41. Official History, vol. 3, p. 384.
42. Ibid., p. 382.
43. Ibid., p. 383.

44. Ibid., p. 386.
45. Montgomery, p. 99.
46. Official History, vol. 3, p. 388.
47. Ibid., p. 388.
48. Ibid., p. 389.
49. Montgomery, p. 99.

50. Official History, vol. 3, p. 389.
51. Ibid., p. 389.
52. K. Ford, *El Alamein 1942* (Oxford, Osprey, 2001), p. 59.
53. Official History, vol. 3, p. 391.
54. Ibid., 391.

CHAPTER FIVE

1. Quoted in D. Jefferson, *Tobruk – A Raid too Far* (London, Robert Hale, 2013), p. 112.
2. P. C. Smith, *Massacre at Tobruk* (London, W. Kimber, 1987), p. 16.
3. Ibid., p. 40.
4. Ibid., p. 16.
5. Ibid., p. 17.
6. Ibid., p. 18.
7. Ibid., p. 19.
8. Smith, p. 9.
9. Ibid., p. 10.
10. F. Maclean, *Eastern Approaches* (London, Jonathan Cape, 1949), p. 184.
11. Ibid., p. 184.
12. http://en.wikipedia.org/wiki/Special_Boat_Service, retrieved 22 April 2013.
13. Smith, p. 20.
14. Ibid., p. 21.
15. Ibid., p. 23.
16. Ibid., p. 24.
17. Ibid., p. 24.
18. Ibid., p. 27.
19. Ibid, p.27.
20. Ibid., p. 29.
21. Ibid., p. 30.
22. Ibid., p. 31.
24. TNA: CAB 44/152 in Wynter, pp. 339–40.
24. TNA: CAB 44/152 in Wynter, p. 340.
25. TNA: CAB 44/152 in Wynter, p. 341.
26. TNA: CAB 44/152 in Wynter, p. 341
27. TNA: CAB 44/152 in Wynter, p. 342.
28. TNA: CAB 44/152 in Wynter, p. 342.
29. TNA: CAB 44/152 in Wynter, p. 342.
30. Operational History, vol. IV, p. 21.
31. Smith, p. 35.
32. Ibid, p. 35.

33. Ibid., p. 36.
34. Major Con J. Mahoney, quoted in Smith, p. 36.
35. Gunner Rating 'Tug' Wilson, quoted in Smith, p. 37.
36. Fitzroy Maclean, p. 184.
37. M. Smith, *Station X – The Codebreakers of Bletchley Park* (London, Channel 4 Books, 1998) pp. 97–98.
38. Jim Rose, one of Hut 3 Bletchley Park's air advisors, quoted in Smith, p. 99.
39. Ibid., p. 100.
40. Ibid., p. 102.
41. Bill Williams, quoted in Smith, p. 103.
42. Ralph Bennett one of Hut 3's intelligence officers, quoted in Smith, p. 197.
43. Smith, p. 38.
44. Ibid., p. 39.
45. Ibid., p. 53.
46. Ibid., pp. 54–55.
47. Ibid, pp. 54–55.
48. Ibid., p. 41.
49. Smith, p. 53.
50. Ibid., p. 49.
51. Ibid., pp. 44–45.
52. Smith, p. 51.
53. TNA: WO 201/749 SIG is described as the Special Detachment G(R); see Sugarman, p. 163.
54. Sugarman, p. 164.
55. Ibid., p. 166.
56. Ibid., p. 164.
57. Ibid., p. 166.
58. Smith, p. 52.
59. Ibid., p. 58.

CHAPTER SIX

1. Lloyd Owen, p. 54.
2. T. Moreman, p. 24.
3. Ibid., p. 24.
4. Lloyd Owen, p. 105.
5. Kennedy Shaw, pp. 78–79.
6. Wynter, pp. 46–47.
7. Lloyd Owen, pp. 105–06.
8. Smith, p. 82.
9. G. Landsborough, *Tobruk Commando* (London, Cassell, 1956), p. 11.
10. Ibid., p. 18.
11. Ibid., p. 19.
12. Smith, p. 81.
13. Landsborough, p. 24.
14. Ibid., p. 25. Trollope was a descendant of the famous novelist.
15. Ibid., p. 25.
16. Kennedy Shaw, p. 187.
17. T. Moreman, p. 35.
18. Ibid., p. 34.
19. Morgan, pp. 98–99.
20. Kennedy Shaw, p. 90.
21. Morgan, p. 42 and following.
22. Lloyd Owen, p. 19.
23. Smith, p. 84.
24. Smith, p. 85.
25. Kennedy Shaw, pp. 188–89.
26. Ibid., pp. 188–89.
27. Ibid., pp. 189–90.
28. Jefferson, p. 159.
29. Ibid., pp. 161–62.
30. Smith, p. 80.
31. http://en.wikipedia.org/wiki/Fairmile_B_motor_launch, retrieved 3 May 2015.
32. Jefferson, pp. 164–65.
33. Ibid, p. 167.
34. Ibid., p. 168.
35. Ibid., p. 183.
36. Ibid., p. 183.
37. Kennedy Shaw, p. 190.
38. Ibid., p.190.
39. Ibid., p. 191.

CHAPTER SEVEN

1. Jefferson, p. 187.
2. Jefferson, pp. 188–89.
3. Ibid., pp. 188–89.
4. Ibid., pp. 188–89.
5. Smith, p. 91.
6. Ibid., p. 91.
7. Smith, p. 93.
8. Smith, pp. 93–94.
9. Ibid, p. 167.
10. Ibid., p. 168.
11. Ibid., p. 168.
12. Ibid., p. 168.
13. Landsborough, pp. 98–99.
14. Ibid., p. 103.
15. Ibid., p. 104.
16. Ibid., p. 105.
17. Ibid., p. 106.
18. Sugarman, p. 168.
19. Landsborough, pp. 108–09.
20. Ibid., pp. 114–15.
21. Ibid., p. 116.
22. Jefferson, p. 9.
23. Jefferson, p. 10.
24. Ibid., p. 37.
25. Ibid., p. 38.
26. Ibid., p. 39.
27. Ibid., p. 39.
28. Ibid., p. 39.
29. Ibid., p. 40.
30. Smith, p.?
31. Jefferson., p. 40.
32. Smith, p. 98.
33. Smith, p. 148.
34. Ibid, p. 148.
35. Ibid., p. 148.
36. Ibid., p. 147.
37. Smith, p. 148.
38. Ibid., p. 148.
39. Ibid., p. 149.
40. Smith, p. 150.
41. Ibid., p. 150.
42. Smith, p. 125.
43. Ibid., p. 126.
44. Ibid., p. 126.
45. Ibid., p. 128.

46. TNA: ADM1/12771 – this was rather long-windedly described as 'the circumstances of the landing at Tobruk by 11th Battalion RM from HM Ships 'Sikh', and 'Zulu' on the night of 13/14 September 1942 (Operation *Agreement*)'.

47. TNA: ADM1/12771 and Jefferson, p. 193.
48. TNA: ADM1/12771 and Jefferson, p. 194.
49. TNA: ADM1/12771 and Jefferson, p. 197.
50. TNA: ADM1/12771 and Jefferson, p. 197.
51. TNA: ADM1/12771 and Jefferson, p. 199.

CHAPTER EIGHT

1. TNA: WO/201/815 and Kennedy Shaw, p. 190.
2. TNA: WO/201/815 and Kennedy Shaw, p. 191.
3. TNA: WO/201/815 and Kennedy Shaw, p. 192.
4. TNA: WO/201/815 and Kennedy Shaw p. 193.
5. Kennedy Shaw, p. 183.
6. Ibid., p. 183.
7. Ibid., p. 194.
8. Smith, p. 109.
9. Ibid., p. 109.
10. Ibid., p. 109.
11. Ibid., p. 111.
12. Ibid., p. 110.
13. Ibid., p. 111.
14. Ibid., p. 133.
15. Jefferson, p. 219.
16. Smith, p. 133.
17. Ibid., p. 135.
18. Ibid., p. 135.
19. Quoted in Jefferson, p. 214.
20. Ibid., p. 214.
21. Ibid., p. 214.
22. Ibid., p. 215.
23. Smith, p. 135.
24. Jefferson, p. 215.
25. Quoted in Smith, p. 137.
26. Ibid., p. 138.
27. Smith, p. 136.
28. Jefferson, p. 216.
29. Ibid., p. 216.
30. Jefferson, p. 217.
31. Smith, p. 130.
32. Ibid., p. 130.
33. Ibid., p. 131.
34. Ibid., p. 132.
35. Smith, pp. 158–59.
36. Ibid., p. 160.
37. Ibid., p. 150.
38. Ibid., p. 151.
39. Ibid., p. 152.
40. Ibid., p. 153.
41. Ibid., p. 153.
42. Ibid., p. 156.
43. Ibid., pp. 153–54.
44. Ibid., p. 154.
45. Ibid., p. 154.
46. Landsborough, p. 151.
47. Sugarman, p. 169.
48. Ibid, p. 169.
49. Ibid, p. 169.
50. Landsborough asserts Steiner pulled Berg clear (p. 162) though Sugarman (p. 169) insists it was in fact Buck.
51. Landsborough, p. 158.
52. Ibid., p. 165.
53. Ibid., p. 167.
54. Ibid., p. 168.
55. Ibid., p. 169.
56. Ibid., p. 183.
57. Smith, p. 154.

CHAPTER NINE

1. TNA: ADM1/1277, Jefferson, Appendix three and Smith, pp. 120 and 161.
2. TNA: ADM1/1277, Jefferson, Appendix three and Smith, pp. 120 and 161.
3. TNA: ADM1/12771 and Jefferson p. 226.
4. TNA: ADM1/12771 and Jefferson, p. 226.
5. Smith, p. 196 and Jefferson, p. 226.
6. TNA: ADM1/12771, Jefferson, p. 226 and Smith, p. 123.
7. TNA: ADM1/12771, Jefferson, p. 226 and Smith, p. 123.
8. TNA: ADM1/12771 and Jefferson, p. 227.
9. Landsborough, p. 180 and Jefferson, p. 227.
10. This was set out in a report six months after the operation submitted to the CO of HMS *Mosquito* the coastal forces' HQ at Alexandria. TNA: ADM1/12771 and Jefferson, p. 228.
11. TNA: ADM1/12771, Jefferson, p. 229 and Smith, p. 122.
12. TNA: ADM1/12771, Jefferson, p. 229 and Smith, p. 122.
13. TNA: ADM1/12771, Jefferson, p. 229 and Smith, p. 122.
14. Smith (p. 112) says Russell, Sillito and Hillman [Steiner]. Sugarman (p. 113) asserts Buck was with them, but this may not be correct. I tend to think not as the other accounts don't mention him and he may have been captured.
15. Smith, pp. 112–13.
16. Ibid., p. 113.
17. Ibid., p. 114.
18. TNA: CAB 44/151 in Wynter, p. 346.
19. Smith, pp. 115–16.
20. Ibid., p. 163.
21. Ibid., p. 164.
22. Smith, p. 165.
23. Ibid., p. 165.
24. Landsborough, p. 188.
25. Smith, p. 167.
26. Ibid., p. 167.
27. Ibid., p. 169.
28. Ibid., p. 171.
29. Ibid., p. 174.
30. Ibid, p. 174.
31. Landsborough, p. 192.
32. Smith, p. 175.
33. There were 63 fatalities on *Coventry*: see IWM: HU89607 and Smith, p. 176.
34. Smith, p. 177.
35. Smith, p. 180 and Landsborough, p. 193, based on the unfortunate experience of HMS *Centurion* during an earlier convoy run. Whenever the ship had a near miss, the force blew some of the scuttling charges, which nearly sank her!
36. Smith, p. 83.
37. Smith, p. 186.
38. Ibid, p. 186.
39. Ibid., p. 190.
40. Ibid., p. 191.
41. Ibid., p. 193.
42. Ibid., p. 194
43. Ibid., p. 195.
44. TNA: CAB 44/151 in Wynter, p. 346.
45. TNA: CAB 44/151 in Wynter, p. 346.
46. TNA: CAB 44/151 in Wynter, p. 346. He was later found by Tommy Langton's group.
47. Smith, p. 170 and Landsborough, p. 215.
48. TNA: CAB 44/151 in Wynter, p. 347.
49. TNA: CAB 44/151 in Wynter, p. 347.
50. TNA: WO/201/740, TNA: WO/21897 (Langton's report).
51. TNA: WO/201/740, TNA: WO/21897 (Langton's report).
52. Jefferson, p. 224.
53. Official History, vol. IV, pp. 22–23.
54. Ibid., p. 23.

CHAPTER TEN

1. CAB 44/152 in Wynter, p. 338.
2. CAB 44/152 in Wynter, p. 335.
3. CAB 44/152 in Wynter, p. 335.
4. CAB 44/152 in Wynter, p. 336.
5. CAB 44/152 in Wynter, p. 336.
6. CAB 44/152 in Wynter, p. 337.
7. CAB 44/152 in Wynter, p. 337.
8. CAB 44/152 in Wynter, p. 337.
9. CAB 44/152 in Wynter, p. 338.
10. CAB 44/152 in Wynter, p. 348.
11. CAB 44/152 in Wynter, p. 348.
12. CAB 44/152 in Wynter, p. 348.
13. T. Moreman, pp. 49–50.
14. Kennedy Shaw, p. 200.
15. Ibid, p. 200.
16. Ibid., p. 201.
17. Ibid., p. 201.
18. Ibid., p. 202.
19. Ibid., p. 202.
20. Ibid., p. 202.
21. Morgan, p. 74.
22. Kennedy Shaw, p. 205.
23. Ibid., p. 206.
24. Ibid., p. 206.
25. CAB 44/152 in Wynter, p. 339.
26. CAB 44/152 in Wynter, p. 339.
27. CAB 44/152 in Wynter, p. 348.
28. ADM 339/335.
29. ADM 339/335.
30. ADM 339/335.
31. ADM 335/339.
32. Sugarman, note on p. 177.
33. Jefferson, pp. 248–49.
34. Sugarman, p. 171.
35. Ibid., pp. 172–74.
36. Jefferson, pp. 260–62.

GLOSSARY

AA – Anti-aircraft

AFV – Armoured Fighting Vehicle

AP – armour-piercing

A&SH – Argyll and Sutherland Highlanders

AT – Anti-tank

BEF – British Expeditionary Force

bir – well, cistern

BTE – British Troops in Egypt

CO – Commanding officer

CP – Command post

CSM – Company Sergeant-Major

DAF – Desert Air Force (RAF)

DAK – Deutsches Afrika Corps

DMO – Director of Military Operations

DSC – Distinguished Service Cross

DSO – Distinguished Service Order

folbot – folding kayak

FUBAR – Fucked up beyond all recognition

gebel (Jebel) – mountain or hill

gilf – cliff, plateau

GHQ – General Headquarters

GOC – General Officer Commanding

hatiet, hatiya – patch of vegetation

HE – High Explosive

HF – High frequency

HQ – Headquarters

IDF – Israel Defence Force

IED – Improvised explosive device

IFF – Identification, friend or foe

ISLD – Inter-Service Liaison Department

JPS – Joint Planning Staff

KD – Khaki drill

kebir – large, big

K.I.S.S. – Keep it simple, stupid

LAF – Libyan Arab Force

LRDG – Long Range Desert Group

LRP – Long Range Patrol (forerunner of LRDG)

MC – Military Cross

MEF – Middle East Forces

MG – Machine gun

ML – Motor launch

MNBDO – Mobile Naval Base Defence Organization

MO – Medical Officer

MT – Motor Transport

MTB – Motor Torpedo Boat

NAAFI/EFI – Navy, Army and Air Force Institutes/Expeditionary
   Forces Institute

NCO – Non-commissioned officer

OH – Official History

OKH – Oberkommando des Heeres

OKW – Oberkommando der Wehrmacht

ORBAT – Orders of Battle

PRU – Photographic Reconnaissance Unit

quaret, gara – hill

QM – Quartermaster

RA – Royal Artillery

RAF – Royal Air Force

RAP – Regimental Aid Post

RAMC – Royal Army Medical Corps

RANVR (Royal Australian Naval Volunteer Reserve)

RAOC – Royal Army Ordnance Corps

RASC – Royal Army Service Corps

RDF – Radio Direction Finding (radar)

RE – Royal Engineers

recce – reconnaissance

'Regt' – 'Regiment'

RM – Royal Marines

RN – Royal Navy

RNF – Royal Northumberland Fusiliers

RNVR – Royal Naval Volunteer Reserve

RTR – Royal Tank Regiment

RV – Rendezvous

SAS – Special Air Service

SBS – Special Boat Service

SD – Sicherheitsdienst

SDF – Sudan Defence Force

serir – gravel desert

SIG – Special Interrogation Group

SMG – Sub-machine gun

SOE – Special Operations Executive

SOO – Staff Officer Operations

SS – Schutzstaffel

USAAF – United States Army Air Force

USAMEAF – United States Army Middle East Air Force

wadi – watercourse, normally dry

WD – War department

VC – Victoria Cross

BIBLIOGRAPHY

PUBLISHED SOURCES

Adair, R., *British Eighth Army, North Africa 1940–1943* (New York Avco, 1974)

Agar-Hamilton, J. A. I. and Turner, L. C. F., *Crisis in the Desert May–July 1942* (Oxford University Press, Cape Town, 1952)

Alexander, Field Marshal the Earl, *The Alexander Memoirs 1940–1945* (Frontline, London, 1962)

Arthur, M., *Forgotten Voices of the Second World War* (Ebury Press, London, 2004)

Bagnold, R., *Libyan Sands* (Eland Publishing, London, 1935)

_____,'Early Days of the Long Range Desert Group' in the *Geographical Journal,* Vol. 105 (Jan -Feb 1945), pp. 30–42

_____, *Sand, Wind & War: Memoirs of a Desert Explorer* (University of Arizona Press, Tucson, 1990)

Bailey, J. B. A., *Field Artillery and Firepower* (Routledge, London, 1989)

Barnett, C., *The Desert Generals* (Cassell, London, 1960)

_____, *Engage the Enemy More Closely: The Royal Navy in the Second World War* (Hodder & Stoughton, London, 1991)

Barr, N., *Pendulum of War, The Three Battles of El Alamein* (Pimlico, London, 2004)

Battistelli, P. B., *Rommel's Afrika Corps Tobruk to El Alamein* (Osprey, Oxford, 2006)

Beale, P., *Death by Design, British Tank Development in the Second World War* (Tempus, Stroud, 1998)

Bennet, R., *Ultra and Mediterranean Strategy 1941–1945* (Hamish Hamilton, London, 1989)

Bidwell, S., and Graham, D., *Firepower, British Army Weapons and Theories of War 1904–1945* (Pen & Sword, London, 1982)

Bierman, J. and Smith, C., *Alamein, War Without Hate* (Penguin, London, 2002)

Bingham, J., Wordsworth, K. and Haupt, W., *North African Campaign 1940–1943* (TBS, London, 1969)

Bishop, C. and Drury, I., *Guns in Combat* (Book Sales, London, 1987)

Braddock, D. W., *The Campaigns in Egypt and Libya* (Gale & Polden, Aldershot, 1964)

Bradford, E., *Malta 1940–1943* (Pen & Sword, London, 1985)

British Troops Egypt, *Official Handbook for British Troops in Egypt, Cyprus, Palestine and the Sudan* (BTE, 1936)

British Troops Egypt, *Official Handbook for British Troops in Egypt, Cyprus, Palestine and the Sudan* (BTE, 1936)

Bruce, C. J., *War on the Ground 1939–1945* (BCA, London, 1995)

Bryant, Sir Arthur, *The Turn of the Tide*, vols I and II (Reprint Society, London, 1957–59)

Bull, S., *World War II Infantry Tactics: Squad and Platoon* (Osprey, Oxford, 2004)

_____, *World War Two Infantry tactics: Company and Battalion* (Osprey, Oxford, 2005)

Carver, M., *El Alamein* (Wordsworth, London, 1962)

_____, *Tobruk* (Wordsworth, London, 1964)

_____, *Dilemmas of the Desert War* (Wordsworth, London, 1986)

_____, *The Apostles of Mobility: The Theory and Practice of Armoured Warfare* (Holmes & Meier, New York, 1979)

Chalfont, A. J., *Montgomery of Alamein* (Littlehampton, London, 1976)

Churchill, W., *The Second World War* (Penguin, London, 1951)

Clark, A., *The Fall of Crete* (Efstathiadis Group, London, 2008)

Clayton, P., *Desert Explorer: A Biography of Colonel P. A. Clayton* (Zerzura Press, 1998)

Connell, J., *Auchinleck: A Biography of Field-Marshall Sir Claude Auchinleck* (Cassell, London, 1959)

Cooper, M., *The German Army 1933–1945* (Zebra, London, 1978)

Cowles, V., *The Phantom Major – The Story of David Stirling and the SAS Regiment* (Ballantine, London, 1958)

Crawford, R. J., *I was an Eighth Army Soldier* (London, 1944)

Crichton-Stuart, M., *G Patrol* (Tandem, London, 1958)

Crimp, R. L., *The Diary of a Desert Rat* (Macmillan, London, 1971)

Crisp, R., *Brazen Chariots: An Account of Tank Warfare in the Western Desert, November–December 1941* (Bantam Doubleday, London, 1959)

Cruickshank, C., *Deception in World War Two* (Oxford University Press, Oxford, 1979)

Defence Operational Analysis Centre, *The Combat Degradation and Effectiveness of Anti-Tanks Weapons – Interim Analysis,* vols. I and II, Study 670

_____,*The Effectiveness of Small Arms Fire in Defence* Study no. M 83108

_____,*Historical Analysis of Anti-Tank Battles – The Battle of Snipe*, Study N 670/201

De Guingand, Major General Sir Francis, *Operation Victory* (Natnaj Publishers, India, 2006)

Delaney, J., *Fighting the Desert Fox* (Weidenfeld & Nicolson, London, 1998)

Die Oase – Journal of the Afrika Corps Veterans Association

Douglas, K., *Alamein to Zem Zem* (Faber & Faber, London, 1979)

Eighth Army Weekly

Ellis, J., *Brute Force: Allied Strategy and Tactics in the Second World War* (Andre Deutsch, London, 1980)

_____, *The Sharp End of War: The Fighting Man in World War Two* (Andre Deutsch, London, 1980)

Farran, R., *Winged Dagger* (Collins, London, 1948)

Fergusson, Sir Bernard, *Wavell, Portrait of a Soldier* (Collins, London, 1961)

Fletcher, D., *The Great Tank Scandal: British Armour in the Second World War*, Part 1 (HMSO, 1989)

Ford, K., *El Alamein* (Oxford University Press, Oxford, 2001)

_____, *El Alamein 1942* (Osprey, Oxford, 2005)

Forty, G., *The Royal Tank Regiment – A Pictorial History* (Spellmount, Tunbridge Wells, 1989)

_____, *World War Two Tanks* (Osprey, London, 1995)

_____, *The Armies of Rommel* (Osprey, London, 1997)

_____, *British Army Handbook 1939–1945* (Tempus, Stroud, 1998)

Fraser, D., *Alanbrooke* (Hodder & Stoughton, London, 1982)

_____, *And we Shall Shock Them: The British Army in the Second World War* (Hodder & Stoughton, London, 1983)

_____, *Knights Cross: A Life of Field Marshal Erwin Rommel* (Hodder & Stoughton, London, 1993)

Garret, D., *The Campaign in Greece and Crete* (HMSO, 1942)

Gordon, J. W., *The Other Desert War: British Special Forces in North Africa 1940–1943* (ABC Clio, New York, 1987)

Greacen, L., *Chink: A Biography* (Macmillan, London, 1989)

Greenwood, A., *Field Marshal Auchinleck* (Pentland Press, London, 1990)

Griffith, P., *World War II Desert Tactics* (Osprey, Oxford, 2008)

Hamilton, N., *Monty: The Making of a General 1887–1942* (London, 1982)

_____, *The Full Monty: Montgomery of Alamein 1887–1942* (London, 2001)

_____, *Master of the Battlefield 1942–1944* (Sceptre, London, 1983)

Harris, J. P. and Toase, F. H. (eds), *Armoured Warfare* (Sceptre, London, 1990)

Harrison, F., *Tobruk: The Great Siege Reassessed* (Brockhampton, London, 1996)

Harrison-Place, T., *Military Training in the British Army, 1940–1944: From Dunkirk to D-Day* (Tempus, Stroud, 2000)

Henry, C., *British Anti-Tank Artillery 1939–1945* (Osprey, Oxford, 2004)

Hinsley, F. H., *British Intelligence in the Second World War* (HMSO abridged ed. London, 1993)

Humble, R., *Crusader: Eighth Army's Forgotten Victory November 1941 to January 1942* (Leo Cooper, London, 1987)

Hogg, I. V. and Weeks, J., *The Illustrated Encyclopedia of Military Vehicles* (Book Sales, London, 1980)

Horrocks, Lieutenant General, Sir B., *A Full Life* (Collins, London, 1960)

Irving, D., *The Trail of the Fox* (HarperCollins, London, 1977)

James, M., *Born of the Desert – SAS in Libya* (Greenlist, London, 1945)

Jefferson, D., *Tobruk: A Raid too Far* (Robert Hale, London, 2013)

Jenner, R., List, D., Sarson, P. and Badrocke, M., *The Long Range Desert Group 1940–1945* (Oxford University Press, Oxford, 1999)

Johnson, M. and Stanley, P., *Alamein: The Australian Story* (Oxford University Press, 2002)

Joslen, Lieutenant-Colonel H. F., *Orders of Battle: Second World War* (HMSO, 1960)

Kay, R. L., *Long Range Desert Group in the Mediterranean* (Wellington, 1949)

Kennedy-Shaw, W. B., *Long Range Desert Group* (London, 1945)

Kippenburger, Major-General Sir Howard, *Infantry Brigadier* (Oxford University Press, Oxford, 1949)

Landsborough, G., *Tobruk Commando* (Cassell, London, 1956

Latimer, J., *Alamein* (Macmillan, London, 2002)

_____, *Deception in War* (Macmillan, London, 2001)

Lewin, R., *Rommel as Military Commander* (Batsford, London, 1968)

_____, *Montgomery as Military Commander* (Batsford, London, 1971)

_____, *The Life and Death of the Afrika Korps* (Batsford, London, 1977)

Lewis, P. J., and English, I. R., *Into Battle with the Durhams: 8 DLI in World War II* (London Stamp Exchange, London, 1990)

Liddell Hart, Captain B. H., *The Tanks: The History of the Royal Tank Regiment and its Predecessors, Heavy Branch Machine Gun Corps, Tank Corps and Royal Tank Corps, 1914–1945*, 2 vols. (Cassell, London, 1959)

Lloyd Owen, Major-General D., *The Long Range Desert Group – Providence Their Guide* (Pen & Sword, Barnsley, 2000)

_____, *The Desert My Dwelling Place* (Cassell, London, 1986)

Lucas, J., *War in the Desert – The Eighth Army at El Alamein* (Arms and Armour, London, 1982)

_____, *Panzer Army Africa* (Arms and Armour, London, 1977)

_____, *Hitler's Enforcers; Leaders of the German War Machine 1939–1945* (Arms and Armour, London, 1996)

MacDonald, C., *The Lost Battle: Crete 1941* (Macmillan, London, 1993)

Maclean, F., *Eastern Approaches* (Cape, London, 1949)

Macksey, K., *Rommel: Battles and Campaigns* (London, 1979)

Majdalany, F., *The Battle of El Alamein* (Weidenfeld & Nicolson, London, 1965)

Molinari, A., *Desert Raiders – Axis and Allied Special Forces 1940–1943* (Osprey, Oxford, 2007)

Montgomery, Field Marshal the Viscount B. L., *Memoirs* (Collins, London, 1958)

Moorehead, A., *Mediterranean Front* (Cedric Chiltern, London, 1942)

_____, *Years of Battle* (Cedric Chiltern, London, 1943)

_____, *The End in Africa* (Cedric Chiltern, London, 1943)

Moreman, T., *Desert Rats: British 8th Army in North Africa 1941–1943* (Osprey, Oxford, 2007)

Morgan, M., *Sting of the Scorpion* (Sutton, Stroud 2000)

Myatt, F., *The British Infantry 1660–1945: The Evolution of a Fighting Force* (Blandford, Poole, 1983)

National Archives, *Special Forces in the Desert War 1940–1943* (London, National Archives, 2001)

Neillands, R., *The Desert Rats: 7th Armoured Division, 1940–1945* (Weidenfeld & Nicolson, London, 1991)

Nicolson, N., *Alex: The Life of Field Marshal Earl Alexander of Tunis* (Macmillan, London, 1971)

Norris, J., *88 mm Flak 18/36/37/41 and Pak 43 1936–1945* (Osprey, Oxford, 2002)

O'Carroll, B., *Bearded Brigands: The LRDG in the Diaries/Photographs of Trooper Frank Jopling* (Pen & Sword, London, 2003)

_____, *Barce Raid, the Long Range Desert Group's Most Daring Exploit in*

World War II (Ngaio, Wellington, 2005)

_____, *The Kiwi Scorpions: The Story of the New Zealanders in the Long Range Desert Group* (Ngaio, Wellington, 2000)

Parkinson, R., *Blood, Toil, Sweat and Tears* (Hart-Davis McGibbon, London, 1973)

_____, *A Day's March Nearer Home* (Hart-Davis McGibbon, London, 1974)

_____, *The War in the Desert* (Hart-Davis McGibbon, London, 1976)

Peniakoff, V., *Popski's Private Army* (HarperCollins, London, 1950)

Perrett, B., *Panzerkampfwagen IV Medium Tank 1936–1945* (Osprey, Oxford, 1999)

Philips, C. E. L., *Alamein* (Macmillan, London, 1962)

Pitt, B., *The Crucible of War 1: Wavell's Command* (Cassell, London, 1986)

_____, *The Crucible of War 2: Auchinleck's Command* (Cassell, London, 1986)

_____, *The Crucible of War 3: Montgomery and Alamein* (Cassell, London, 1986)

Playfair, Major General I. S. O., Official History, UK Military Series, Campaigns: *Mediterranean and Middle East*, vols. 1–4, (HMSO, London, 1962–66)

Quarrie, B., *Afrika Korps* (Patrick Stephens Ltd, Cambridge, 1975)

_____, *Panzers in the Desert* (Patrick Stephens Ltd, Cambridge, 1978)

Rommel, E., *Infantry Attacks* (Greenhill, London, 1990)

Rottman, G., *World War Two Infantry Anti-Tank Tactics* (Osprey, Oxford, 2005)

Salmond, J. B., *The History of the 51st Highland Division* (Bishop Auckland, 1994)

Samwell, H. P., *An Infantry Officer with the Eighth Army: The Personal Experiences of an Infantry Officer During the Eighth Army's Campaign Through Africa and Sicily* (Blackwood, London, 1945)

Schmidt, H. W., *With Rommel in the Desert* (Constable, London, 1951)

Smith, M., *Station X – The Code Breakers of Bletchley Park* (Channel 4, London, 1998)

Smith, Peter C., *Massacre at Tobruk* (W. Kimber, London, 1989)

Stewart, A., *The Eighth Army's Greatest Victories: Alam Halfa to Tunis 1942–1943* (Pen & Sword, Barnsley, 1999)

_____, *The Early Battles of Eighth Army: 'Crusader' to the Alamein Line 1941–1942* (Pen & Sword, Barnsley, 2002)

Strawson, J., *The Battle for North Africa* (Pen & Sword, Barnsley, 2004)

_____, *A History of the SAS Regiment* (London, 1986)

Terraine, J., *The Right of the Line* (Wordsworth, London, 1997)

Toase, F. H., and Harris, J. P., *Armoured Warfare* (London, 1990)

US Command and General Staff College – Selected Readings in Tactics, vols. I and II, April 1974

Van Creveld, M., *Supplying in War: Logistics from Wallenstein to Patton* (Cambrige University Press, Cambridge, 1977)

Verney, G. L., *The Desert Rats: History of 7th Armoured Division 1938–1945* (Greenhill, London, 1954)

War Office: *Military Report on the North-Western Desert of Egypt* (HMSO, London, 1937)

Warner, P., *The Special Air Service* (Kimber, London, 1971)

_____, *Alamein – Recollections of the Heroes* (Kimber, London, 1979)

Wynter, Brigadier H. W., *The History of the Long Range Desert Group June 1940–March 1943* (National Archives CAB 44/151, 2008 edition)

Young, D., *Rommel* (Collins, London, 1950)

Zaloga, S. J., *M3 Lee/Grant Medium Tank 1941–1945* (Osprey, Oxford, 2005)

_____, *M3 and M5 Stuart Light Tank 1940–1945* (Osprey, Oxford, 1999)

UNPUBLISHED – DEFENCE ACADEMY SHRIVENHAM

TRDC 02954; Notes from Theatres of War, vol 1: Cyrenaica November, 1941

05407; The Retreat to El Alamein, 22 June 1942–30 August 1942

05408; The German Assault on the Alamein Position 31 August 1942–7 September 1942

05408; The Battle of El Alamein part II – Opr. Lightfoot

05408; Campaign in the Middle East Part 3, September–November 1942

05889; Defence in the Land Battle

06347; Tactical Deception

07315; Charles Turner Saga

08225; Pace of Operations

09153; The Battle of Snipe

09657; Engr. Aspects of N. Africa 1940–1943

09787; Battle of El Alamein

09995; Passage Operations, El Alamein 1942

10728; Culminating Points

11964; The Manoeuvrist Approach

12114; Tactical Handling of Artillery

12274; AFM vol. 4, part 3, Historical Desert Supplement

12374; Ibid

12546; El Alamein BFT

12686; Armour in Battle 1939–1945

13054; The Battle of El Alamein Part III

13535; Info. Brief on Tactical Deception

13711; Conquest of North Africa

13846; North Africa Extracts

14118; Air Power at El Alamein

14221; Desert Warfare: The German Experience of WWII

14258; Effectiveness of Anti-Tank Weapons in Combat vols. 1, 2, and
3, parts A and B

14543; Breakthrough and Manoeuvre Ops vols. 1 and 3, parts A and B

14903; Exercise Sphinx Ride – JFHQPXR

75123; Air Power at El Alamein

INDEX

OPERATION AGREEMENT